RATIONAL APPROACH TO ISLAM

RATIONAL APPROACH TO ISLAM

Asghar Ali Engineer

GYAN PUBLISHING HOUSE
NEW DELHI-110 002

RATIONAL APPROACH TO ISLAM
(Religion)

ISBN: 81-212-0725-8

© Asghar Ali Engineer

Published in 2001 in India by
Gyan Publishing House
5, Ansari Road,
New Delhi-110 002
Phone : 3282060, 3261060 Fax : 3285914
E-mail: gyanbook@del2.vsnl.del.in
Visit Our Web Site At http:\\www.gyanbooks.com

Laser Typesetting at: Power Photocomposers, New Delhi
Printed at: Mehra Offset Printers, New Delhi

Contents

	Preface	7
1.	Religion and Peace in Twenty-First Century	11
2.	On the Key-terms in the Qur'an	21
3.	Maulana Abul Kalam Azad and His Concept of Unity of Religion	31
4.	Islam and Secularism	43
5.	Islam, Reason and Revelation	53
6.	Islam and Modernity	63
7.	Islam, Muslims and Philosophy—An Introductory Note	75
8.	Globalization, Islam and Threat to Diversity	87
9.	Islam and Other Religions	97
10.	The Concept of Islamic State	107
11.	Islamic Ethic	119
12.	Islam, Women and Gender Justice	129
13.	Islam and Pluralism	147
14.	*Ikhwanus Safa*—A Rational and Liberal Approach to Islam	157
15.	Muhammad (PBUH) as Liberator	169
16.	The Concept of Ijtihad in Islam	179
17.	Sir Syed and his Commentary on Qur'an	191
18.	On Religious and Intercultural Dialogue	203
19.	Islam and the Concept of Jihad	211
20.	On Methodology of Understanding Qur'an	221
21.	Qur'an and Isma'ili Ta'wil	231
22.	Reconstruction of Islamic Thought	241
23.	What I believe	251
24.	The Intra-Community Violations of Rights—The Bohra Case	261
25.	Imam Bukhari—His Life and Contribution to Science of Hadith	271
26.	Sighting of Moon and Problems of Muslim Calendar	283
	Index	293

Preface

Islam is a world religion and there are Muslims today practically in every country be they in majority or minority. There are Muslims belonging to practically every race, linguistic and ethnic group. Thus it will be seen that Islam belongs to various civilisational groups and its followers actively participate in shaping the world event. Also, it is the religion of overwhelming majority of people in oil rich areas of the world, particularly in the Middle East. Thus this area becomes highly strategic for the West. This part of the world, like other parts of Asia and Africa was part of the western colonies during the nineteenth and twentieth centuries. Still the Western powers consider it highly important area to be controlled for their own interests.

Thus Islam is both respected and feared by the Western rulers. They want to politically cultivate these Islamic countries and also fear the explosive situation there for number of reasons not to be analysed here. There are different trends among the Western scholars as far as Islam is concerned. Some view it sympathetically like Prof. John L. Sposito and others fear it like Prof. Huntington. Prof. Huntington developed the theory of "clash of civilisations" and says that Western Civilisation and Islamic civilisations clash with each other. It is highly dubious theory based on complete misunderstanding both of Islam and of civilisation.

Similarly in India too there are different trends both among scholars as well as political propagandists and theorists. Some view Islam positively and approve of its rich contribution to Indian culture and civilisation. Many others, on the other hand, view it with great suspicion and think that it brought nothing but violence and conflict. These propagandists believe that Islam teaches demolition of others' religious places and the Muslim rulers demolished the temples of Hindus and converted them to Islam forcibly.

The Muslim fundamentalists too add to this by their writings and actions be they in Afghanistan, Pakistan or in India. It sends wrong message to both Muslims and non-Muslims. What Muslim fundamentalists do

strengthens the impression on non-Muslims that Islam is a fanatical
religion, which urges its followers to indulge in violence and suppression
of women's rights. Apart from fundamentalists the orthodox Muslims
believe in medieval theology as final and vehemently oppose any attempt
to rethink issues in the light of contemporary experiences. They while
approving of hermeneutics look down upon critical reason. They consider
role of critical reason as destructive and hence reject it. They worship the
text (*ibadat al-nass*) and refuse to entertain creative ideas and role of critical
reason.

Keeping all this in view these essays on Islam have been written and
collected in this volume. I have tried to cover various topics in these essays
concerning Islamic ethics, question of gender justice, Islam and other
religions, the core values of the Qur'an, Islam and the concept of *jihad*
(holy war) and Islam and question of *ijtihad* (creative interpretation of the
text) and such other issues. I believe that reason and faith for consistent
to each other and, on the contrary, supplement each other. Faith, though
very fundamental to leading a meaningful life, is insufficient by itself. It
needs to be enriched and propped up by reason. I believe that faith and
reason are two wheels of religion and both are equally necessary. The
Qur'an, therefore, rightly stresses the role of critical reflection, thought and
reason—what it calls *tafakkur, tadabbur* or *hikmah*. Hikmah is a key term
in the Qur'an which can be translated as wisdom—reason synthesised with
justice and benevolence. Qur'an says that human being has been created
in the best of mould *(ahsan- e-taqwim)* but he degenerates into *asfalas
safilin* (lowest of the low) as he is ruled by his or her desires rather than by
higher values and reason.

Islam, it should be noted, is not merely *ibadaat* (worship) but also
provides a framework of interpersonal behaviour *(mu'amalat)*. While
ibadaat are unique practices of acts of worship and hence immutable,
mu'amalaat greatly depend on changing circumstances and hence cannot
be treated as immutable. New problems keep o.: arising and one has to find
answers to these problems. Thus constant reexamination of issues become
necessary. One cannot live in past, life being a dynamic process. New
scientific discoveries raise new ethical issues and one can hardly ignore
these issues. Ones mind cannot be anchored in the past while living in the
present.

Also, one cannot continue to treat women in the same way as in the
medieval ages. The Qur'an is great champion of gender equality but the

medieval theologians framed rules of the Shari'ah keeping ethos of their own times in mind. It could not have been otherwise. The understanding of text cannot be torn out of the context in which one lives. Today there is great need for radically re-thinking issues relating to women. Women cannot be confined to four walls of home any more. Also, they cannot be veiled from head to feet. The Qur'an does not prescribe restrictive veil; rather it admonishes both men and women to wear dignified dress so as not to expose sexual charms publicly. It belongs strictly to private domain. A woman, as far as the Qur'anic prescriptions are concerned, is free to participate in all social, political, cultural and economic activities along with man. It was nothing more than medieval theologising which prescribed highly restrictive role for women. Thus the gender issues also need to be radically rethought today.

I also like to stress through these essays that modernity need not be worshipped and should not be treated uncritically. The role of reason as far as modernity is concerned is instrumental rather than value-oriented. Modernity with its emphasis on reason as a servile instrument of vested interests has brought about more woes than happiness to the people. It is therefore necessary to have faith in core values. A constructive critique of modernity and emphasis on values like compassion, justice and equality of all human beings and their dignity and worthiness is highly necessary. Modernity *per se* should not be our goal; modernity as enabling factor to enrich our lives with its much wider reach to technological means for problem solving should be welcomed. Thus it will be seen that healthy faith in core values is the greatest asset for us and hence religion, with its emphasis on faith would provide meaningfulness to our lives. Reason and science, on the other hand, would ensure success and enable us to solve problems. One must thus attempt a creative blend of meaningfulness and successfulness. Life cannot be bereft of the either.

What these essays on Islam present here is an attempt to create this blend. In the collection of essays written from time to time some degree of repetition is inevitable. The repetition is necessary to some extent to strengthen the argument. I plead with my readers to bear with me in this respect. I hope they will. These essays are based on my conviction and it is unnecessary that all will agree with me. I would welcome any constructive debate on the subject.

Bombay
2.8.200

Asghar Ali Engineer

CHAPTER 1

Religion and Peace in Twenty-First Century

In this new millennium, it would be interesting to see how religion faces new challenges in this present century. The World Conference for Religion and Peace (WCRP), an international organization based in New York organized a four-day international conference in Amman, Jordan (November 25-29, 1999), to define the role of religion in promoting world peace in the twenty-first century. Some fifteen religions leaders from 100 odd countries represented in this conference. Top religious leaders and heads of religious communities participated in the discussion. What was most interesting was that the Jewish, Christian and Muslim leaders from the conflict-torn Bosnia and Kosovo were also present. They talked to each other face to face and vowed to promote peace in their respective regions.

Raisul Ulama Mustafa Cervic, the Chief Mufti of Bosnia-Herzegovina made some interesting remarks. He pointed out that it was too dangerous to leave politics to politicians alone and similarly too hazardous to leave theology to theologians alone. It was, needless to say, professional politicians and theologians who were at the root of the problem. It was true that politics or theology should not be left to professionals. Any common man had the right to be involved both in politics as well as in theology. When it was left to only the professionals, they ignored interests of the common people and promoted their own interests.

Another important question to be answered, 'Is religion alone responsible for the conflict in the world?' Conflicts in many parts of the world like Bosnia or Kosovo appear to be due to religion. Prince Hassan bin Talal of Jordan maintained that it was not religion, but politics that was the cause. Hassan Talal said, "We believe in positive engagement as partners in a world which is becoming increasingly interconnected and interdependent, and where borders are becoming less meaningful, rather disintegrating." He further said "We are moving towards a 'single world' with a single agenda. We want all people and all cultures to contribute to the formulation of this agenda' so that it will reflect our mutual interests and concerns." He made a significant remark, "For a 'single world' with a single agenda formulated according to the value system of one culture—to the exclusion of others—will be a world in which injustice and marginalization will inevitably lead to conflict and further, to war. However, a 'a single world' built upon ten thousand cultures, a world in which commonalties are the foundation and particularities are the cornerstones, will be characterized by cooperation. This is the only basis for common living and a joint effort necessary for the construction of a brighter future in which all individuals and all communities have the means to achieve their potential."

There is much truth in what Hassan bin Talal observed. The problem is precisely what he pointed out. The West has its own agenda and wants to impose it on the unwilling peoples of Asia and Africa. All those who participated in the conference felt that mutual respect for each other's religious traditions and cultures is very necessary for peace. It is when the West determines the agenda for the whole world that Usama bin Laden are born who, in order to fight western hegemony, promote religious hatred and extremism. The likes of Usama use religious vocabulary that is as dangerous as armament. In a lighter vein Mustafa Cervic of Bosnia suggested that there should be disarmament of extremist vocabulary, like 'holy war' and 'holy peace' should take its place.

Rabbi David Rosen from Israel was of the opinion that, though it is important that one should love ones neighbour, but sometimes this principle can be applied negatively—say if my neighbour hates me I will also hate him. This will again promote conflict and bloodshed. So he felt it is essential to emphasize that regardless of how the other behaves and regardless of the pain of your own experience, one must not loose sight of the fact that every human being, regardless of race, colour, creed or sex, is of inestimable transcendent divine value. Accordingly, we must respect for each person's life and dignity, regardless of whether or not they behave correctly and regardless of one's own bitter experiences. However, this is too moralistic to work successfully in the world of ordinary mortals. One wishes all human beings were like the ones Rabbi David Rosen suggests. Rabbi also said, "The challenge of common living is precisely the ability to overcome our own sense of pain and alienation so that we may see the other as a child of God." He was right in pointing out that an overwhelming number of the members of our religious communities are trapped in their own very real historic and even contemporary sense of victimhood. This is true in Northern Ireland, in the former Yugoslavia, in Sri Lanka, in the Middle East, and throughout the world where territorial conflicts exist involving human identities, inextricably bound up with religious cultural factors. In all such contexts and beyond them, the various protagonists feel that they have been someone's victims and they are not genuinely accepted and respected by the other."

This is, needless to say, unless we accept the other with all sense of his/her dignity there cannot be peace. Mutual acceptability and respect for other's dignity is what is lacking and we often end up blaming the religion. Religion and religious values can only be a guide for us. What is important is to bring a revolution within us and develop a culture of respecting the other and accepting him/her as he/she is. It is sense of our superiority that brings us in headon conflict with. We think that others threatens our existence, our domination and hence, we seek to maintain our domination through assertion of our superiority which is often imaginary. It results in rejection of the other and hence conflicts.

Archbishop of Canterbury Carey posed a question, like Prince Hassan bin Talal, "Do religions cause conflict?" But at the same time he also posed another question, "Can religion resolve conflict?" While the answer for former is negative, the one for the later can be positive if religion is not made an instrument of promoting selfish interests. Though, to promote selfish interests is quite contrary to the very spirit of religion. Similarly, the Grand Mufti of Al-Azhar Sheikh Tantawi profusely quoted from the Qur'an and the Prophet's traditions to show that Islam means peace and there is no place for belligerence of any kind.

What role religion can play in the present century? Will religion be sidelined in view of the breathtaking technological progress or will it be a valuable resource for peace in the coming years or a source of conflict? These are the questions which have to be grappled with and one has to find answers to them. Religion is not a source of conflict, but it can be a valuable resource for peace. Religious identities clash as these identities signify much more than mere religious beliefs. A religious identity signifies, cultural and territorial hegemony, a conflict with the other who competes for these cultural and territorial spaces. Also, religious identities are, more often than not, the signifiers of specificities that are sought to be contested by other cultural identities. The battles for political or cultural supremacy are fought through assertion of religious identities. This possibility has tremendously increased in view of globalization. Globalization seeks to steamroll all other cultures and impose western secular and consumerist values over the people of Asia and Africa who not only are rich in their own traditional cultures, but also are having a feeling of deprivation vis-à-vis the developed western world which has pushed them to the margin of existence.

It is this marginalized sense of existence and acute sense of exploitation that fuels violent conflicts in the region. Unless this imbalance is corrected, there cannot be hope of meaningful coexistence. One also has to bear in mind that today's world is basically pluralist in character. Rapid means of transportation cause mass migration both within and outside the country. Large number of people are migrating to other (western countries) countries for better prospects. The migrants either compete with the local people for jobs or become a source of cheap labour causing deep resentment among the natives. These battles are often fought under the garb of religious or cultural identities. Thus, globalization and mass migration are fuelling religious and cultural conflicts both in Asian and African countries as well as in western countries.

In coming days this process will be more intensified causing more religio-cultural conflicts. More the conflict, greater the need for coexistence. However, coexistence will be difficult if there is no sincere attempt to build a just society. It is in this respect that religion can become an important resource for justice and peace. If religious values, rather than religious rituals, are asserted, there will be greater possibility of building a just and peaceful society. It must be noted that the core values of all religions are complimentary rather than contradictory. If Hinduism and Jainism stresses non-violence, Buddhism stresses compassion, Christianity stresses love, Islam stresses justice and equality, these core values can become an important resource for a more meaningful and peaceful society.

Besides this there will be more important challenges facing the religion in coming days. These challenges are already surfacing. One of the greatest challenges is that of gender justice. There is not a single gender just society today, neither in the 'advanced' western society nor in traditional Asian and African societies. Unfortunately the World Conference for Religion and Peace (WCRP) also did not address this question adequately. Though, some people did refer to it, it was only in passing. The women in this conference did not even have important role to play. The question of gender justice will be the most fundamental question in coming years. Without addressing this question it will not be possible to build a just society, much less a peaceful one. Gender justice is quite rampant in all the countries of the world, particularly in the developing countries of Asia and Africa. In many societies the problem is very acute. There is what is known as 'honour killings' Those women who marry against the will of the parents or even develop some kind of relationship with men of their choice are killed in the name of honour of the family. This is quite rampant in tribal areas of Pakistan. Recently when a married woman from Northwest Frontier Area of Pakistan wanted divorce from her husband it was thought to be against the honour of the family and was shot dead at the instance of her own parents in the office of her lawyer. The parents were highly educated and well off. This is called 'honour killing' and the culprits escape clutches of law.

It is legally condoned in many Muslim countries like Egypt and even in a liberal country like Jordan. When a bill was brought in the Jordanian Parliament to amend the criminal procedure Code 360 to punish the guilty of 'honour killing' as ordinary culprits, the conservatives opposed it tooth and nail, saying it will increase the cases of illegitimate sex and corruption of morals and threaten the very basis of family life. The amendment of course could not be passed. The conservatives carried the day. In Sindh, Pakistan, the feudal lords have devised ingenious way to save their land being divided through inheritance of their daughters. They marry off their daughters to holy Qur'an and thus deprive them of their legitimate right to marry a man. The woman has to lead a life of virginity and 'piety' She cannot even protest, let alone break the shackles of her 'marriage' with the holy book.

Such killings and such marriages have, of course, no justification in the Islamic law and is, yet, widely practised in several Islamic countries. And even when these practices are totally contrary to Islamic teachings the ulama either keep silent or lend their support to them in the name of 'purity of morals' and sanctity of family life. Now with greater democratization of societies and greater awareness of women of their fundamental rights such antediluvian practices are causing grave social tensions and great injustice to women. The theologians and Islamic jurists have to meet this challenge and banish such grossly unjust practices. No religion, much less Islam, comes in the way of gender justice. It is only customs and traditions of patriarchal society, which have accorded the status of sanctity to these practises. In view of increased awareness of rights among women these practices cannot and should not be perpetuated. However, our traditional societies are still not prepared to abolish them. And, yet, we are boasting of preparing ourselves to face challenges of the present century or present millennium.

In India too, if a woman marries with a man of inferior caste—she is often beheaded in villages in front of all. At times even a man is executed for daring to marry the woman of higher caste. Also, in certain parts of India there is the custom of child marriage. Infants still in the lap of their mother are married off. In these cases also it is the woman who suffers more in her adulthood as the man is free to marry a woman of his choice, if he does not like the one whom he married in his infancy, but a woman cannot do that. Of course such marriages are not sanctioned by the scriptures, but are part of social baggage. Also, there is more horrifying tradition of *sati* (burning the wife on the funeral pyre of her husband). Though not widely prevalent, still one comes across instances of *sati* what is more painful is its celebration by men and women and even constructing a temple on the site to worship the *sati*. There are more widespread instances of bride burning for the sake of dowry. These are of course legally punishable but yet glorified by the society or condoned by it. It is a great challenge before the religious people. They must see that these practices are abandoned being basically against the spirit of religion. No religion, much less, Hinduism, would permit taking human life. Religious people, being compassionate, should not withstand taking of human life. If they want religion to survive with dignity in the present millennium they should bring about psychological as well as spiritual revolution and restore the right of women to live with full dignity and honour. Compassion for life and full honour and dignity for all human beings including women, is the part of basic religious attitude.

The environmental destruction is one of the gravest challenges before humanity today and religious people cannot escape their responsibility in this regard. Industries and motor vehicles have made our environment unfit for healthy life. It is greed of the few rich who pollute, so that they can live in luxury and consume far more than others. It is the rich countries who are consuming beyond all limits. In fact their lust knows no limit. It is also the rich in developing countries who imitate the ways of their counterparts in the West. It is having adverse effect especially on the poor. Many schemes of industrialization or of big dams bring immense misery to the people living in that area. The forests are also indiscriminately destroyed by launching such schemes. Religious people would not approve of such destruction of nature and resultant problems. Universe is the creation of God and God's creation must be respected as well as loved. In fact, as pointed out above, it is over consumption of the rich, which is responsible for the grave danger to our environment. However, all religions in the world stress austere living and avoid overindulgence. It is this fundament of religion that must be propagated by truly religious people. Again, over consumption, apart from polluting the environment, deprives the poor of their right to livelihood. And every religion sensitises its followers to the needs of the weaker sections of society.

Thus, religious people in the world should come together to protect the environment and to uplift and empower the weaker sections of society. While there is so much production and much more potential for more, the poor continue to suffer. The science and technology has great potential to solve the problems of poverty and hunger, but the vested interests come in its way. The WTO regime is also essentially against the poor of the world and it is precisely for this reason that trade unions and other NGOs are demonstrating against the WTO meeting in Seattle in USA. The people of religion, whatever religion they belong to, should throw their weight behind those fighting against the WTO and similar other regimes. But it is unfortunate that the religious heads either consider it beyond the scope of religion or keep silent in order to serve the needs of the powerful rather than those of the poor. The religious establishments should disassociate themselves from these interests. Either they can serve these interests or the interests of religion. The poor are becoming more and more aware of their rights and would question the religious authorities if they ignore their interests. In the present millennium the poor are likely to increasingly question the religious authorities on their attitude about the interests towards them.

There is another most important question—the question of faith and reason which has to be tackled to the satisfaction of the people in this twenty-first century. The medieval age was the age of faith and nineteen and twentieth centuries, the centuries of reason. However, our experience in twentieth century, particularly towards the end shows that reason alone cannot meet the challenges of human existence. Human existence is full of complex challenges and these challenges cannot be met with the help of reason alone. Reason, it must be noted, is a tool, not the goal. Goal is meaningful human existence in this world. Faith is equally necessary to achieve this goal. Neglecting faith results in more complex problems. Nowadays we witness religious extremism throughout the world. The revivalist and fundamentalist movements surface posing great challenge. These movements become violent, as they cannot persuade those at the helm of affairs to listen to their point of view. This violence, it is important to note, is the violence of frustration. And violence in the age of technology can be much more devastating than one can imagine.

Faith, in human existence, plays a very important role. Without faith in values, or for many in higher reality or God, life would be devoid of meaning. Life without faith would be mere hedonism for some and mere animal existence for many. But faith alone cannot, like reason, enable human beings to live purposeful life. Blind faith cannot only be exploitative, but also superstitious. Faith to many is mere solace and comfort of mind. An inquirer's mind, on the other hand, is restless and devoid of comfort which a believer experiences. Nietzsche, in a letter to his sister in 1865, wrote, "...if you wish to strive for peace of soul and pleasure, then believe; but if you wish to be a devotee of truth, then inquire." However, Nietzsche made this observation in nineteenth century which was essentially a century of reason and revolt against blind faith. But by the end of twentieth century we can say that neither superstitious faith nor instrumental reason can serve our purpose. It is creative synthesis of faith in values and reason as an enlightening tool of inquiry that is needed for purposeful human existence.

Thus, religion has to lead the twenty-first century with a new agenda: a creative blend of comforting faith in values and an inquiring reason to construct a meaningful and humane society. A truly religious person should not escape from the responsibility of inquiry after truth. While faith determines the purpose and meaning of life reason unfolds the hidden mysteries of universe. Also, new technological breakthroughs have raised new ethical questions which people of faith have to tackle. Be it cloning or be it unravelling the genetic code, new ethical problems are arising and in coming years many more will arise. The people of faith will have to meet them in the light of their values and with an open and liberal mind, a mind that accepts truth, not mere dogmas, a mind that is dynamic, not static, a mind that is rooted in faith, not in past traditions. People of faith should have a mind free of traditional encumbrances, a mind that is fearless and free. The people of faith should serve the twenty-first century with such a mind.

CHAPTER 2
On the Key-terms in the Qur'an

Every scripture, every religion and every ideology has its own terminology, some terms among them being, what can be described as key-terms. These terms play a very important role in understanding the particular scripture, religion or ideology. In case of a religion it is certain scriptural terms which play a fundamental role. Some of these terms even influence the hermeneutics of the scripture and help formation of basic dogmas of the religion. To understand the key terms of a religion, it is essential to understand properly the underlying spirit of that religion or ideology.

However, all these terms do not play a very seminal role as some particular terms do. But again there may be differences of opinion as to which terms constitute the key terms. These differences may always be there. The selection of these terms will also reflect the ideological inclination of the person who selects. But despite these differences some terms are bound to be common among various selectors. And, as long as these terms are derived directly from the scripture, one should not and cannot object to selection of these terms.

The Islamic terminology is basically derived from the Qur'an which is a revealed scripture according to Muslim belief. This terminology plays significant role not only in understanding the Qur'an, but also deeply influences the lives of Muslims both in terms of beliefs and practices. Though, of course the selection of the key terms matters, as pointed out above, but whatever the terms—as long as they are derived directly from the Qur'an—they leave their impress on the Muslim beliefs and practices. We have selected a few key terms for discussion in this Chapter which involve not only the Muslim beliefs, but also the Islamic value-system.

The most basic term of course is *din*. It is generally translated as 'religion' in English. It is, of course, not entirely correct. This term is so basic that Allah says in the Qur'an, "Today have I perfected your *din* and have bestowed upon you the full measure of My blessings, and willed that Islam shall be your *din.*" Thus, one can understand how important is this term *din* in the Qur'an.

What is the meaning of the term *din* in Arabic language? We come to know from the lexicographers that it is used in various ways. Some of the senses in which *din* is used are to conquer, power, governance, regime, law, constitution, law and order, judgement, reward and punishment, etc. It also means, obedience and acceptance, according to lexicographers, *Taj* and *Muhit.* We also find in *Lata'if al-Lughat* that *din* means accountability, overpowering and managing. In *Kitab al-Istihqaq*, its given meanings are obedience and community (*millat*).

In the Qur'an this word *din* has been used in all these senses. In 2:131 it has been used in the sense of submission to the law of the nourisher of this universe (*aslamtu li Rabbil Alamin*). And in 3:18 *din* is equated with Islam, i.e., *din* means Islam which in turn means surrendering to the will of Allah. In 56:86 it has been used in the sense of authority. Similarly in 9:29 it has been used as submission to the divine system. And in 12:76 it has been used in the sense of law *Din al-malik* (law of the king). In 24:2 the words (*Dinillah*) Law of Allah has been used. But in 24:25 the word *din* has been used in the sense of reward.

In the first chapter of the Qur'an we have the term *yaum al-din.* It can mean the day of accounting, the day when Allah will dominate and His servants will surrender. It can also mean the day of rewards and punishments. In 82:18-19 the Qur'an first asks, How do you know what is *yaum al-din*" and then replies, "The day when no soul controls aught for another soul. And the command on that day is Allah's." Thus, the day of *din* is in fact the day of complete domination by Allah and Allah's set laws. Everything will be judged according to that law alone and rewards and punishments will be dispensed without any partiality or injustice. No soul can escape on that day if it has done wrong and no soul can be deprived of its reward if it has done good. Thus, *din* also means domination and absolute power which rests with Allah alone. The Qur'an also describes Allah as *malik-e-yaum al-din*, i.e., Allah will be the master of that day and it will be Allah's power, Allah's law which will prevail. *Yaum* in Arabic does not necessarily mean one day, but a whole period. In that sense *yaum al-din* does not necessarily refer to one day, but a whole period, a period when Allah's law will prevail and in that period as in the verse 82:18-19 no human being will be dominated by another human being, but by Allah's law alone which will be just. Thus in that period absolute justice will prevail and it will be an ideal period. Every human being will be free and subject only to the just law of Allah.

Din, also means system and according to *din Allah* it means the system given by Allah and this system fixes limits of our freedom and determination, our latitude and dependence. If human beings follow this system strictly they will be emancipated from slavery of selfish desire and will experience real spiritual freedom and contentment. In the first chapter *Al-Fatihah*, Allah has been described as *Rabb* and *Rahim*, Sustainer and Merciful or Compassionate. Thus Allah, in His capacity as sustainer and merciful has provided abundantly for all living beings, be they humans or animals or plants. But it is human greed which destroys the just system of Allah and its sustenance for all and enslaves other human beings and misappropriates their share and also destroys the ecology of the system as well. The humanity can be freed and *yaum al-din* can be enforced only if Allah's law dominates and absolute justice prevails and everybody is rewarded or punished only according to this divine system called *din*.

The word *madinah* according to some authorities is also derived from *din*, i.e., place of *din*. Thus, *madinah* is the place where justice is dispensed according to divine law and where every one obeys the divine system. Madinat-un-Nabi was the city of the Prophet where the Prophet enforced the *din* of Allah. He made it a just place. Ibn Faris says that *madinah* is derived from *din* because in city one has to follow the law of the government. No city can experience law and order without proper governance.

It is also important to note that no where the Qur'an describes Islam as *madhab*, but it describes Islam as *din*. *Madhab* means a way, whereas *din* as pointed out, is much more comprehensive term. Various schools of jurisprudence are referred to as *madhab*, but not Islam. Islam can be described only as a *din*. *Madhab* can divide, but not *din*. *Din* unites. That is why the Qur'an makes it clear that *din* is one, i.e., the Qur'an talks of *wahdat-e-din* unity of *din*. If one follows *din*, or divine

commands and divine system there will be no differences between
religions. These differences have been brought about by human beings
for their own vested interests.

The next term we want to take up is 'Islam'. It is derived from the
root s.l.m. It is interesting to note that salama from which Islam has been
derived means to be purified from all defects and evils or to be protected
from them. It means one has avoided these defects. For example, we
read in 2:71 about the cow belonging to Bani Israel that it is "sound
without any blemish in her". Thus, *salama* basically means to be perfect
without any blemish and to bring all our good abilities into action rising
above all weaknesses.

The second root meaning of it is to be protected from all eventualities, accidents and difficulties. This meaning of the word pertains
more to health and security. It is in this sense that in Urdu language
we say *salamat* (to be secure). It is interesting that in Philipino language
the word for thanks is *salamat* that is the sentiment of obligation is
expressed by wishing desire for security of the obliging person. In
Arabic also it is said *salima min al-afaati*, i.e., he remained secure from
all troubles. In Qur'an one of the names of Allah is *Salam* (59:23),
i.e., one who is perfect and above all defects. But the compiler of
Taj al-'Urus does not agree with this meaning at all and maintains that
Salam is one who can provide security to others and *Saalim* is one who
is protected by others. Thus, according to *Taj al-'Urus*, Allah is *Salam*
because he protects all others and he saves His creation from disorder
and disturbance.

It is used in, yet, another sense, i.e., peace and order. One who lives
in complete harmony and peace with others is called *al-silm*. To live in
peace and harmony and create such possibility for others. In other
words to create peace and security for the world. Yet, another meaning
is to surrender oneself. It is only when one surrenders to the forces of
law and authority, when human beings surrender to the laws of Allah
and of nature that there can be peace and harmony in the world. It also
means to adopt the middle path avoiding all extremes as extremes bring
about disturbances and disorder. It also means to avoid what is absurd
and meaningless. Also in Arabic usage *al-salemah* is a woman who is
very delicate and beautiful. Thus, it would also mean what is beautiful
and appealing.

In this sense *al-Islam* would mean, as pointed out by Parvez in his *Lughaat al-Qur'an* that system of life which (1) removes all the defects in human beings and his capacities can flower to perfection; (2) in which he remains secure from all troubles and disorders; (3) and which ensures that he goes on developing himself and keeps on rising higher and higher in station; (4) and that he finds himself secure and peaceful and ensures peace and security for others and he does not create trouble or disturbance for others thus, destroying the harmony in the social system; (5) that he obeys the divine laws to the utmost and surrenders himself to Allah with heart and soul; (6) he should adopt the middle way and never resort to either extreme; (7) thus, he will create balance not only within himself, but also in the society.

Thus, it will be seen that to be a Muslim is not just to profess a set of beliefs and perform certain rituals, but much more than that. This is also reflected in *hadith* literature wherein the Prophet has elaborated on ethical conduct. One of the Prophet's pronouncement is that a true Muslim is one in whose hands everyone is safe. This is possible only if one not only consciously strives for peace and harmony, but also never desires what belongs to others and follows an upright path.

Another key term of the holy Qur'an is *rahmah* which is translated as mercy or also as compassion. The Qur'an lays great emphasis on compassion. Two of the Allah's names are *Rahim* and *Rahman*, i.e., Merciful and Compassionate or Dispenser of grace. Mercy for Allah is so fundamental that "He has ordained mercy on Himself" (6:12). Which means that one cannot think of Allah without mercy. The Qur'an also describes the Prophet as *Rahmatul lil Aalamin*, i.e., mercy of the worlds. Thus, both Allah and His Messenger represent mercy and compassion.

It is quite interesting to note that *rahem* means mother's womb and while in mother's womb it is protected from all external influences. Mother's womb nourishes the foetus and it grows within its protected shell. Thus, Allah is also nourisher and sustainer of the whole universe. Every species in the universe grows and flourishes under His protection and because of His *rahmah*. According to *Taj al-'Urus*, *rahmah* is that innate quality which brings about hidden and manifest perfection in a being and it is available freely without any direct or indirect cost.

The Qur'an also uses this word in various ways signifying nour-
ishing, sustenance, growth, compassion, and mercy. It also describes
the food crops which grow as *rahmah* (see verse 30:46). If parents bring
up children it is also described as *rahmah* by the Qur'an (17:24). It is
also important to note that in the very first chapter of the Qur'an, i.e.,
Surah Fatihah, Allah is described as *Rabb al-Aalamin* and *Al-Rahman
al-Rahim*, i.e., He is the Sustainer of the whole world and also the
Compassionate and Merciful. Thus, these are very fundamental attributes of Allah. Mercy and compassion are closely related with sustenance and nourishment.

In fact *Rahim*, according to *Taj al-Urus* is one who generally
provides with the material for sustenance and growth in general and
rahman means one who provides with all intensity and power the help
with sense of compassion in an emergency situation. Thus, it will be
seen that Allah is provider and sustainer of life under all conditions to
ensure growth and development. *Rabb* itself means one who ensures
growth through various stages to perfection.

Rahman also means softness and sensitivity as mercy can flow
from one who is not hard hearted. Thus, a person who has quality of
mercy and compassion is quite sensitive to others suffering. This sensitivity is a sterling quality for a human being. One who is not sensitive
to others suffering cannot qualify to be a good human being. The
Qur'an wants to inculcate this sensitivity to suffering in human beings
to its utmost degree. The Prophet is also reported to have said that it
is more meritorious to feed a hungry person than to pray. The message
is clear. If a person who prays does not develop sensitivity to others
hunger, his/her prayer is an empty ritual. Allah guarantees sustenance
of the whole universe to avoid this suffering of living beings.

It will thus, be seen that Islam is deeply associated with compassion and mercy rather than violence. It is unfortunate that Islam, for
historical and other reasons, has come to be associated with *jihad*
rather than mercy and compassion, peace and harmony. As pointed out
above, Islam itself means peace and security and hence, mercy and
compassion too, are very fundamental aspects of it. Those who associate Islam with *jihad* and violence are hardly aware of the real spirit of
this religion. *Jihad*, as we have shown in our Chapter on "The Concept
of *Jihad* in Islam" itself does not mean war. It means to make efforts

for truth and goodness to prevail. It is only in an extraordinary situation that *jihad* shall take the form of war. The Qur'an, in fact, does not mention the word *jihad* in that sense at all. It only is used in the sense of making efforts.

Yet, another key term in the Qur'an is *hikmah* which is generally translated as wisdom. The Qur'an also uses *'aql, tafakkur,* and *tadabbur* which mean reason, thinking and reflection. Thus, it will be seen that the Qur'an does not encourage blind following of any dogma or belief at all. It appeals to reason, thinking and reflection. It has also been pointed out by some that the Qur'an emphasizes inductive reason and encourages study of nature. The Qur'an says that accept divine guidance after proper thinking and reflection.

Hikmah (wisdom) in a way is a higher form of reason. Reason is not sufficient by itself as it has no criteria to judge. Thus, reason can be used both ways for good as well as for evil. One can use reason to promote self-interest also, as is often done. Reason, it must be noted, is an instrument, not a goal. There is thus, great emphasis in modern civilization on reason, but not on values. Modern society has thus, become totally directionless and the only concern is growth, development and increased gross product. The multi-nationals put reason to their own selfish ends. They do not even hesitate to use unfair means for their own growth.

But *hikmah* (wisdom) is reason synthesized with higher values. *Hikmah* is no mere concern with reason as an instrument, but promotion of higher values as a goal. Justice, equity, equality, human dignity, compassion, humanism are some of these higher values which reason should strive to promote. Thus, *hikmah* is higher than reason. *Hikmah,* however, can never degenerate into unreason. Reason remains its important component. Thus, Allah is described by the Qur'an as *Hakim, 'Alim* and *Khabir,* i.e., Wise, Knower and Informed. Wisdom, knowledge and proper information can never lead to unreason. If any religious belief is based on unreason or irrationality, it must be rejected. Any religious belief must fulfil the criteria of reason and higher values. Such beliefs alone can be compatible with spiritual growth, human values and inner peace and richness.

The root of the word *hikmah* is h.k.m. which basically means to control and stop crossing the limit with firmness. Thus, *hakamat* in

Arabic means reining in the horse in a way which will not allow horse to get out of control (see *Kitab al-Ishtiqaq*). The root of *hakama* also conveys the sense of stopping within the limits so that one does not commit excess. One should know what is the limit beyond which one should not go. And a *Haakim* is one who properly judges the limit and does not allow the people to cross this limit. Thus, one who is appointed to judge and arbitrate is also called *hakam* and government is called *hukumat* because its function is to judge the behaviour of the people and to restrain them from crossing the limits of law.

Allah has been described by the Qur'an as *Ahkam al-Hakimin* (justest of the just) because He lays down the rules of justice and exhorts people not to transcend limits. He is the source of justice and just guidance. And *al-hikmah* carries the sense of judgement which is just and takes into account the rights of every one and does not violate any ones rights. *Hikmah* is that which bridles our unjust tendencies and brings about and promotes what is based on proper balance and would stop disorder and mischief. *Hikmah* is prevention of all that is bad, evil or unjust and violative of what is judged to be right by all.

Qur'an has also been described as *Hakeem* as it provides guidance to us so that a just social order can be brought into existence which is not violative of descent limits. This alone can lead to a stable society. Thus, *istihkam* (firmness, stability) is also derived from this root because it is only just and balanced society which can remain firm and stable. A society which is not based on these values will experience repeated upheavals and instability.

Thus it will be seen that the Qur'an lays great emphasis on *hikmah* (wisdom) as it intends to establish a properly balanced society based on values which ensures growth and development of all human beings and this growth is as much spiritual as material, it should be as much inner as outer material growth. It is this balance between spiritual and material growth which will ensure a humane society. Thus, *hikmah* becomes very fundamental to the Qur'anic discourse. It is, as pointed out before, a synthesis of reason and higher values.

Another key term of the Qur'an is *'adl* and *ihsan* (justice and benevolence). Of course a society based on *hikmah*, as pointed out above, would include *'adl* and *ihsan*, but the Qur'an separately emphasizes these terms. Allah is described by the Qur'an as *'Aadil* and

Muhsin (just and benevolent). *'Adl* has root meaning of balance. What is loaded on the camel has to be equal on both the sides of its hump to balance it and hence, it is called *'idl* and balancing the balance is called *'addal al-mizaan*. Thus, the word *i'tidaal* is also derived from this root and means middle path.

'Adl is very central to the Qur'anic values. The Qur'an gives the concept of a just society. A society whatever the form of its governance, has to be just. The Prophet is reported to have said that a society can survive with unbelief (*kufr*), but not with oppression or lack of justice (*zulm*). The Qur'an, for this reason, does not approve of concentration of wealth in few hands (59:7). Such a course will be violative of justice. Allah, therefore, desires that there should be proper opportunities for all human beings to sustain themselves and grow.

'Adl is not only a key word of the Qur'an, but also the central value of Islam. It is so central that the Qur'an commands Muslims to do justice even to the enemies. The Qur'an says (5:8), "O' you who believe, be upright for Allah, bearers of witness with justice; and let not hatred of a people incite you not to act equitably. Be just; that is nearer to being God-consciousness..." It will be seen from this verse that justice is at the very centre of Islamic ethics. One cannot be a Muslim without being just. It is in this spirit of justice that Allah favours the weaker sections of society and promises them to make leaders and inheritors of this earth. (28:5). The other term used for justice in the Qur'an is *qist*. Like *'adl* it also means balancing. It carries the sense of fulfilling with justice that is someones due without any favour to any one. Thus, a true Muslim will never curtail in what is others due.

Ihsan is another key term in the Qur'an. Its root is h.s.n. We find in *Muhit* that *hasan* means correct balance in the limbs of the body and popularly what appeals to the eyes is called *hasan*. Thus, *hasan* means beauty which is basically due to proper balance in body. And *ihsan* would mean to correct the balance and to restore the beauty. According to Raghib *ihsan* is of two types, i.e., to do favour to someone and restore beauty and balance in him or to create balance in ones own self through good conduct. Raghib also says that *'adl* means to give others what is their due, but *ihsan* means to give more than that. In popular usage *ihsan* means doing good to others.

Thus, according to the Qur'an one should not only do justice to others, but also good to others. One should be benevolent and Allah has been described as *Muhsin*—the Benevolent. Doing *ihsan* is part of higher ethics. To keep our society running smoothly both *'adl* and *ihsan* is necessary. It is only through *'adl* and *ihsaan* that human fellowship will be strengthened.

Thus, it will be seen that the key terms in the Qur'an besides *din* and Islam are *rahmah, hikmah, 'adl* and *ihsan,* i.e., compassion, wisdom, justice and benevolence. It is these terms which represent the true spirit of Islam, not *jihad* and blind faith. These are the higher moral concepts and the Qur'an is infused with the spirit of these higher morals. *Jihad* also has to be non-violent as far as possible. Violence is permitted only to defend oneself. The Islamic *da'wah* (call) also has to be based on goodly exhortation and wisdom (16:125), in no sense it could be aggressive, let alone violent. The misconduct of some Muslim rulers should not be confused with the Qur'anic injunctions.

CHAPTER 3

Maulana Azad and His Concept of Unity of Religion

Maulana Abul Kalam Azad's *Tarjuman al-Qur'an* has its own place in the *Tafsir* literature of India. The Maulana wrote *Tarjuman al-Qur'an*, first during his internment in Ranchi during late twenties, which was destroyed by the British police, while raiding his house before arresting him in order to scour 'subversive literature'. Maulana Azad wrote it again during late thirties, but could not complete it, being very busy with political affairs. What we have today is an incomplete commentary. It is interesting to note that Sir Syed also could not complete his commentary, though for different reasons. Both commentaries are of great value, despite being incomplete.

Maulana Azad was greatly influenced by Sir Syed and his modern religious outlook. He used to wait for any of Sir Syed's books with great keenness and would finish reading it as soon as he received one. Maulana Azad was a great religious thinker in his own right and while writing *tafsir* struck his own original path. There are similarities and differences between Sir Syed's religious views and those of Maulana Azad. Both were influenced by modern liberalism and both differed from classical commentators, particularly on social and political issues. Both had great regard, though within certain limits, for women's rights. Also both stood in favour of inter-religious harmony. But they profoundly differed from each other on their approach to the British rule—Sir Syed almost favouring it and Azad completely rejecting it.

Maulana Azad made seminal contribution to the *tafsir* literature through his concept of what he called *wahdat-e-din* (the unity of religion) with which we would like to deal here in this chapter. It must be however, emphasized, that Azad was not the first to do so. Earlier, other Muslim religious thinkers too had dealt with this concept in the pre-modern period both in India and outside. The sufis, it is well-known, had struck their own path in this respect and believed in truth of all religions. The sufis particularly belonging to the *Chishti Silsila* (the Chishti school) to which Khwaja Moinuddin, Baba Farid and Nizamuddin Awliyah belonged. They all laid great stress on the respect for religions other than Islam. Muhiyuddin Ibn Arabi, the great promoter of the Sufi concept, referred to *wahdat al-wujud* goes as far as describing his heart as the centre of love for God and hence, terms it as a church, a synagogue, a temple, and a mosque. The holy Qur'an also maintains that Allah's name is remembered in all religious places of worship be they of Christians, Jews or Muslims. Thus, the Qur'an says, "And if Allah did not repeal some people by others, *cloisters, and churches, and synagogues, and mosques in which Allah's name is much remembered,* would have been pulled down." (22-40) (Emphasis mine). Thus, it is clear that the Qur'an considers all places of religious worship wherein Allah's name is remembered (though in different forms) as worthy of respect and hence, needs to be protected. Some Islamic thinkers have even pointed out that in this verse, *masjid* has been mentioned last and other religious places precede it. No wonder than Muhiyuddin Ibn Arabi considered his heart as church, synagogue and masjid wherein Allah's name is remembered.

But apart from sufi tradition, other Islamic thinkers like Shah Waliyullah of Delhi who was a great Islamic theologian and a thinker of eminence also refers to certain verses of the Qur'an to maintain that all religions are worthy of respect. He also subscribes to the concept of *wahdat-e-din* (unity of religion) which he discusses in his magnum opus *Hujjatillahil Balighah.*

The question arises, what is the contribution of Maulana Azad in this respect? The difference lies in the way he presents the concept. He presents it very systematically and quotes profusely from the holy Qur'an to support his contentions. He also quotes from scriptures of different religions, including Hinduism to prove his point. His knowledge in comparative religious studies is also quite sound. He also tries to find support for his theory of unity of religion in various other ways. Thus, compared to other theologians Maulana Azad is the most systematic propounder of the concept of *wahdat-e-din* in modern times in India. Thus, he, among Islamic theologians is closest to the sufis of medieval period.

Maulana Azad also points out that the prevailing thought system of every period of time (*har ahad ka fikri asar*) influences the commentator of the Qur'an. Thus, the Qur'anic commentary cannot be written in vacuum. He also points out that it is a matter of great pride that the Islamic thinkers, the 'ulama never compromised the principles of Islam under political pressures, but the influence of prevalent thought system in a given period does not exercise itself only through political structures, but also through countless other ways including psychological and social. And once these doors of influence are opened it is very difficult to close them even if one wants. No mind, Azad points out and rightly so, can remain safe from these influences. Thus, it is not true to maintain that there is only and only one way of understanding the Qur'an. Moreover, it is also important to note that often the scriptural language is rich in symbolism which can be interpreted in a number of ways depending on one's mental capacity, background and experience. New meanings unfold themselves with new developments and new experiences. Maulana Azad was open to new interpretations and was receptive to new developments. And that is why he could grasp richness of the Qur'anic symbolism.

The Maulana was also aware that after the 10-11th century and particularly after the sack of Baghdad in 1258, there began a sharp decline in the creative interpretation and the Muslim theologians began to stick to earlier interpretations. Thus, it was almost an end of *ijtihad* in Islam. The theologians took pride in imitating their predecessors and any deviation from this path came to be condemned and was considered almost heretical. Now began the period of *taqlid* (blind imitation). Thus, since that period there was no worthwhile contribution by any *mufassir* (commentator). According to Azad now what all the commentators did was to write few notes on the margin of existing exegesis. He even considers the classical exegesis by *Baidawi* and *Jalalain* as nothing more than painting the existing house rather than constructing a new one.

Maulana Azad of course does not approve of what is called *tafsir bi' al-ra'i* exegesis or explanation of the Qur'anic verses by one's own personal opinion. But, at the same time, he points out that it does not mean that one should not use ones intellect and vision (*basirat*) in explaining the meaning of the verses. He cites the Qur'anic verse to substantiate his point. "Do they not reflect on the Qur'an? Or, are there locks on the hearts?" (47:24) This verse clearly demonstrates that the verses should be understood with the power of ones intellect and vision. Constant reflection on the contents of the Qur'an is most desirable. It is only through deep reflection on these verses that new meanings will dawn on the exegetes.

However, Azad is also aware of the dangers of such a course. If one stretches such a process to another extreme, it can result in importing such meanings which do not accord with the intention of the revelation at all. He gives example of some sufis who tried to discover hidden meanings in these verses and strayed far away. They did not leave any portion of the Qur'an from this exercise. And it is this which should be construed as exegesis based on ones personal opinion (*tafsir bi' al-ra'i*). Such an exegesis has done considerable harm. The Muslims also used the Greek knowledge of various sciences including the knowledge of Greek astronomy to understand the verses of the Qur'an referring to stars and other heavenly objects. This is also, according to the Maulana *tafsir bi' al-ra'i*. (For these remarks see Maulana Azad's Preface to the First Edition of *Tarjuman al-Qur'an* written in the Meerut Jail on 16th November, 1930).

We have thrown some light on the methodology of exegesis adopted by Maulana Azad so that we can understand his approach to understanding of the Qur'an. He carves out a delicate path of his own which is different from that of the classical commentators and, yet, is not alien to the spirit of the Qur'an. Though, many might differ from Azad's understanding of the Qur'an, but no one can challenge his sincerity, integrity and scholarship. His is a fresh and profound approach. Maulana Azad was no mere theoretician or a theologian. He was much more than that. He was deeply involved in the freedom struggle and gave great importance to throwing away the yoke of foreign rule. It was this profound involvement with great emotional intensity in his country's freedom from foreign rule that shaped his understanding of the text of the Qur'an.

He also had to strike partnership with members of other faiths particularly Hindus to succeed in his struggle and hence, his fundamental emphasis on Hindu-Muslim unity, and on unity of all religions (*wahdat-e-din*). He evolved this concept on the basis of his own struggle. The Qur'an, it is important to note, did not lay emphasis merely on the philosophical interpretation and the world to come (*aakhirah*), but also on transforming it, on changing it and hence, its emphasis on justice, equality, freedom, and human dignity. It strongly favours weaker sections of society so much so that it says: "And we desired to bestow a favour upon those who were deemed weak in the land, and to make them the leaders and to make them the heirs. And grant them power in the land..." (28:5-6) Azad grasped this spirit of Qur'an and engaged himself in transforming the destiny of his country, land of his ancestors. He could not see it enslaved by foreign rulers.

Any scholar of the eminence of Azad who is also engaged in transforming and rebuilding destiny of his country could not have accepted the existing exegetic (*tafsir*) literature. He was bound to bear his vision which evolved from his own social and political struggle to bear on understanding the text of the Qur'an. He was fighting for the oppressed, for the enslaved and for exploited. And all the oppressed, irrespective of their religious faith must unite to overthrow the yoke of enslavement and exploitation. To fight for the weak and oppressed is stressed in the Qur'an which says, "And what reason have you not to fight in the way of Allah, and of the weak among the men and the women and the children, who say: Our Lord, take us out of this town, whose people are oppressors, and grant from Thee a friend, and grant us from Thee a helper." (4:75) Thus, the Maulana did not base his understanding of the Qur'anic text on mere speculation or opinion, but on his own struggle for the weak in keeping with the directives of the Qur'an. In doing so he was following the example of the Prophet and his companions who engaged themselves in transforming the world to make it worthy of human dignity. The Prophet had led life full of struggle to establish sense of dignity, justice, brotherhood, and equality. He rejected all comforts in favour of struggle. Thus, action (*'amal*) is the central theme of Qur'an. The Prophet's life was full of action and in this action-oriented transformative project the Prophet sought help of all across religious faith. Thus, he brought about a pact with the Jews, Christians and Pagan tribes of Madina (known as the *mithaq-e-madina*) for realization of the transformative project. Allah, according to the Qur'an, sent His messengers to the different parts and to people of the world for the same purpose. The Qur'an thus, accepts the truth of

all other religions sent prior to Islam. Azad lays stress on this aspect
of the Qur'anic teaching while stressing his concept of *wahdat-e-din*.
Also, in keeping with the Qur'anic teaching he also maintains that,
though *shari`ah* may differ the essence of *din* cannot. While rituals,
customs and traditions differ, *din* is one.

Mualana Azad emphasizes, in keeping with the teachings of the
Qur'an, that one of the most essential element of *din* is the doctrine of
unity of God what the Qur'an refers to as *tawhid*. Azad brings to bear
his vast knowledge of other religions, including most primitive ones, to
show that in all these religions the doctrine of unity of God was very
fundamental. Thus, he refers to various anthropological and sociological
studies done in the nineteenth century and examines the evolution of
beliefs of various tribes and nations to show the presence of the
doctrine of oneness of God. He refers, in this connection to the beliefs
of people of Mohenjodaro also. Thus, he points out that the people of
Mohenjodaro believed in *tawhid*, i.e., unity of God. They were not,
according to Azad's research, idol worshippers. They called their God
as, 'Oun' which resembled the Sanskrit word 'Undwan'. According to
their belief this One God rules all over the world and His laws are
supreme.

Similarly, all the Semitic tribes from which various other tribes in
West Asia and Africa, including 'Aad, Thumud, Assurians, Sumerians,
Aramians, etc., formed, believed, according to Azad, in oneness of God.
Azad says, "...a study of Semitic group of languages—Hebrew, Syriac,
Aramaic, Chaldean, Himyarita and Arabic—discloses that a special style
of word formation and of sound had been in vogue among the Semitic
peoples to denote the Supreme Being. The alphabets *A*, *L*, and *H*
combined in varied form to constitute the term by which this Supreme
Being was to be styled. The Chaldean and Syriac term '*Ilahia*', the
Hebrew '*Ilaha*' and the Arabic '*Ilah*' are of this category. It is the *Ilah*
in Arabic which assumed the form *Allah* and was applied exclusively
to the Creator of the Universe." (See English Tran. Of *Tarjuman
al-Qur'an* by Syed Abdul Latif, Vol. I, Asia Publishing House, 1965,
pp. 14-15)

Thus, Azad, among other things, shows that the concept of unity
of God which is essence of *din* has existed among all human beings,
including those who lived in pre-historic times. This should constitute

the basis of unity of religion apart from other aspects. Azad, quoting the Qur'anic verses, tries to show that all human beings were one on the basis of guidance received from Allah and it was later that some strayed from the right path creating differences and destroying the basis for unity. Thus, he quotes the Qur'anic verse—"And (all) people were but a single people (i.e., they were not lost on different paths) then they differed." (Azad's words in parenthesis) (10:19)

He quotes another verse from the Qur'an to buttress his argument. The Qur'an says, "Mankind was a single nation (i.e., they were on one path of natural guidance, then they differed). So Allah sent prophets as bearers of good news and as warners, and He revealed with them the Book with truth, that it might judge between people concerning that in which they differed" (Azad's words in parenthesis) (2: 213). Thus, at one time entire humanity was united on the right path and it was later that some went astray and differed and whenever they differed God sent his prophets to judge their differences with justice according to the revealed book.

In this connection Azad's concept of *rububiyah* (sustenance or divine providence) is also quite significant. He derives this concept from the first chapter of the Qur'an *Surah Fatihah* which refers to *Rabb al-'Alamin* (one who nourishes or sustains all). Allah is the nourisher of entire universe which includes not only plant, animal and human life, but all other objects. Allah makes no distinction between one or the other as far as His function of sustenance is concerned. Azad goes to the extent of saying that God not only sustains and develops all, but does so in uniform way. Thus, he says, "The strangest thing about this scheme of Providence, though the most patent, is its uniformity and the harmony underlying it. The method and manner of providing means of sustenance for every object of existence are the same everywhere."

This concept of *rububiyah* as developed by Azad has bearing on the unity of humankind too. Allah sustains everyone, even misguided ones. One should not discriminate between human beings on the basis of ones belief. It is against the divine function of *rububiyah*. The sufis go even further. They maintain that even one who does not believe in God should also not be discriminated against. Here I am reminded of a story from the Sufi lore. Prophet Ibrahim (Abraham) did not eat without a guest. Once it so happened that no guest came for three days. Ibrahim

suffered pangs of hunger, but did not eat without a guest. When pangs
of hunger became unbearable he went out in search of a guest. He
found an aged person sitting alone. Ibrahim invited him to dine with
him. On the way home prophet Ibrahim while conversing with him came
to know he is an atheist. Prophet Ibrahim was angry learning about his
atheism. On this the divine voice told him, "O' Ibrahim you could not
tolerate this old man for few minutes whom I tolerated for seventy
years!" The lesson is that one should be patient and tolerant and if
necessary, dialogue with the person with wisdom to make him aware of
his erroneous views while respecting his integrity as a person.

Azad, as pointed out above, was a profound scholar of not only
Islam but also of comparative religion. It takes detailed study of the first
volume of his *Tarjuman al-Qur'an* to gauge the depth of his scholarship
in comparative religion. He had studied almost all the religions of the
world and has thrown light on their teachings in his *magnum opus*.
While trying to demonstrate truth of religions other than Islam he
throws light on the teachings of Hinduism also. On the concept of unity
of God while examining the contents of *Rig Veda*, he says that in the
early *slokas* of *Rig Veda* one finds concept of nature worship, but one
also feels the concept of *tawhid* emerging side by side. In the *slokas*
of section 10 in particular one clearly perceives the prominence of the
concept of *tawhid*. Now in this section the concept of polytheism was
evolving into monotheism. But he also maintains that even in the earlier
sections one can clearly discern the existence of concept of monotheism.
The number of deities which spread over three hundred and thirty-three
became limited to three spheres, i.e., to earth, atmosphere and sky. And
then it developed into one sustainer *al-Arbabi* (Henotheism). Then this,
'Henotheism' further contracts and the greatest being taking others into
its fold emerges. This being can be seen at times in *Varun* and at other
times in *Inder* or in *Agni*. But at last one sees the emergence of one
creator called *Prajapati* or *Vishwakarman* (Creator of All). He is the
reality behind all creation. He then quotes from the 10th section. "He
is the Spirit of Universe, source of all Energies, He is Eternity, never to
decay, that which breathes without breathing, We cannot see Him, We
cannot cognise Him in a comprehensive way. He is Ekam Sat (One
Truth)" (Section 10:2-121).

Maulana Abul Kalam also draws our attention to the Hindu refined concept of the 'Ultimate Reality' which can neither be known, nor defined, i.e., the concept of *neti, neti* (not this, not this). He calls it the concept of negative attributes of God. The God cannot be defined through positive attributes, i.e., in terms of what He is, but what He is not. This is very sophisticated concept. Abul Kalam explains its significance thus: whatever attributes we ascribe to God will be product of our limited mind and our mind is imprisoned in possibilities and relativities and is, therefore, incapable of conceiving an unlimited Reality. And when such a mind conceives it will concretise the Absolute.

He draws our attention to another aspect of Hinduism that is *Upanishad* which also tries to give positive attributes to Brahman and gives it the form of Ishwar with certain attributes and once Brahman (Absolute Reality) became Ishwar imaginative intellect carved out beautiful attributes and thus, the belief in Unity of Being was transformed into a Being with positive attributes, i.e., *nirgun* (a being without attributes) became *sagun* (a being with attributes). When we study these attributes, Azad says, we come accross a higher concept which synthesizes both negative and positive attributes. Thus, in the Hindu theology, God is one, without any parallel, none is like Him, He is above all the limitations of time and space, He is eternal, He is imperishable, He is the Creator, He is the Protector, He is the Destroyer, He is the Prime Cause, all creations are from Him, are in existence because of Him and will return to Him, He is Light, He is Ultimate, He is Beauty, He is Purity, He is Merciful, and He is the object of all worship and love. Azad then goes on to discuss the causes of development of polytheism in the Hindu tradition. He says that this refined concept of *tawhid* got mixed up with polytheistic ideas and the concept of unity of Being and unity of attributes could not strike deeper roots and polytheism became so rooted in the hearts and minds of Indians that it was impossible to uproot it and many gods and goddesses came into being under the over all suzerainty of one God.

After throwing light on Hindu concept of God, he also discusses the Buddhist approach. He maintains that Buddha's silence about God should not be construed to mean his negation of God. His silence was more akin to what he calls *nafi' sifat* (negating attributes of God) and not negating God Himself (*nafi' zat*) and he emphasizes that negating attributes of God is such that human being is totally helpless in defining or comprehending God and there is no way except to keep silent. Thus, Abul Kalam Azad interpretes Buddha's silence about God in his own characteristic way. Azad also thinks that another reason for Buddha's silence about God was the widespread practice of idol worship in various forms in his time. Buddha's refined intellect could not approve of it as a means to reach the ultimate Reality. Buddha, according to Azad tried to remove such block to ultimate Reality and concentrated on the nobility of deeds in life. The natural outcome of this, Azad says, was to reject the Brahminic dogmas of gods' worship and to emphasize that the salvation does not lie in worshipping these gods, but in the knowledge of truth and in truth-oriented action (i.e., the eightfold way). Azad thinks that this relative rejection of God by Buddha (i.e., negation of popular idol worship) gradually took the form of absolute rejection of God due mainly to exaggeration in opposition to Brahmanic religion. Azad then also throws light as to how Buddha's personality and simple teachings were transformed into divine personality and acquired the complex form of religious dogmas, something Buddha himself had negated. He also quotes some authorities to show that Buddha's statue began to be worshipped after the Ashoka period as until then one does not find Buddha's statues. Buddha until Ashoka's time was represented either through lotus or an empty chair. Then he came to be represented by two feet and then ultimately his whole statue appeared which became the object of worship.

It will thus, be seen that Azad had deep study of various Indian and non-Indian religions and he bases his thesis on unity of religion on the Qur'anic concept of unity of God *tawhid*. He thinks as per the Qur'anic doctrine that all prophets and seers brought the message of unity of God and that later the followers of these prophets and seers corrupted the message. Thus, according to Azad *din* which comprises the doctrine of *tawhid*, belief in the angels, in the Day of Judgement and in prophets is one everywhere and this he tries to show through his study of the process of development of teachings of various religions as we have shown above. But he concedes differences in *shari'ah* (in rituals of worship), in laws pertaining to marriage, divorce, inheritance, etc.

He maintains that the *shari'ah* laws do not represent the essence of any religion but depend on time and space, local customs and traditions. Thus, differences in *shari'ah* laws should not lead us to think that there are fundamental differences in *din* itself. One can say that Azad judges all religions and their evolution in the light of the Qur'anic teachings and that he does not judge these religions on their own merit and does not base the acceptance of the truth of these religions on the beliefs of their followers. This can be said to be the limit of Azad's doctrine of *wahdat-e-din*. He tries to trace the concept of *tawhid* in all religions to accept their truth.

Well, this is limitation of Azad's thought, but it would be unfair to accuse him of not accepting the truth of religion as the followers of those religions themselves accept. This is one way of thinking which has its own merit. However, Azad certainly tries to examine the beliefs of other religions in the light of the Qur'anic teaching that all religions are true and were originally based on the revelation sent down from time to time through prophets and seers. A Muslim thus, is supposed to believe in all the prophets sent by Allah and should not make distinction between one prophet and the other. Thus, the Qur'an says, "The Messenger believes in what has been revealed to him from his Lord, and (so do) the believers. They all believe in Allah and His angels and His Books and His messengers. We make no difference between any of His messengers." (2:285) Thus, these words of the Qur'an are quite clear that several messengers (though all of them have not been named in the Qur'an) came for the guidance of humanity from time to time. Since they all were sent by Allah their fundamental teachings could not have differed from each other. Only the *shari'ahs* differed in view of differences in local customs and traditions. Azad, thus, not only stresses truth of other religions in the light of this Qur'anic doctrine, but also proceeds to examine evolution of the teachings of these religions and finds elements of *tawhid* in these religions to prove the Qur'anic assertion that Allah sent his messengers for guidance of all the peoples in the world. The Qur'an also asserts that the apparent differences in various religions are not on account of contradictory teachings of these religions, but because of corruption of original teachings by the vested interests later. Thus, Azad also tries to examine how changes were introduced over period of time by their followers for various reasons during the course of time. Thus, Azad's concept of *wahdat-e-din* is based entirely on the teachings of the Qur'an. One may call it his profound faith in Qur'an or his limitation of approach, whatever ones perspective.

Even if one differs from Azad's approach, one can hardly deny his deep study of world religions and their evolution. This has to be further appreciated in the light of the fact that he led very busy life since his adulthood and got involved in the freedom movement from very young age. It is also amazing that he wrote commentary on the Qur'an during his captivity in Ranchi when he was quite young. It must also be appreciated that Azad studied other religions from a very broad perspective and never indulged, like other narrow-minded theologians, in proving them wrong. On the contrary, he quite objectively examined their teachings like a scholar of comparative religion. This is the strength of Azad's scholarship. Thus his strength is his liberalism and openness of mind. And he derives his openness from the Qur'an.

CHAPTER 4
Islam and Secularism

Many people feel that Islam is quite incompatible with secularism. Some even maintain that as long as one is Muslim he cannot be a secularist. This is further reinforced by the propaganda by some Muslim countries like Saudi Arabia that secularism is *haram* and that all secular nations are enemies of Islam. Maulana Maududi, the founder chief of Jamat-e-Islami said while leaving for Pakistan in 1948, that secularism was *haram* and all those who participated in secular politics in India would be rebels against Islam and enemies of the messenger of Allah.

How far is it true? Are Islam and secularism really incompatible? Is Saudi propaganda against secularism justified? Was Maulana Maududi right? These are some important questions and we must search for the answers. We must bear in mind that in every religion there are different intellectual trends—both liberal as well as conservative. Both quote scriptures in support of their respective positions. Since a scripture or religious tradition for that matter has to deal with complex social situation, one finds differing or even contradictory statements responding to the contradictory situations.

In scriptural hermeneutics one has to take situation in totality and develop certain keys to deal with the evolving situation. The commentators often deal with the situation as if it is static. Social situations can never be static. It continually evolves and changes. The way scriptural statements were understood by early commentators conformed to their own socio-cultural situation. Their hermeneutics should not be binding on the subsequent generations as it will not conform to the changed situation. For every age there are some keys which help us understand the scripture in our own age. Also, a commentator should have a vision of society and this vision evolves from ones own social situation. Allah's creative power cannot be treated as static. The Qur'an also refers to His dynamism when it states, "....every day He manifests Himself in, yet, another (wondrous) way. Which, then, of your Sustainer's powers can you disavow?" (29:55). Thus Allah manifests Himself every day in new state *(sha'n)*. And the word *yaum* literally means day but figuratively it can also mean a whole epoch, a period. Taking the word *yaum* in this sense, the verse will mean Allah manifests His glories in new ways from period to period, from epoch to epoch.

The early commentators of the Qur'an, on which depends the conservative view of the 'ulama', were product of their own socio-religious and socio-cultural situation. In the early days of Islam, particularly in the period of four caliphs succeeding the holy Prophet, state was very closely identified with religion of Islam. In the Arabia of early days there did not exist even a state before advent of Islam, let alone any laws associated with the state. However, a state came into existence when Islam united people of Arabia transcending tribal bonds.

The state needed laws to deal with fast evolving situations. First, they took help of the Qur'an and then *sunnah* of the Prophet. Even then if they could not solve the problem they held the assembly of the companions of the Prophet and tried to solve the problem in consultation with them. Their collective wisdom was often of great help. But it is quite obvious that they heavily drew from their own experiences in the social milieu they lived in. This social milieu also heavily influenced their understanding of the Qur'anic verses. And some Qur'anic verses were integrally related to the situation obtaining there.

The problem really arose when the subsequent generations treated the understanding of the Qur'anic verses by the companions of the Prophet or the early commentators who drew their own understanding heavily from the pronouncements of these companions and their followers *(tabi'in)*. The companions were thought to be—and rightly so—as great authorities as the Qur'an was revealed during their lifetime and in their presence and who could understand it better than these companions. Most of the subsequent commentators simply referred to these companions and their followers' pronouncements became the only source of understanding the Qur'anic verses. Until today the commentators of the Qur'an are repeating those very ideas and these

ideas have become sacred and any deviation is considered heresy by
most of the orthodox commentators of the Qur'an.

The Islamic state which came into existence after the death of the
Prophet, as pointed out above, also became a model for the subsequent
generation, though this model was hardly followed even in early period
of Islamic history. The Umayyad and the Abbasid empires which came
into existence after what is called *khilafat-e-rashidah* (the rightly guided
period of *khilafat*, Islamic state) never followed this religious model.
Both the empires were based on personal and authoritarian rule and
were Islamic only in name. The Umayyad and the Abbasid caliphs
followed their own personal desires rather than the Qur'anic injunctions
or the *shari'ah* rules. They just symbolically made their obeisance to
religion and followed what was in their personal interest. Thus, theirs
were what we can call a 'semi-secular' states.

And the states which came into existence after the Abbasid state
were even more secularized except the Fatimid state which was more or
less based on the Isma'ili theology. Even the Fatimid Imams had to face
serious problems as their Isma'ili followers were very few in their domain
and the vast majority belonged to the Sunni faith. Thus, they often
separated affairs of the state from Isma'ili theological considerations.
A separate department of Isma'ili theology (Fatimi *Da'wah*) had to be
established.

Though, the *khilafat* model was never repeated in the history of
Islam, in theory, it remained the objective of all the Islamic theologians
to establish the state on the model of early *khilafat* and any state which
did not follow that model came to be condemned as un-Islamic and it
was even more strongly condemned if the state claimed to be secular.
Maulana Maududi opposed Jinnah vehemently because his vision of
Pakistani state was based on secular concept giving all citizens equal
rights irrespective of their religious faith. The Maulana refused to support
the Pakistan movement as Jinnah would not agree to set up an Islamic
state.

Now the question is whether Islam as a religion is compatible with
secularism? Does it aim at setting up an Islamic state? Can there be a
Muslim country with a secular state? These are some of the crucial
questions one has to answer in order to deal with the subject of Islam
and secularism. Of course, we should remember that there cannot be
uncontested answers. Every answer that we attempt would be and

could be, contested by those with differing viewpoint. Ours is a liberal and inclusive approach and we will, of course, attempt answer from this viewpoint.

Before we deal with the question of Islam and secularism, we would like to throw some light on religion and secularism. Here too there are differing views. There are rationalists and atheists who consider religion and secularism quite contrary to each other. For them the two are quite incompatible. Secularism is a non-religious, if not altogether anti-religious philosophy. A secular political philosophy should have nothing to do with any religious tenets or doctrines. A secular state then would not take any religious beliefs or practices into account while legislating on any issue and in some extreme cases even citizens would not be free to have religious faith and declare it and practice it publicly. Religion, in other words, would be almost a taboo in such a political set up. The former Soviet and Chinese states came close to this model.

Then there is western liberal secular model where religion is not a taboo but is also not a basic factor as far as state affairs are concerned. State affairs are conducted quite independently of any religious considerations. In the UK too, where Anglican Christianity continues to be state religion and the King or Queen of England is considered head of the Anglican Church, religion plays hardly any role in the matters of state. All state legislations are quite independent of the tenets of the Anglican Church. The Church cannot oppose any law passed by the House of Commons and approved by the House of Lords.

In other western countries too positions are more or less similar. The state remains quite independent of the church. In fact church and state have totally independent domains and do not interfere in each others sphere. This western model comes closest to the political philosophy of secularism. The Islamic world has its own features and uniqueness. When we deal with the question of Islam and secularism we have to keep this in mind. It should, however, be kept in mind that the Islamic world is also not homogenized one. One comes across fundamental differences in Islamic countries from Algeria to Indonesia, though, all of them follow religion of Islam. Commonality of religion does not necessarily mean commonality of social or political traditions. These traditions are as different as their societies and social realities.

Algeria, for example, is a modern westernized state and hence it is undergoing a great religious turmoil as a section of citizens want it to be an 'Islamic state' of their vision. Then there are countries like Malaysia and Indonesia with mixed populations, though with Muslim majority and they too have secular states. The movements for setting up Islamic states in these countries by the Islamic groups did not succeed. Both these countries have adopted models of polity suited more to a pluralist society. So is the case with Malaysia. Though, it is a Muslim majority country it is also pluralist in character and hence, has chosen to be secular in character.

Turkey is overwhelmingly a Muslim country and yet, it chose to be a secular country since Kamal Pasha's revolution in 1924 and it has stayed secular ever since. Though, there have been attempts at religious revival, they did not register much success. Turkey has gone to the extent of abolishing Islamic personal laws and have replaced them with secular Swiss Code. Perhaps Turkey is the only country to do so.

Among Arab countries, besides Algeria, Tunisia and Morocco also have brought about considerable modern reforms, though technically they are not secular states. Their state religion continues to be Islam. Jordan is another moderate country with 10 per cent Christian population. Iraq, on the other hand, is ruled by the Baath Party which is socialistic in character. Iraq, until the Gulf war in 1990, was quite secular in character. However, the compulsions of the Gulf war and earlier war with Iran in eighties brought about some changes in its character and Saddam Husain, in order to win a degree of legitimacy, started mild measures of Islamisation. Some of the gulf countries like Bahrain, the Yemen, are also Islamic in character, but with liberal dispensation unlike the Saudi Arab and Kuwait. In fact the fast process of modernization is also affecting hard Islamic countries like Saudi Arabia and Kuwait.

Thus, it will be seen that all Islamic countries are not same in political and even religious character. Among them there are great deal of differences. We find the whole range of political shades—from rigid Islamic character of Saudis to liberal Islamic character of the countries like Iraq to secular country like the Turkey. There is not and there cannot be, any homogeneity. As far as orthodoxy or liberalism or secularism is concerned, much depends on the proclivities of the ruling classes in a particular country. It also depends on the interests of the ruling classes and their political alliances.

Now the important question, can Islam and secularism go together? We have already said above that whether religion and secularism can go together or not depends on the interpretation of both religion as well as secularism. If religion is interpreted in keeping with very conservative traditions, it may be difficult for it to go along with secularism which demands more liberal disposition and not only tolerance, but also promotion of pluralism. If secularism is interpreted too rigidly, i.e., if it is equated with atheism, as many rationalists do, then also the two (religion and secularism) will find it difficult to go together.

Islam too, as pointed out above, can be interpreted rigidly, or liberally. If both Islam and secularism are interpreted liberally there should not be any problem with Islam in a secular set up. In fact if one studies the Qur'an holistically one can find strong support for 'liberal or non-atheistic secularism'. No religion will support atheistic secularism for that matter. If we talk of liberal secularism what do we mean by it? We must clearly define it. Liberal secularism does not insist on belief in atheism. It promotes pluralism and respect for all faiths and also it guarantees full freedom of religion for all citizens. Secularism guarantees equal rights for all citizens irrespective of caste, creed, race, language or faith.

Islam can hardly clash with this liberal secularism. The Qur'an, in fact, directly encourages pluralism vide its verse 5:48. This verse clearly states that every people have their own law and a way, i.e., every nation is unique in its way of life, its rules, etc. It also says that if Allah had pleased He would have created all human beings a single people, but He did not do so in order to test them (whether they can live in harmony with each other despite their differences in laws and way of life). Thus, it is clear assertion of pluralism. One must respect others faith and belief and live in harmony with them.

The Qur'an also asserts that every people have their own way of worshiping God (see 2:148). One should not quarrel about this. Instead one should try to excel each other in good deeds. In the verses 60:7-8 we find that Allah will bring about friendship between Muslims and those whom you hold as enemies. And Allah does not forbid you from respecting those who fight you not for religion, nor drive you forth from your homes and deal with them justly. Allah loves doers of justice.

The above verse is a good example of secular ethos. If others do not fight you in matters of your faith and allow you to profess, practice and propagate your faith you should respect them and deal with them justly. This is precisely what our own secular Constitution says and this what secular constitutions world over emphasise. Also, in 6:109 the Qur'an prohibits Muslims from abusing people of other faiths or their gods as in turn they will abuse Allah. This verse also makes much more significant statement that Allah has made for every people their deeds fair-seeming i.e. every community thinks its beliefs and deeds are fair and good and social harmony lies in accepting this situation rather than quarreling about each others beliefs and practices.

The Qur'an also states in 22:40 that no religious place should be demolished as in all religious places be it synagogue, or church or monastery, the name of Allah is remembered and hence all these places should be protected. This is another tenet of liberal secularism which is upheld by the Qur'an.

The Islamic tenets, it will be seen, do not disapprove of composite or pluralistic way of life. Even the Covenant of Madina (called *Mithaq-i-Madina*) clearly approves of pluralistic set up. When the Prophet migrated from Mecca to Madina owing to persecution in Mecca at the hands of Meccan tribal leaders, he found Madinese society a pluralistic society. There were Jews, Pagans and Muslims and also Jews and Pagans were divided into several tribes, each tribe having its own customs and traditions. The Prophet drew up a covenant with these tribes guaranteeing them full freedom of their faith and also creating a common community in the city of Medina with an obligation to defend it, if attacked from outside.

This was in a way a precursor of modern secular nation, every citizen free to follow his/her own faith and tribal customs and their own personal laws, but having an obligation towards the city to maintain peace within and defend it from others. The Prophet clearly set an example that people of different faith and traditions can live together in peace and harmony creating a common bond and respecting a common obligation towards the city or country.

It is interesting to note that the Muslim theologians belonging to the *Jamiat al-'Ulama-i-Hind* (the Association of the 'Ulama of India) drew the inspiration for creating a composite secular nation in India from the Prophet's Covenant of Madina. These 'ulama opposed two nation theories and maintained that Islam is not against composite secular nationalism. Different religious communities can exist together in a country. The only condition for this is that all should be guaranteed to freely profess, practice and propagate their religion. Since the Indian Constitution allows this, the 'ulama happily accepted the liberal secular political disposition in India and did not find any justification for a separate state for Muslims of the sub-continent.

Yet, another question which remains to be answered is about equal rights to all citizens in a country with Muslim majority. It is often argued that Muslims are reluctant to accord equal citizenship rights to religious minorities. No doubt there is some truth in this assertion, but not the whole truth. Some Muslim majority countries certainly do not allow non-Muslims equal rights, but many other countries do. We have already given examples of countries like Indonesia and Malaysia. Both countries, though have Muslim majorities, do allow all their citizens, including the non-Muslims, equal political rights. In Pakistan too, until Zia-ul-Haq's time, enjoyed equal citizenship rights and joint electorate. It was Zia who created separate electorate for non-Muslims.

In Qur'an, as pointed out elsewhere, there is no concept of state, nor of territorial nationalism. In fact religious scriptures are hardly supposed to deal with such questions. It nowhere states that it is obligatory for Muslims to set up a religious or a theocratic state. Qur'an does not refer, not even indirectly, to any concept of state. Its whole emphasis is on truth, justice, benevolence, compassion, tolerance, and wisdom as far as life in this world is concerned. As long as people conform to these values, it does not matter what religious faith they belong to. They can coexist in peace and harmony. Thus, the concept of a purely Islamic state is a historical construct attempted by Muslim jurists over a period of time. It is these jurists who laid down detailed rules of *Shari'ah* and also drew up a configuration of an Islamic state defining the rights of non-Muslims in such state. Moreover, it was very different historical situation and the Qur'anic verses were interpreted under the influence of their own social and religious ethos.

The rights of non-Muslims, in other words, will have to be rethought and reformulated. The Qur'an nowhere states that religion can be the basis of political rights of the people. This was the opinion of Muslim jurists of the medieval period when religion of the ruler determined the status of the ruled. Such a formulation cannot be considered a necessary part of the political theory of Islam. The only model for this purpose can be the *Mithaq-i-Madina* and this Covenant, as pointed out above, did not make any distinction between people of one religion and the other in matters of political rights. This Covenant, at least in spirit, if not in form, provides a valuable guidance for according political rights to citizens of modern state irrespective of ones religion. It is unfortunate that the later political theorists of Islam wholly neglected this significant political document drawn up by the Prophet of Islam. In fact he was far ahead of his time in relation to non-Muslim's equal religious and political rights. The theory of political rights in the modern Islamic state should be based on this document.

There is great deal of emphasis on freedom of conscience and human rights in the modern civil society. It is highly regrettable that most of the Muslim countries do not have good record in this field. Freedom of conscience, human rights and democracy are quite integral to each other. In most of the Muslim majority countries today which have declared themselves as 'Islamic countries' even the democratic discourse is banished, let alone human rights discourse. It is not right to maintain that an Islamic society cannot admit of human rights. The lack of democracy and human rights is not because of Islam or Islamic teachings, but due to authoritarian and corrupt regimes which totally lack transparency in governance. Again, if we go by the *sunnah* of the Prophet and record of governance of the rightly guided caliphs, we see that the principle of accountability and transparency in governance was quite fundamental. The people who had experienced the conduct of the Prophet were so sensitive to the doctrine of accountability that there was great uprising when the regime of the third caliph deviated from this doctrine for various reasons not to be discussed here. The Prophet of Islam and his companions had sensitised the Muslims to such an extent in respect of accountability and transparency in governance that any deviation from it was strongly protested. But when authoritarian regimes came into existence and *khilafat* turned into monarchy beginning with the first Umayyad monarch Yazid, this doctrine vanished into thin air.

Those who respect the doctrine of accountability would never maintain that Islam is against democracy and human rights. In fact almost all Islamic countries—with few exceptions—signed the UN Human Rights Declaration of 1948. Some countries who refused to sign had objection only on one clause—on freedom of conscience and right to convert to any religion of ones choice. They felt it was against the tenets of Islam and one who renounces Islam should be punished with death. This is of course not the place to discuss this controversial question of the right to convert, but suffice it to say that the Muslim jurists had instituted this punishment more for political than religious reasons. In the modern nation states, the punishment for *irtidad* (renouncing Islam) cannot be death and the individual must be given right to belief of what he/she desires. One cannot be made to follow any religion under the threat of death. A religion is certainly a serious matter of conscience and commitment.

From all this it will be seen that Islamic teachings as embodied in the Qur'an and *sunnah* of the Prophet (and not opinions of the jurists) are not against the concept of human rights and individual freedom (freedom of conscience). It is authoritarian rulers of some Muslim countries who denounce the concept of human rights as alien to Islam. Islam, in fact, is the first religion which legally recognized other religions and gave them dignified status and also accepted the concept of dignity of all children of Adam (17:70) irrespective of their faith, race, tribe, nationality or language (49:13).

The verse 2:213 is also quite significant on the unity of all human beings. All differences are human and not divine and these differences should be resolved in democratic and goodly manner (29:46). These are the norms laid down by the Qur'an, but the rulers of Muslim countries deviate from these norms to protect their hold on power and blame it on Islam.

Islam upholds pluralism, freedom of conscience and human and democratic rights and thus, does not clash with the concept of secularism. It is also interesting to note that in a secular set up like India the 'ulama accepted the secular principles of governance and never objected to it. In fact, the 'ulama in India stress secularism and urge upon Muslim masses to vote for secular parties. Maulana Husain Ahmad Madani had taken lead in this respect by legitimizing composite nationalism (*Muttahida Qaumiyyat*) and rejecting two nation theory. Of late the *Jama'at-e-Islami-i-Hind* has also accepted secular democracy and has even set up a secular democratic front of its own, particularly after demolition of Babri Masjid and the riots that followed it. Thus, it will be seen that the Indian 'ulama' have shown a way in this respect by accepting secularism. Islam and secularism can and should go together in the modern world.

CHAPTER 5

Islam, Reason and Revelation

During my recent visit to USA for a conference on 'What Men owe to Women', two scholars of Islamic Studies and myself were engaged in a discussion on the concept of revelation. The two young scholars, both product of western universities, were arguing that revelation is highly problematic and that the Qur'an contains human words. The fact that it is in Arabic language, itself shows that the words are human. I tried to argue otherwise and maintained that Qur'an is a divinely revealed book and since it is addressed to human beings, it naturally has to use a human language like the Arabic. Then the discussion started on mode of revelation, but the two young scholars were not persuaded and maintained that revelation is, on many account, highly problematic. This persuaded me to write a chapter on this subject to clarify issues.

In fact thaere has been for long a debate about reason and revelation in the history of Islam. There never was any unanimity among theologians, philosophers and scholars on the concept of revelation, though all of them were unanimous on the contents of the holy Qur'an. No theologian has ever differed on the compilation of the Holy Book, though a small section of Shi'ahs have maintained that some parts of Qur'an which contained praises of Hazrat Ali were excluded from the compilation known as *Mushaf-e-Uthman*. However, even this section of the Shi'ahs never challenged the authenticity of what is contained in the *Mushaf*. Thus, there has been no contention about the present book in entire history of Islam, though there has been, as pointed out before, great deal of discussion about the mode of revelation.

It is also important to note that despite these debates among the scholars and theologians no one had ever challenged the concept of divine revelation. All have been unanimous in their opinion that the holy Qur'an is a divinely revealed book. I would like to throw some light in this study on both reason and revelation. Some of the questions which I want to discuss relate to the concept and mode of revelation and its relations with human reason. Are they mutually complimentary or contradictory?

As far as the Qur'an is concerned the word *wahy* occurs number of times. It is used in number of ways in the Qur'an. Allah also makes revelation to a bee on making hives in the mountains and in the trees and in what they build. (16:68). Here of course *wahy* does not mean what is implied by it when a messenger of Allah receives revelation. Muhammad Asad in his *The Message of the Qur'an* says, commenting on this verse, "The expression 'He has inspired' (*awha*) is meant to bring out the wonderful quality of the instinct which enables the lowly insect to construct the geometrical masterpiece of a honeycomb out of perfectly proportioned hexagonal, prismatic wax cells—a structure which is most economical and therefore, most rational, as regards to space and material. Together with the subsequently mentioned transmutation, in the bee's body, of plant juices into honey, this provides a striking evidence of 'God's ways' manifested in all nature." (Mohommad Asad, 1964, pp. 404-45).

Thus, it will be seen here that *wahy* means an instinctual act which is a gift of Allah and whole nature works in this way. It is *sunnat al-Allah* (Way of Allah) which does not change, otherwise, nature will witness arbitrary functioning again and again and its laws will keep on changing on purely arbitrary basis. Much of scientific discoveries depend on induction and induction can work only if there is no arbitrary change. Here the concept of *wahy* has been used in a very different sense, but nevertheless it is the Qur'anic usage.

Similarly, this word is used in different ways in different places in the Qur'an. If we consult Imam Raghib's *Mufradat al-Qur'an* we find different meanings of this word. He says that the word *wahy* has been conveyed in different modes by Allah. It is conveyed through limbs (*jawareh*) or through gestures (*ramz*). Sometimes it is in single syllable without forming a word and sometimes it is revealed as a book or through written word. The Imam cites verse 11-19 and says that in this verse '*awha*' (revealed) either means 'made a gesture' or according to others means '*kataba*' (wrote).

In the verse 6:113 the word *wahy* has been used in negative sense. The enemies of prophets inspire (*yuhi*) each other with gilded speech to deceive. Similarly in 6:122 it is used in the same way ("And certainly the devils inspire their friends to contend with you..."). But in Shar'i terminology, according to Imam Raghib *wahy* means the word of Allah put into the heart of prophets and His friends as for in the verse 42:51.

This verse says, "And it is not vouchsafed to a mortal that Allah should speak to him, except by revelation or from behind a veil, or by sending a messenger and revealing by His permission what He pleases." Here *wahi* is used in the sense in which Muslims understand Qur'an to be a revealed Book of Allah." (Imam Raghib, 1971, p. 1098)

Also, there are different modes of *wahy* mentioned in the Qur'an as far as human word is concerned. It is sent through an angel called *rasul* in the Qur'an. Muslims believe this angle to be Jibra'il (Gabriel). Allah also speaks to humans from behind a curtain (*min wara'i hijabin*) as he spoke to Hazrat Musa (Moses). According to a *hadith* it also means to inspire something into ones heart.

According to the Qur'an all prophets have been recipients of *wahy* (revelations). The Qur'an also talks of Allah having sent revelation to the *hawwariyun*, i.e., companions of Christ. (see 5:111). However, there is a controversy as to whether they were given revelation directly or through Christ. The words of Qur'an give an impression as if they received inspiration directly. Similarly in the verse 21:73 it is stated, "And We made them leaders who guided (people) by our command, and We revealed to them the doing of good and the keeping up of prayer and the giving of alms..." Here also it seems the Qur'an refers to the leaders of people who receive *wahy* from Allah.

The Qur'an, it is obvious from all above references, is a compilation of revelations from Allah through His last Messenger. The Prophet Muhammad received this revelation and recited to those around him and these companions reduced it to writing. These verses, revealed from time to time for a period of 23 years, were later compiled together during Prophet's own lifetime and there has been no indication of any deletion or addition until *Mushaf-i-Uthman* was compiled which is what is amongst us today. This final compilation was needed in view of different diacritical marks being used by people in different areas of Arabs due to variation of dialects. This could have led to serious differences and hence, one final *Mushaf* was compiled.

However, the seminal statement of the Qur'an about *wahy* as sent to the Prophet of Islam is in the verse 53:3 which says, "Nor does he speak out of desire. It is naught, but revelation that is revealed." Thus, whole of Qur'an is a revelation in this sense. Whatever is contained in the Qur'an has been revealed from Allah; naught that has been spoken out of human desire has been included in it. Thus, the prime quality of revelation is that it is above human desire (*hawa'*). It alone is capable of providing true guidance. One that is mixed with human desire cannot have this quality. Whatever the Prophet of Islam spoke through revelation was not as human being, but only as the Messenger of Állah.

Now there are of course differences among theologians as to the mode of revelation as pointed out before. One prevalent view among the 'ulama is that literally an angle appeared before the Prophet and conveyed the message from Allah literally in those very words. All prophet did was to repeat those words. According to this view the Prophet was a conveyor without any interpretation of his own. It was not that the substance was caste into his heart and then he put it into his words. But the very words were inspired into his heart through Jibra'il.

Another view, held by Sab'iyins (seveners), Batinis (those who believe in esoteric meaning of the holy Qur'an) and Isma'ilis is that there is no separate existence of Jibara'il outside the existence of Prophet, but it is ingrained ability of the Prophet to receive revelation. According to this view the Arabic word *malak* or angle is derived from the root *m l k,* i.e., to possess, to own. All words derived from this root carry this sense in one way or the other. For example, a king is called *malik* as he owns the country and rules over. Similarly, the word for property is *milk* as it is owned by someone. And similarly one who owns or possesses is called *malik.*

According to this view the word *malak* for angle means certain abilities which some chosen people are possessed of. It is also referred to *quwa' malakutiyah,* i.e., divine powers which are gifted to Allah's chosen people and His Prophet has highest degree of such divinely gifted capabilities. Only such chosen person has capability to receive revelation from High On. This interpretation implies that the divine message was conveyed to the Prophet, through the ability he was gifted by Allah in the form of inspiration and not through an angle existing out there. In other words, it was an innate divine capability.

The M'utazila, the rationalists in Islam, also held more or less same position. The Mu'tazilites called themselves a party of *Tawhid* and *'adl* (party of Unity of God and Justice). They, unlike *Mutakallimun* (dialecticians) of Islam, depended more on reason and intellect in understanding the issues of Islam. They are, therefore, popularly known as rationalists of Islam. They also believed in the doctrine of *khalq-i-Qur'an* (createdness of Qur'an) and persecuted those who rejected this doctrine and believed instead, in the opposite doctrine of the Qur'an being coeternal with God and hence, indestructible. This was a major controversy between the rationalists and orthodox in the early history of Islam. As the M'utazalites were early collaborators of the Abbasids, they had political authority and used their authority to enforce the doctrine of createdness of Qur'an.

Similarly the Mu'tazilites believed in the doctrine of revelation through *ilqa' 'alal qalb* (God throws on the heart) of the Prophet what He desires and the Prophet recites it before the people. Thus, the Prophet has been gifted with special ability as stated above. Sir Syed Ahmad Khan, who was a reformer of nineteenth century in India was modernist in approach and also holds similar view. He maintains that prophethood (*nubuwwah*) is not like any office assigned to any man as an king assigns certain offices to certain people, but it is a natural thing (*fitri amr*) which he refers to as *malkae nubuwwat* (gift of prophethood). Only one who has been given this quality by God can have it. He says that right from the beginning of Islam, 'ulama have held two views: (1) All men are equal and Allah selects someone and gives him the office of prophethood and (2) Allah creates some people specially with the quality of prophethood. He then quotes from *Tafsir-i-Kabir* of Imam Fakhruddin Razi to prove his point. According to Al-Razi there are men who have divine light within them (*anwar-e-Ilahiyyah*) and there are those who have no spiritual inclination and love materialism. The people of first category are capable of receiving revelation whereas people of later category are barred from it. However, there can be difference of degree among the people of first category. Some have it upto the degree of perfection, whereas others to lesser degree. Thus, the essence of what Imam Razi says is that the prophets have created in them that innate capability (*malkae nubuwwah*) which makes them capable of receiving revelation from Allah. Sir Syed quotes Shah Waliyullah also to this effect from his *Tafhimat.* (Sir Syed, 1995, Vol. I, pp. 56).

It is obvious from the foregoing that there have been different interpretations as to how one becomes prophet and as to how revelation is received by the incumbent. These are intellectual controversies and will go on forever. But what is important is that no one, among believers, have ever doubted the authenticity of the Qur'anic text. There were some differences in diacritical marks, rendition and recitation, but never in the text of the revelation. These differences were also eleminated by compilation of what is known as *Mushaf-i-Uthman* which is the prevalent Qur'an unanimously accepted by all.

However, there are differences in interpretation of the text and this has given rise to not only numerous commentaries of the Qur'an, but also to numerous sects. From Asha'irah to Isma'ilis to Batinis, there are fundamental differences in interpretations, almost irreconcilable differences. Hence, despite Qur'an being one, there has never been unity among all Muslims in the entire history of Islam except during the Prophet's lifetime. The Prophet, a keen observer of socio-religious scene, himself seems to have been aware of this possibility and hence, predicted through a *hadith* that there will be seventy-two sects after me.

However, this should not in any way lead to controversy about the authenticity of the revealed text or about revelation itself. In fact whole of Qur'an is witness to the authenticity of the text. The inner evidence is quite redoubtable in the case of the Qur'an. No wonder than that the Qur'an itself claims inner evidence to be a conclusive evidence of its authenticity. In fact it claims to be the only miracle of the prophethood of Muhammad. The Arabs with their poetic and oratorial skills of which they were immensely proud, were dumbfounded when they listened to the recitation of the Qur'anic text. Its overwhelming poetic and prose qualities along with its divine message could not be duplicated by the greatest of elocutionist of Prophet's contemporaries. The Qur'an challenged the non-believing master orators of their time to bring anything remotely resembling the verses of the Qur'an, but this challenge could never be met (see the verse 2:23, 10:38, for example).

Our wonderment further increases if we learn that the Prophet was not formally literate and he is often referred to as *ummi* which means, among other things one who can neither read nor write. *Ummi*, of course also means belonging to mother or to *Umma*, i.e., people and there have been differences of interpretation about the word *ummi* itself. But most of the Muslims maintain that the Prophet was not literate and this enhances the authenticity of revelation which, in that case, could only be result of either highly perfected inner capability (*malkae nubuwwat*) of the Prophet or through an external agency of Jibra'il existing out there.

Also, it was not mere question of eloquence of the Qur'anic language. It was of course very important quality of the text and was universally acknowledged. But the revelation through the Prophet was much more than that. The quality of its guidance was far more important than its linguistic eloquence. The guidance was again not restricted to the spiritual field alone. It embraced all those fields in which human activities are located and the futuristic dimension of its teachings.

Bearing in mind that the Prophet had never been to any university or to any institution of higher learning in any field or discipline, let alone be accomplished in any of these fields, the contents of the revealed text makes us wonder. In Arabian desert as well as the primitive Meccan urban environment one could hardly think of the subjects dealt with by the Qur'an, let alone make profound observations about them. The Qur'an has put it in its inimitable style as *wala ratabin wala yabisin illa fi' Kitabin mubin* (6:59) ("there is no anything fresh or dry but is in the clear book"). This itself should make any doubter believe in the innate revealed qualities of the text of the Qur'an and its integrity.

This brings us to the innate relationship of revelation and reason. Many rationalists would like to believe that the two are antagonistic which it is not, except if one takes very superficial view. Reason and revelation—if revelation be authentic and not based on mere pretensions, as it often happens, will be found to be complementary in senses more than one. Reason, although a very important human faculty in its perfected form, a great boon for humanity—I would not hesitate to say—is not, by itself, a goal. It is rather an essential instrument to reach the desired goal. Goal is laid down by fundamental values and values are arrived at either through intuition or revelation.

The faculty of reason, it is important to note, is highly worthy of respect as it enables us to question and critique with an open mind with several options before us. It enables us to liberate ourselves from ignorance and blind imitation. It also enables us, through acquisition of knowledge, to emerge from darkness to light. But, in view of its possible instrumentality, it cannot be a value guidance. It can tell us how to do, but not why to do, it can enable us to reach a goal, but cannot fix the goal by itself. In view of its instrumentality, it can lead us to negativity, disaster and destruction as much as to positivity, avoidance of disaster and constructive acts. In other words it is a double-edged sword. It often leads us to rationalization and shows us ways of legitimation rather than legitimacy itself.

Intuition and revelation, on the other hand, help us to search for value goals and enrich our spiritual and intellectual quality. While reason may induce us to achieve selfish ends which includes personal, communal or national its marriage with revelation makes us transcend selfishness (in collective and national sense too) or self-oriented achievements. Revelation lifts us spiritually and makes us highly sensitive to others suffering rather than our own. A spiritually sensitive person would never achieve anything at the cost of suffering of others. In other words, he achieves higher wisdom what the Qur'an calls *hikmah* and repeatedly describes Allah as *Hakim* (Wise).

Hikmah is a complex concept in the Qur'anic terminology which has *'adl, ihsan, rahm.* and *'aql* (justice, benevolence, compassion, and intellect) as its components. Thus, Allah is *Hakim* in the sense that He is embodiment of justice, benevolence, compassion, and intellect. Thus, Allah is *'Adil* (just), *Muhsin* (Benevolent), *Rahman* (Compassionate) *and 'Alim* (Knower). These are the attributes of Allah in the Qur'an. And thus the ideas and concepts of higher morality is proof, if any is required, of Qur'an's revealed status.

The Qur'an deals with number of subjects. Above all it is a book of moral guidance. One finds most exalted moral concepts in it. The very second verse of second chapter calls it a "guide to those who keep their duty". It repeatedly exhorts believers to "enforce what is good and banish what is evil". It makes everyone accountable for ones deeds and stresses the concept of the 'Day of Judgement' (*yaum al-Din*). Basically the Arab society was tribal, sociologically speaking, but the Qur'an does not talk of collective, but individual responsibility. It talks of individual rights and duties.

The Qur'anic teachings and precepts are astonishingly modern. It is Muslim practice, not Islamic teachings, which is feudal and past-oriented. The Islamic teachings fulfill all the modern parameters. The modern socio-political system has following parameters: (1) Democratic form of governance; (2) concept of individual rights (also referred to as human rights) as well as individual accountability; (3) women's rights, and (4) freedom of faith.

It will be seen, on objective examination of the Qur'anic teachings that these parameters are fulfilled. The Qur'an had instructed the Prophet to consult his companions in worldly matters (*wa shawirhum*) and the first Islamic government was based on the Covenant of Madina (*Mithaq-i-Madina*) which the Prophet signed with different religious and tribal groups. This covenant granted full religious freedom to all the residents of Madina. The Qur'an had earlier pronounced this principle when it said, "For you is your religion and for me is mine" (109:6) and also "There is no compulsion in matters of religion" (2:256). Subsequently, after the death of the Prophet also, the caliph was elected by the believers.

The first caliph, on being elected, stressed the principle of accountability and asked the Muslims to remove him from the seat of authority if he failed to protect the weaker sections of society from the hands of powerful ones. The Qur'an shows its sympathy for weaker sections of society (*mustad'ifun*) and exhorts the believers repeatedly to take care of the poor, needy, widows, orphans and pay off the debts of the indebted and bring about liberation of slaves. Islam also gave the concept of welfare state by establishing *bait al-mal* (state treasury for helping weaker sections of society). Thus, it will be seen that Islam gave the concept of most modern system of governance. Democratic and welfare state came into existence in Europe only in 20th century.

The Qur'an, as pointed out earlier, fixes responsibility of individual acts on individuals, not on tribes or other collectivities. It has been forcefully mentioned in the verse 99:7-8, "One who does an atom's weight of good will see it. And he who does an atom's weight of evil will see it." None, but the doer will account for his/her deeds. This principle is, needless to say, most modern in its concept. Similarly, every individual has been guaranteed the rights contained in the United Nations' Charter of Human Rights. For lack of space we will not be able to go into its details. I have written in detail on this issue in my book *Rethinking Issues in Islam.*

It is generally thought that the Qur'an deprives women of her rights and subjects her to the authority of father or husband. It is far from the Qur'anic teachings. In fact Qur'an was the first revealed book in the world which accorded women the concept of legal entity and she was given rights as an individual which itself is a most modern concept. Qur'an treats men and women quite equally in all matters of rights and duties. If there is any doubt in this respect let him/her examine the verses 2:228, 33:35 and 3:194. The Qur'an clearly accepts women's right to property, inheritance, marriage, divorce, alimony, custody of children and also allows her to earn her own living. Polygamy has been most reluctantly permitted putting severe restrictions very difficult to overcome. Also, the Qur'an prescribes dignified way of dressing both for men and women and not to display sexual charms publicly. These are most modern rights and became available to women in Europe only after nineteenth century or early twentieth century.

Another important criterion of modernity is use of reason and the power of intellect. Qur'an has never devalued reason, but has accorded it a central place in the human affairs. It repeatedly calls upon the people to reflect deeply and to think with their own intellect and not merely follow blindly the traditions of their forefathers. It gives example of Prophet Abraham who refused to follow his forefather's traditions and reflected deeply over movements of stars and laws of nature and acquired knowledge of creator of this universe. Thus, reason is quite central to the acquisition of knowledge and knowledge is quite central to the teachings of Qur'an. Knowledge is likened to light and ignorance to darkness and Qur'an dramatically poses the question. Can you equate light with darkness? Can seer be equated with the blind? Also acquisition of knowledge, according to one *hadith*, is obligatory for both men and women.

Thus, it will be seen that Qur'anic teachings are astonishingly modern and encourage values of equality of all human beings irrespective of caste, creed, colour or sex (49:13). Equality of all human beings is very central to the teachings of the Qur'an and Islam is quite modern in this respect too. Qur'an makes absolutely no distinction on the basis of caste, colour or creed. Hardly any legal or moral system has laid so much emphasis on equality of human beings as the Qur'an. Is it not astonishing that Mohammad brought about such radical change in the economic, social, and political system of the world and gave it to the humanity fourteen hundred years ago? Was it not miracle of Qur'an? Can we doubt its being a revealed book, though we may differ on mode of revelation?

Thus, it will be seen that the Qur'an gave most modern legal system as well as system of governance. In spiritual field it gave exalted concepts of morality and spiritualism. The sufis who were practitioners of spiritualism found their inspirations only in the treasure house of the Qur'an.

CHAPTER 6

Islam and Modernity

What is the relation between Islam and modernity. Generally it is thought to be negative. But it is very superficial approach. In fact one has to go deeper both into Islamic theology and history as well as into the meaning and significance of the term 'modernity'. Modernism and modernity have evoked great deal of controversy in India as well as in the Islamic world. The response of Islamic world also has not been uniform to the project of modernity.

Before we go into the question of response of Islamic world to modernity, we should discuss the meaning and significance of modernity. Modernity has several dimensions. It is unfortunate that some people begin to worship modernity as blindly as some people reject it blindly. Modernity is neither all boon for everyone (except perhaps for the west to some extent) nor unmitigated curse as staunch supporters of traditions make it out to be. One must thoroughly and critically examine the concept of modernity as propounded by the western scholars.

Bernard Lewis, a noted American scholar has attempted to give definition of modernity in his article "The West and the Middle East" published in *Foreign Affairs* (1997). According to Madhavi Santanam Sondhi, "Lewis uses a definition of modernity designed to dissipate the reservations of non-western, particularly Islamic cultures, to enable them to shed their inhibitions and embrace much of modern western civilization."

If one reads Lewis's article carefully, it emerges that in one way or the other modernization implies westernization. European modernity thought of Graceo-Roman origins owes much to Judeo-Christian civilization also. Europe reached its destination of modernity via complex route which also include impact of Islam. Islam, Lewis points out was first to create a multi-racial, multi-cultural, inter-continental civilization and to "borrow, adapt and incorporate significant elements from the remoter civilizations of Asia". Bernad Lewis includes, in his definition of western modernity, experimental sciences, aspects of commerce and banking, mathematics, and astronomy. Then he concludes, "In every era of human history, modernity, or some equivalent term, has meant the ways, norms and standards of the dominant and expanding civilization. Every dominant civilization has its own modernity in its prime...over a wide area and radiated (its) influence over a much broader one still, far beyond (its) imperial frontiers...Today, for the time being...the dominant civilization is western, and western standards therefore, define modernity."

He also suggests, "There have been other dominant civilizations in the past, there will doubtless be others in the future. Western civilization incorporates many previous modernities that is to say, it is enriched by the contributions and influences of other cultures which preceded it in leadership. It will itself bequeath a western cultural legacy to other cultures, yet, to mature."

In other words, Bernard Lewis emphasizes two important aspects of western modernity: its science and technology, commerce and banking and its domination over non-western cultures and civilizations. While the former, i.e., science and technology, commerce and banking have been readily accepted by Islamic countries (as well as other countries), the later, i.e., its dominance is being rejected by many countries both Islamic and non-Islamic in Asia and Africa, though the response, as pointed out above, has been far from uniform.

Some other western scholars have also included democracy, human rights, individual freedom and gender equality among the criteria for modernity. Prof. Huntington, lays emphasis on these aspects of modernity. He, however, does not mention scientific experimentation or technology among the parameters of modernity of his concept. Keeping these criteria in mind, there are fundamental differences between various Islamic countries.

Before we take up the question of Islamic countries and their varied response to western modernity, we would like to consider Islam and its attitude to modernity. The most important question is: is Islam opposed to modernity? Again there might be different responses from different people depending on their own bent of mind. In a way such questions are quite subjective and their responses too. If a person is rigid and orthodox in his/her approach the response will be that Islam is opposed to modernity as modernity or objective inquiry into someone's beliefs leads to 'atheism', according to them. Someone else with liberal bent of mind may respond favourably and may find modernity in conformity with Islam with some conditions. Interestingly, a person on the other extreme, i.e., an atheist, might also dismiss Islam as opposed to modernity.

As I subscribe to liberalism I feel Islam is not opposed to modernism. Modernism cannot be separated from change. In fact Islam, like many other religions, was a product of fundamental social and economic changes which were occurring in the Arabian society. Tribal relations were breaking down in and around Mecca and a trans-tribal mercantile class was emerging on the scene, quite greedy for wealth and totally neglectful of higher human values like compassion, alleviation of poverty and misery of weaker sections of society, mitigation of woes of slavery, recognition of socio-legal status of women, equality of all human beings transcending all barriers of caste, creed, colour, race, and tribe.

Islam laid great emphasis on these values while welcoming the change taking place in the society. But it provided human face for the change and exhorted people not to neglect their duty towards human suffering. It not only accepted mercantile operations as opposed to tribal socio-economic structure, it laid down proper guidelines for honest mercantile transactions. The Qur'an also laid down proper procedure for taking loan, reducing it to writing with two witnesses so as to avoid disputes. Before this loan operations, as in any tribal society of Arabs, were verbally transacted.

Education is highly necessary for any modern society. Even scientific experiments cannot be conducted without ability to read and write. In pre-Islamic society, literacy was extremely low, some historians even maintain that before Islam there were only 17 persons in Mecca (the birth place of Islam) who could read and write. Though this appears to be an exaggeration, the fact remains the percentage of literacy was very low. The Qur'an, through its first revealed verse, encouraged reading and writing. Allah also swears by *qalam* (pen) giving it great importance, making it sacred to swear by.

Also, as pointed out by philosopher-poet Iqbal in his *Reconstruction of Religious Thought in Islam* the Qur'anic approach is inductive (as opposed to the deductive approach of Greek philosophy).

While inductive approach leads to encouragement of scientific observations of the universe, deductive approach leads to speculative thinking. While western philosophers like Descartes stuck to deductive reasoning, western scientists like Darwin and others adopted inductive approach which led to great discoveries. Physics, astronomy, chemistry, biology and their different branches all depend on observations and the process of induction. Using Bernard Lewis's criteria of modernity mentioned at the outset of this Chapter, i.e., scientific experimentation, etc., is quite in keeping with the Qur'anic spirit. In some chapters of the Qur'an crucial questions have been raised about this universe and the faithfuls have been encouraged to observe the animals, plants, moon, sun, stars, and other heavenly bodies. For example, see verses like: 2:164; 3:190; 10:6; 30:22; 35:27; 2:22; 25:49; 80:25; 86:6, etc. It is true the language of these verses is theological and naturally so. The Qur'an, after all, is the book of religious guidance. It is not fundamentally a book of science. However, it is not against scientific observations and experimentations; it encourages it. And in the verse 3:190, it encourages people to reflect on the creation of God. And it is only through this reflection and study that they can conclude that nothing has been created in vain; everything has been created with a purpose.

Scientific Developments in the Early History of Islam

No wonder than we see a spurt of scientific activities in the early period of Islam. The Abbasid empire in its early period gave full impetus to flowering of knowledge, particularly secular knowledge. For spread of science and philosophy a house of wisdom Bait al-Hikmah was established in Baghdad. And this institution became a centre of learning in philosophy and various natural sciences. The Greek works of Plato, Aristotle and other great thinkers, scientists, philosophers, mathematicians, astronomers and others were translated into Arabic and it was through Arabs that this knowledge reached Europe. The noted historian H.G. Wells calls the Arabs the 'foster fathers of knowledge'. The medieval universities of Europe taught the works of Arab philosophers like Avicena (Ibn Sina), Averros (Ibn Rushd) and others who borrowed much from Greek thought and also enriched it through their own creative and critical thinking.

The M'utazelites were rationalists of Islam and in a political fight between the Umayyads and the Abbasids, they sided with the Abbasids. When the Abbasids came to power they gave important positions in administration to M'utazelites. Since the M'utazelites were rationalists, they started the controversy about the Qur'an's creation. They maintained that the Holy Book is a created one and not coeternal with God. The orthodox Muslims argued that it is not created but co-eternal with God. The M'utazelites thought that since it is God's speech, it cannot be eternal. Only God is eternal, not His speech.

The M'utazelites were widely known as a party of *tawhid* and *'adl* (i.e., Unity of Godhood and justice). They believed in rational interpretation of the word of God. They also believed, human being is a free agent as against the *jabriyas* (determinists) who thought human person is not a free agent. It is interesting to note that this debate between the *Jabriyas* and *Qadriyas* (i.e., those who believed human person is not a free agent and those believed he/she is) was not merely a philosophical debate, but basically a political debate.

Those who opposed freedom of human agent were supporters of highly exploitative and oppressive regime of the Umayyads and those who upheld human freedom were supporters of those who opposed Umayyads. Hasan al-Basri, a great Islamic savant and a sufi saint of great eminence, supported the cause of human freedom as he was opposed to the Umayyad regime. He cited a letter of Imam Hasan, the grandson of the holy Prophet in support of his position.

The M'utazelites, as pointed out above, were also opposed to the Umayyads and supported the Abbasid's struggle against them and hence, they also supported those who upheld human person to be a free agent. Both the parties quoted the relevant Qur'anic verses in their support. The political nature of the debate can be understood from some of the *Jabriyas* book. They maintained that since everything happens as per the will of God, oppression and exploitation too, is in keeping with His will and hence, one cannot question it. They thus concluded that even if the Umayyads are tyrants and oppressors, their actions are determined by God and hence, we should accept them as they are and not try to overthrow them. The *Qadriyas* on the other hand dismissed this argument.

M'utazelites, the rationalists of Islam, sided with the Abbasids in their struggle and fully supported the point of view of human freedom.

Later on, this debate became purely philosophical after the political controversy was over. In fact it is rationalists in Islam i.e., M'utazelites who persecuted their detractors. The orthodox Imams who rejected the M'utazelite contention that the Qur'an is created by God and not coeternal with Him, were flogged publicly and jailed. However, later on, when the Abbasid regime began to decline, al-Mutawakkil became caliph and began to support the orthodox position and then the rationalists came to be on the receiving end.

Bernard Lewis maintains in his essay in *Foreign Affairs* (1997), that one which is dominant and ruling power which represents modernity. Thus, he says, "In every era of human history, modernity, or some equivalent term, has meant the ways, norms and standards of the dominant and expanding civilization. Every dominant civilization has its own modernity in its prime...over a wide area and radiated (its) influence over a much broader one still, far beyond (its) imperial frontiers." Thus, from what Bernard defines, and what Prof. Toynbee calls Abbasid state as the Universal State of Islam, it (the Abbasid state) had all the elements of modernity. Though, the Abbasid state declined and its caliphs adopted Islamic orthodoxy as their creed, its influence extended far beyond its imperial frontiers and far beyond its being in political power.

The great philosophers of Islam like al-Farabi, Averros and Avicina rose to the height of their fame after the Abbasid power began to decline. Of course the encyclopedic work like *Ikhwanus Safa* (The Brethren of Purity) was written and compiled during the hey days of the Abbasids. There is great deal of controversy as to who compiled the work which could be described as most modern of its time for its liberalism, openness and sweep. The Isma'ilis claim that the work was compiled by their Imam Husain al-Mastur to effectively reply to the Abbasids through their own weapon. However, others feel that there was a society in Basra which met secretly and discussed the most burning religious and philosophical questions of the time and written records of these were maintained and these records were later on compiled under the title *Ikhwanus Safa*. Whatever the truth the fact is that this encyclopedic work was very comprehensive and it runs into 52 volumes, each volume devoted to some subject or the other. It adopted the then most modern approach to the problems and discussed everything in the light of reason and proved their contentions, even of faith, by rational arguments and not blind belief.

It will be interesting to quote here from some philosophical and theological works to show how philosophical and theological controversies were debated in the light of reason. I quote passages from Al-Ghazali's *Al-Munqidh min al-Dalal* (that which Delivers from Error) to show the nature of debates. It should be born in mind that al-Ghazali was an orthodox theologian and opposed to any kind of philosophical reasoning. He wrote a book *Tahafut al-Falasifa* (Bewilderment of Philosophers). Ibn Rushd, a great philosopher and the contemporary of Ghazali replied by writing *Tahafut, Tahafut al-Falasifa* (Bewilderment of the Bewilderment of Philosophers).

Thus, al-Ghazali says in one of his passages in his *Munqidh min al-Dalal*: "In this and similar cases of sense-perception the sense as judge forms his judgements, but another judge, the intellect, shows him repeatedly to be wrong; and charge of falsity cannot be rebutted."

To this I said: "My reliance on sense-perception also has been destroyed. Perhaps only those intellectual truths which are first principles (or derived from first principles) are to be relied upon, such as the assertion that ten are more than three, that the same thing cannot be both affirmed and denied at one time, that one thing is not both generated in time and eternal, nor both existent and non-existent, nor both necessary and impossible."

Further Ghazali continues: "Sense perception replied: 'Do you not expect that your reliance on intellectual truth will fare like your reliance on sense-perception? You used to trust in me, then along came the intellect-judge and proved me wrong; if it were not for the intellect-judge you would have continued to regard me as true. Perhaps behind intellectual apprehension there is another judge who, if he manifests himself, will show the falsity of intellect in its judging, just as, when intellect manifested itself, it showed the falsity of sense in its judging. The fact that such a supra-intellectual apprehension has not manifested itself is no proof that it is impossible.'

Ghazali then gives the example of dream: "My ego hesitated a little about the reply to that, and sense-perception heightened the difficulty by referring to dreams. 'Do you not see,' it said, 'how when you are asleep, you believe things and imagine circumstances, holding them to be stable and enduring and, so long as you are in that dream-condition, have no doubts about them? And is it not the case that when you awake you know that all you have imagined and believed is unfounded and ineffectual? Why then are you confident that all your waking beliefs, whether from sense or intellect, are genuine?' They are true in respect of your present state; but it is possible that a state will come upon you whose relation to your waking consciousness is analogous to the relation of the latter to dreaming."

The argument goes on. The question is not which point of view was right or wrong; more important question is the quality of arguments, their objectivity and methodology which was quite modern. So the theological and philosophical debates were intellectually rich and based on certain agreed methodology which could be construed as quite modern from the norms of those days.

Another parameter of modernity, though not insisted upon by Bernard Lewis, but by some other western scholars is gender justice and human rights. If we go by the Islamic ideals and not the practice in Muslim societies, Islam stood for gender justice. The Qur'anic pronouncements in this respect were quite revolutionary from the standards of those days. What is most important is that Islam accepted woman as a legal entity with definite rights in terms of marriage, divorce, inheritance, maintenance, property, so on. But the conservative 'ulama, under the influence of their own societies, interpreted, in many cases through inventions of *ahadith* (Prophet's sayings), the Qur'anic verses in such a manner as to rob her of the very rights granted to her, in many cases in the most unambiguous terms, by the divine Book. No other legal system by then had granted her legal individuality, not even the Roman law, which was the most advanced law in the pre-Islamic world.

However, the time was not ripe to practice gender justice as we understand today, much less gender equality. Whatever was given to women was taken away by the Muslim society through backdoor. In that sense too, Islam was modern religion which, at least theoretically, brought about radical change in the status of women. There is, therefore, urgent need to rethink about women's rights related issues in the Muslim world. It is ironical that the Muslim world is charged today with oppressing their women and denying them justice.

As for democracy the Qur'an requires the holy Prophet to consult people in secular matters, or matters relating to the community. (see 3:159 and 42:38). This approach could have produced a democratic culture and the early companions of the Prophet did practice it for a limited period of time. However, soon such efforts were sabotaged by some power hungry people who converted Islamic democracy into dynastic rule. And the tryst with democracy ended there and Muslim society has not known democracy and democratic values ever since. Feudalism and authoritarianism which were totally alien to the Islamic spirit came to be legitimized and at the same time the most oppressive and exploitative regimes came into existence in the Islamic history. The early democratic spirit was never rediscovered. It is only in our time that some Islamic countries have ushered in democracies to varying degrees. But, it must be admitted that most of the Muslim countries are ruled by monarchs or military dictators. Thus, we have to face the odium that Islam is against modernity.

Islamic World and Modernity

The response of Islamic countries to the concept of modernity as it obtains today varies from country to country. One thing in common, again with one or two honourable exceptions, is that all of these countries have excepted domination of the west, particularly the USA. Some of them even consider this domination as the ultimate in modernity although their societies continue to be utterly feudalistic in values. Neither do they have democracy nor any trace of gender justice. However, most of these countries vie one with the other in buying latest weaponry from the west. This also is considered by them as a symbol of modernity.

Saudi Arabia

Saudis are governed by highly authoritarian monarchy with no trace of democracy or gender justice. In this so-called Islamic regime women enjoy no independence worth the name. Though, they are allowed to work in establishments run only by women, they are not free to work anywhere else. They are not allowed to go out alone without being accompanied by a *mehram* (a man within the prohibited degree of marriage). No independent thinking in the fields of religion, philosophy and other social sciences is permitted. In every field there are preestablished official dogmas to which all Saudi citizens have to conform. There is no respect for human rights as there is no democracy. So all parameters of modernity are absent.

Yet, one finds a superficial aura of modernity. The Saudi cities are concrete jungles including the holy cities of Mecca and Madnia. There is so much blind imitation of the West in designing buildings that no trace of Islamic heritage has been left. There is no Islamic ambiance even outside the holiest mosque of the Islamic world to which millions of pilgrims flock every year, i.e., K'aba. Just outside the holiest mosque of the Islamic world there are huge modern concrete buildings. Mecca appears to be like any other Western city. No attempt has been made to preserve its Islamic heritage, not even in architecture. Could this be construed modernity? If it is, it is very superficial. There is no rethinking of Islamic issues, no freedom of thought, no critical evaluation of Saudi practices, but only blind imitation of the west in its worst aspects— mindless urbanization and disruption of old patterns of living. Also, the Saudi rulers buy huge stockpiles of Western arms which only increases their servility to the west. More arms they purchase from the West, more dependent they Iran become on it.

Iran

Earlier the Shah of Iran had also followed similar policies. He tried to impose forcibly the western modernism on a highly traditional society. The Shah also wanted to become regional satrap by stockpiling the Western arms. There was no trace of democracy in Iran during his regime too and no respect for human rights which are important parameters of modernism. Also, women were made to wear mini skirts which was taken as sign of gender justice. In fact women were far from enjoying higher status in the Shah's Iran. After the revolution Ayatollah Khomeini also tried to impose many restrictions on women. *Chador* was made compulsory. Also, the traditional laws as regards women were not changed. However, women in post-revolutionary Iran are becoming quite conscious of their rights. Iran is one of the few Islamic countries which allows women to contest elections and now woman has also become vice-president of Iran. In Kuwait it is still being debated whether women could be given right to vote or not. In appearance Kuwait is one of the most modern cities of the world, but its society still continues to be medieval. In all these countries except Iran there is total dependence on the West—for arms as well as for economic development. They have no ability for developing modern science and technology or independent thinking in social or religious sciences. Egypt produced many modern thinkers, but it is also regressing now and fundamentalism has raised its head. In Egypt also there is lack of democracy and human rights. In relation to women too, the 'ulama of al-Azhar are resisting change. So the record of gender justice is not very bright in Egypt too. However, compared to other Islamic countries, Egypt is relatively more advanced. Pakistan had much better record until Zia's time. Zia's political Islam pushed Pakistan too back to medieval thinking in religious matters. Democracy there is not more than a decade old. In post-Zia-ul-Haq period democracy was striking roots, but it lasted for few years and military rule has been reimposed. Zia's fundamentalist Islam also deprived women of their many rights which otherwise they had gained through their struggles.

Thus, it will be seen that though Islamic society had much better record in terms of modernity during the early period of Islam, the Islamic societies today have regressed to medieval ages, though they claim to be superficially modern. Most of the Islamic societies have neither democracy, nor concept of human rights or gender justice nor capacity for independent development of science and technology.

CHAPTER 7

Islam, Muslims and Philosophy—An Introductory Note

Islam is not only a great religion which liberated human beings from clutches of superstition and made them aware of nature and its laws, but also enriched human culture, thought and philosophy. Its contribution in these fields is immense. The Arabs did not give much importance to learning before Islam appeared on the scene. They were very proud of the science of genealogy. They made immensely rich contribution to poetry. Nothing else interested them much like poetry. They were not even interested in literacy; in fact they took pride in being illiterate. Also like other tribals, they were very proud of oral culture. When Islam appeared on the scene, we are told, by historians, there were only 17 literate persons in Mecca.

However, Islam gave great deal of importance to reading, writing and learning. *'Ilm* (knowledge, science) is repeatedly stressed in Qur'an. Some of the attributes of Allah are *'alim* (knower), *khabir* (informed), etc., 'To read' is one of the commandments of Allah. The Qur'an says, "Read and thy Lord is most Generous, Who taught by the pen, Taught man what he knew not. Nay, man is surely inordinate, Because he looks upon himself as self-sufficient." (Qur'an 3-7:96). And as for *'ilm* and its numerous derivatives we find hundreds of verses. The Qur'an in fact equates *'ilm* with *nur* (light) and *jahl* (ignorance) with darkness. The Prophet also encouraged learning by his famous saying that the ink of a scholar is more precious than the blood of a martyr.

It was because of this encouragement of learning and scholarship that Islam changed the whole scenario and within few years of its existence it created an ocean of knowledge. The illiterate Arabs became great patrons of learning and not only wrote volumes and volumes on religious sciences like *hadith* (Prophet's sayings and doings), commentary on Qur'an, *fiqh* (jurisprudence) and biographical writings on the Prophet but also made very rich contribution to the secular knowledge—be it philosophy, be it art and literature, be it political science, history and sociology or be it geography, physics, chemistry, medicines or optics. They developed such taste for knowledge that they scoured all possible sources of knowledge and translated into Arabic from whatever was available in Greek, Persian and Sanskrit. The Abbasid rulers founded what was known as *Bait al-Hikmat* (House of Wisdom). This institution was the only institution of learning and knowledge of its time in the whole world. It was in this place that the treasures of knowledge from Greece, Persia and India were stored and rendered into Arabic. It was perhaps the biggest and richest library of its time. It is worth noting that when the Muslims were spreading the light of knowledge, Europe was passing through the dark ages. The Islamic world gave humanity to the philosophers like Al-Farabi, Avicina (Ibn Sina), and Avveros (Ibn Rushd). Their works were taught in European Universities during medieval ages. In fact Europe rediscovered Greek treasures of knowledge through Muslims. The Isma'ilis had produced by 9th century AD. *Ikhwanus Safa* what was hailed as the encyclopaedia of knowledge. It was written in 52 volumes. There were volumes on religion, philosophy, psychology, mathematics, and music, apart from many other sciences. Jabir bin al-Hayyan was a great chemist. Imam Ja'far as Sadiq, the great Imam was not only a great expert in Islamic sciences, but also was knowledgeable in various other sciences as we find in his book *Kitab al-Tawhid* which is compilation of his lectures. His great grandfather Ali, son-in-law of the Prophet, also encompassed all available knowledge in his great book *Nahj al-Balagha* which has been hailed by many modern western scholars also. No wonder than that H.G.Wells has described Arabs as foster fathers of knowledge. It is true that Arabs themselves were not so much interested in acquisition of knowledge as other non-Arab Muslims, but they provided full encouragement and needed resources for other Muslims to do so. And these Muslims drew their inspiration from the Qur'an and the sayings of the Propet.

It was not only during the Abbasid period that philosophy and other sciences flowered in the Islamic world. Even during the Umayyad period various schools of philosophy came into existence. It was during the Umayyad period that heated discussions took place on questions like whether human person is free or determined. Those who thought human person was free were known as *Qadriyas* and those who thought human beings were not free were called *Jabriyas*. In fact this question acquired political overtones—the supporters of Umayyads stressing that human persons are not free, but determined by divine will and their opponents maintaining that they are free. Hasan Basari, the great sufi scholar of the first century of Islam was supporter of free will. It was his disciple who became founder of rational school of philosophy called the school of Mu'tazalites in Islamic history. They were the first rationalists of Islam.

The Mu'tazalites were fiercely opposed by the traditionalists known as *mutakallimun* (theological dialecticians or simply dialecticians). Dr. T.J. De Boer observes about them, "The name *mutakallimun*, which was at first common to all the dialecticians, was in later times applied specially to the anti-Mu'tazalite and orthodox theologians. In the latter case it might be well, following the sense, to render the term by dogmatists or schoolmen. In fact while the first dialecticians had the dogma still to form, those who came later had only to expound and establish it." (De Boer, 1967, 43).

The rationalists (Mu'tazalites and other rationalists represented by the great philosophers like Avicena and others) and the *mutakallimun* were, in the history of Islamic philosophy always at daggers drawn and these controversies provided much dynamism to Islamic scholars, but in later times the rationalists lost and the dialecticians won. Thus, the common Muslims followed Ash'arites (named after its founder Ash'ari, 873-935) who were vehemently opposed to rationalists. They are also known as atomists. According to them each atom is created, in each moment, by Allah and destroyed by Him. What we perceive as sensible world is mere passing accidents created by Allah. Thus, according to this theory—which became prevalent among the common Muslims mainly due to support lent to it by Imam Ghazali (d. 1111). Imam Ghazali was one of the greatest dialecticians produced by the world of Islam. His widely read book *Ihya' al-'Ulum* (Revivification of Knowledge) influenced the largest number of Muslims since then. He also wrote a book *Tahafut al-Falasifa* (Bewilderment of Philosophers) to point out the deficiencies of philosophers. But Averos wrote a strong rejoinder to Imam Ghazali and named it *Tahafut Tahafut al-Falasifa* (Bewilderment of Bewilderment of Philosophers).

Thus, it will be seen that various intellectual controversies raged in the intellectual history of Islam and that early history of Islam was intellectually quite dynamic and no formulations—dogmatic or intellectual—ever went unchallenged. Though, it is true that it was dialecticians who ultimately prevailed and rationalists lost out, but it is not unique to the history of Islam. The history of Hinduism, Buddhism, or Christianity is no different. When a religion acquires mass proportions, intellectuals can hardly prevail. The masses find much more security in accepting than in questioning. It is acceptance which creates a sense of inner peace while questioning perpetrates scepticism and a sense of uncertainty. Blind faith is far more soothing for ordinary human soul. This is part of human nature and not of any religion or religious belief system. The revealed word is more often ambiguous and subject to different interpretations. While the people of intellect look for stimulation from this ambiguity the theologians look for fixed meanings and carve out dogmas which are then widely accepted by the unquestioning minds. The great minds refuse to accept these humanly formulated dogmas and by questioning these not only provide stimuli to human thought, but enrich it and develop it.

We find such great minds in the intellectual history of all world religions. Alam Khundmiri, a teacher of philosophy from Usmania University, has tried to portray in his philosophical essays now being collected in the book form, these stimulating controversies in early and modern Islam. Alam was very knowledgeable and has brought to bring depth of his knowledge in these philosophical essays. There is hardly any controversy in medieval or modern Islam which Khundmiri has left untouched. It would, therefore, be of great interest to throw light on some of these essays and critically examine the nature of these controversies. Alam, himself a progressive thinker and philosopher, was deeply interested in these questions which had always occupied the great minds in Islamic history.

Alam touches very important question in his essay on "The Tension between Morality and Law in Islam". It is well-known that jurisprudence and law occupies very significant place in Islamic thought. Islam was first preached in a tribal society which had no written law, but only oral traditions. The Prophet was confronted with many questions pertaining to marriage, divorce, inheritance, property, accumulation of wealth, slaves and so on. His preoccupation was a just society and many prevailing traditions were far from just, specially for weaker sections of the society. The Qur'an also stressed the importance of justice and a just society. Concentration of wealth is also strongly criticized. Women were also among the highly oppressed.

Thus, Alam points out: "An ethical vision might have an historical element whereas the actual legal injunction is necessarily a specific response to an actual temporal situation. The relation between the ethical vision and the latter is more of a psychological nature which colours and influences the universe of human intentions and desires. However, there always remains a gap between the basic ethical vision and the actual commands and injunctions. Later this gap reveals itself in the life-style of those who prefer to act according to the letter of the law and those who prefer to strive to get at the historical vision, the basic piety which might be common to more than one historical religion. A serious study of any religion, its dogma and its legal structure reveals this difference."

Alam goes right at the root of the problem. Those who oppose any change, prefer to go by the letter of the law and totally ignore the ethical vision. For pro-changers it is historical vision which is most important and not the legal injunctions pronounced at a particular historical juncture. The debate goes on in all religious traditions. As far as Islam is concerned, justice is a very important element of its ethical vision. Says the Qur'an, "O' you who believe, be upright for Allah, bearers of witness with justice; and let not hatred of a people incite you not to act equitably. Be just; that is nearer to observance of duty. And keep your duty to Allah. Surely Allah is aware of what you do." (5:8). Qur'an also says that, "...when you speak, be just, though it be (against) a relative". (6:153)

Thus, justice is very important for the ethical vision of Islam, but the *Shari'ah* was a project evolved at a particular historical juncture. The orthodox maintain that it (i.e. *Shari'ah*) is immutable as it is based on divine injunctions. It has been causing lot of problems today in respect of women's rights. Alam also points out in his essay that in Islam religiosity and morality have become synonymous with legality. This position needs to be corrected. In fact religiosity and morality should have an upper hand and not legality. Legality should be subordinate to moral and ethical vision. He also very rightly points out that the principle of *sunnah*, so far as general Muslims are concerned, does not normally include the element of the moral fervour of the Prophet and his strong passion for the liberation of man, translated into action so far as the concrete situations of life could permit. The only way to make *Shari'ah* conform to the moral fervour of the Prophet and ethical vision of Islam is to effect necessary changes in it.

Ghazali, as pointed out before, was the great pillar of-revivalism in Islam in the eleventh century. His revivalist project had profound effect on the Islamic thinking throughout the history of Islam. Ghazali encountered the rational trends in his days and reestablished the Islamic orthodoxy. He influenced the Islamic thinking so profoundly that one of the bold writers of modern Arab world Al-Qusaimi is of the opinion that the Muslim world cannot enter the age of enlightenment unless it rejects the Ghazalian world outlook.

Alam Khundmiri points out that Indian writers on Islamic thought are, however, still under the spell of Ghazali and go to the extent of comparing him to the scientific philosophers like Hume and Kant, as if long ago Ghazali anticipated them. In fact, no less a person than Dr. Mohammad Iqbal, compared Ghazali with Kant in his lectures *Reconstruction of Religious Thought in Islam.*

Prof. Khundmiri says that a careful study of Ghazali shows that he was a fatalist in ethics, an obscurantist in his philosophical method and a justifier of status quo in his political theory. All these elements of his thought, he says, proceed from his philosophical method. Ghazali was a rationalist, even an atheist, at one stage of his life. However, in his search for truth, he was dissatisfied with ratiocination and ultimately turned towards *tasawwuf* for inner peace and spiritual solace. Prof. Khundmiri rightly points out that Ghazali is the acknowledged leader of orthodox Islam. It was he who gave a final and decisive blow to the Islamic scholastic philosophy based on Aristotelian and neo-Platonic sources. This was such a decisive blow that philosophy ceased to remain a respectable term in the Islamic world and even the powerful counter arguments of Ibn Rushd (in his *Tahafut Tahafut al-Falasifa*) were not able to revive the respectability once attached to philosophy. Posterity remembered Ghazali as 'the proof of Islam' (*hujjat al-Islam*). According to Ghazali, rationalism led to scepticism and doubt and doubt is far from reassuring in human life and only way out of these doubts for Ghazali was to base religious doctrine upon an inner, supra-rational illumination. Thus, in search of inner peace, Ghazali turned to mysticism. Alam, therefore, rightly thinks that Ghazali represents the rare combination of a theologian and a mystic in the history of Islamic civilization. No other person before or after him, could achieve this distinction of being equally acceptable to both. He gave to theology a mystic orientation and to mysticism a theological foundation.

Here Alam has somewhat exaggerated the importance of Ghazali. In fact after him, Alf Mujaddid Thani from India achieved such a respectability in both theological and mystical circles. Though one does not find in the writings of Ghazali critique of Ibn Arabi's doctrine of *wahdat al-wujud*, one finds such a critique in the writings of the Mujaddid. The Mujaddid, like Ghazali, changed the course of Islamic thought in India. Though, a powerful critic of *wahdat al-wujud* the Mujaddid, remained a sufi and evolved his own doctrine of *wahdat al-shuhud*. Shah Waliyullah and others largely followed Mujaddid Alf Thani and Waliyullahi School's contribution to Islamic thought in the Indian subcontinent is too well-known to be recounted here.

Ghazali strengthened the Ash'ari doctrine of occasionalism. According to this view, occasionalistic metaphysics with its theory of indivisible atoms and accidents, had made all secondary agents (like human beings) superfluous and philosophically irrelevant. According to Ash'ari God creates accidents each moment and the universe consists of these accidents. Thus, the universe is created, according to this view, by the direct will of God. Human agent has no role to play, no creativity or initiative. He is a determined object and not the active, creative agent. The moment of efficacy of the secondary agents is repudiated, the principle of causality pertaining to the world of events becomes superfluous.

Prof. Alam, however, points out that Al-Ghazali and the Ash'arites did not deny that the world appears as continuous; what they denied was that this continuity is an inherent feature of this world. Their position was that continuity proves the 'grace' of God and the miracles establish his omnipotence.

There has been a long debate among the intellectuals as to why Ghazali could deliver such a knocking out blow to rational philosophic thought in Islam. Was it due to inherent strength and superiority of his theologico-mystical arguments or due to some other external factors. Many argue that it was former and others maintain that it was contingent on the historical circumstances. However, a balanced view should be taken. As far as the *jamhur* (masses) is concerned it, more often than not, opts for certitude of faith than nagging doubts of rational thinking. It is the intellectual elite which can face the hazards of nagging doubts. The masses would opt for certitude of orthodox dogmas. As pointed out before, Ghazali was also initially enamoured of rational philosophy, but he found no inner certitude and solace which he ultimately found in mystic thought. It is also interesting to note that the Mu'tazila also did not survive long in the history of Islam as their approach was rational. It is the Ash'arite doctrines which found wide acceptance.

As for the external factors it is important to note that the Ghazali's period was the period of decline of the Abbasid's empire which was finally dealt its deathblow by the sack of Baghdad in 1258. In such circumstances it is conservatism which thrives and it did. The rational thought reached its glory during the hey day of the Abbasid empire. The Persian intellectuals were the mainstay of the Abbasid rule and the Mu'tazila became their political ally. But during its declining period, the Mu'tazila lost their political influence and were severely persecuted by the Abbasid Caliph al-Mutawakkil. Thus it will be seen that both internal and external factors worked to the advantage of Islamic orthodoxy and Imam Ghazali came to be accepted as the proof of Islam.

It can be argued by some that, though the Abbasid caliphate declined strengthening the conservative school of thought what about the Islamic empires in Spain, Iran and India? Were they not at the height of their glory? In fact they were. Why then Ghazali's thoughts prevailed in these regions also? There is no simple answer, but nevertheless the question has to be confronted and some possible answer attempted. Firstly, the Abbasid empire came to acquire a central position in the world of Islam. Other rulers often derived their legitimacy from their sanction. No other ruler enjoyed such a primacy as the Abassids did, rightly or wrongly. They were looked upon as the real legitimate caliphs. Even the Shiite Buwayhid sultans had to maintain the facade of their (i.e., Abbasid caliphate). The Spanish, the Persian and the Indian Muslim rulers were treated as peripheral and their rise and decline did not have such an impact on the intellectual currents in the world of Islam.

But in these peripheral Islamic empires one finds glorious periods of intellectual enlightenment be it in the Fatimid empire of Egypt, Safavids of Iran, Mughals of India or Islamic rule in Spain. There is a definite relationship between political hegemony and material development and intellectual achievements, though it may not be one to one relationship. However, one must say that, though one may not agree with Al-Ghazali all the way one cannot deny his seminal role in the intellectual history of Islam. He was a towering figure.

Alam also deals with another important question which preoccupied the great minds in the intellectual history of Islam, i.e., man's nature and destiny. He deals with this question in his essay "Man's Nature and Destiny—Philosophic View in Islam". The Ash'arites, as pointed out before, dominated the religious viewpoint in the world of Islam. While the Mu'tazilites emphasized moral freedom and responsibility of man the Ash'arites held the view to the contrary. According to them man was unfree. But, even the Ash'arites could not dismiss the fact of felt freedom and were obliged, Khundmiri points out, "To offer an ingenious explanation of the ultimate freedom in terms of 'acquisition' (kasb), metaphysically derived from the doctrine of 'occasionalism', constant intervention of Allah in the life of cosmos and man. In this scheme man is reduced into an automaton, devoid of will, freedom and even responsibility. Each moment he faces death and extinction and next moment is granted resurrection by the grace of Allah."

In the legal schools also the superiority of the legal category over metaphysical and eschatalogical was established and the legists took horizontal view of man. Ultimately this neglect of vertical, Alam feels, resulted in complete negation of it. Alam goes on to make a very radical statement—though it is difficult to disagree with him on this—that a study of Islam in history reveals a fact of immense importance for study of the religious phenomenon that laicization of religion does not ultimately lead to a secular approach in politics and general human life, but results in a tyrannical theocracy, which happened in the history of Islam after the period of the Khulafa al-Rashidun (the four caliphs after the holy Prophet).

The man who was described by the Qur'an as the viceregent of God on earth became a passive spectator of the divine drama on earth and a mere recipient of the divine commandments as interpreted by the

legists. Salvation in this scheme, points out Khundmiri, largely depends
on the literal obedience to law and the life of the spirit is relegated to
the background.

There has always been a debate on reason and revelation among
the philosophers in Islam. The philosophers though stress the role of
reason in human life, do not reject the supremacy of revelation. They
too accept the consensus of the community that revelation supersedes
reason, though reason by no means is insignificant. They make an
interesting connection between reason and revelation. Revelation, for
them, is more than mere spoken word. Revelation itself is the revelation
of the divine reason. Both Al-Farabi and Ibn Sina assert the essential
unity of reason and revelation. It is interesting to note that the Isma'ilis
(also referred to as *Batinis*) held very similar views with the philosophers.
In fact it is claimed by some scholars that Ibn Sina was a secret Isma'ili.
The philosophers, like the Isma'ilis held that man's existence in this
world is a fall in material sense, but a journey upwards in spiritual sense.
Kathif (material) tends to become *latif* (spiritual) as man achieves higher
and higher degree of perfection. The spirit's association with matter is
its descent, but, it rises upwards through perfection to the highest realm
of spirit. Its highest realm is the first intellect which comprehended the
ultimate reality, i.e., God and it represents ultimate unity between spirit
and pure reason or reason and revelation.

According to this view, points out Alam, man's earthly existence is
both.a tragedy and occasion—a tragedy if he forgets his trans-historical
origins and gets absorbed in history, losing his contact with eternity.
The soul's travel upwards is its travel homewards till its merger with the
first intellect. The Isma'ilis, however, maintain that after the descent the
highest realm one can reach—through refinement and spiritualization—
the realm of the tenth intellect, not the first one. It is only the Prophet
and the Imams who can reach the highest realm of first intellect.

In the Sufi literature the. destiny of man is to be *Insan al-Kamil*
(Perfect Man), the actualization of the hidden treasure, the meeting
point of history and eternity. It is the *Haqiqat al-Muhammadiyyah*
(the reality of Muhammad and his prophethood). He is the perfect man.
It is believed that Abdul Karim al-Jili propounded the notion of *al-Insan
al-Kamil*. But Alam maintains that this idea was not his innovation.
Al-Farabi, much before him, was moving in the direction of unfoldment

of this idea. He says that the philosopher Imam of Farabi is the highest gnostic being, the *Khidr* of the Qur'anic symbolism.

Jalaluddin Rumi is another respectable name in this respect. He stresses the importance of love. For him love assumes the role of mediator between the highest reality and man. If one is absorbed in love and higher its degree of absorption, nearer one will be to the highest reality. Also, interestingly enough, Prof. Alam draws our attention to Ibn Arabi's doctrine that 'Every thing that exists is the object of God's Mercy (*kullu mawjudun marhum*) in *Fusus al-Hikam*' According to Ibn Arabi, the sufficient cause of origination of things is the divine compassion (*rahma*) which mediates between non-being and being. Man's nature, therefore, lies in divine compassion.

Thus, there is identity of views between Rumi and Ibn Arabi. While for Rumi love is the meeting point of the sensible and spiritual, for Ibn Arabi, it is compassion which brings about unity of the two. Love thus, mediates between the sensible and spiritual and completely transforms the human personality.

Alam Khundmiri also discusses the problems of religion and modernity in his essay "Religion and its Application to Modern Life". For all eastern religions, particularly Islam this problem has emerged as a major challenge. Alam, unlike many others, does not see basic contradiction between the two. He points out that the Western world does not face this problem for it has "an unbroken identity from its Greece-Roman past till the present moment, but the Islamic world gained a new identity after it embraced Islam. The problem of the Islamic world is to enter the new age of science without losing its identity, i.e., without renouncing its Islamic past".

Alam is fully aware of the fact that to preserve ones identity is to preserve ones past. Also, in Islam the world of events (*duniya*) and the hereafter (*akhirah*) are regarded as a continuum. Both together provide human beings the opportunity for development to higher stages of reality. Alam points out that the Qur'an regards time and history as real and believes in the irreversibility of time. It does not encourage idea of rebirth or the possibility of man's entry in the world of events. It believes in the law of causality so far as the world of events is concerned. It makes it obligatory to study the physical world and history of mankind. It also discourages pseudo-sciences like astrology and regards universe as indifferent to human destiny. It also denies that there are intermediaries between God and universe and thus, makes a scientific study of universe possible. After recounting these characteristics of Islam he comments that "these few points are enough to suggest that the Qur'anic spirit is not anti-scientific, it rather encourages scientific study of the universe. Dr. Iqbal in his *Reconstruction of Religious Thought in Islam* has pointed out that the Qur'anic spirit is inductive, not deductive and modern science depends on inductive way of thinking. Deductive method leads to speculative reasoning while inductive logic leads to study of empirical facts.

According to Qur'an man is free and can act freely within the limits set by God. Life is described as "striving in the way of God" (*jihad fi sabilillah*). One must strive in conformity with the values and ethical vision revealed by Allah and for him entire world is a stage of activity provided he fixes his gaze towards Allah. Amal is quite central to Islamic way of life. The Prophet, through his actions transformed the whole world and made it obligatory for his followers also to continue to transform it

It is this vision that the Muslims have to recapture if they want to live successfully in the modern world. Science deals with objects out there and Islam in no way opposes this. If Muslims today fit ill with modernity and modern science it is their fault, their failure to come to terms with the changing world.

Thus, it will be seen from what is discussed above that Prof. Alam Khundmiri is a significant modern Islamic thinker from India. Unfortunately, he did not publish much which he was capable of. His ideas deserve much wider dissemination. It is a commendable step to publish his essays in one volume which were written for different journals. These essays deserve to be read very widely both in academic as well as non-academic world.

CHAPTER 8

Globalization, Islam and Threat to Diversity

Every country in the so-called Third World is facing the threat of cultural homogenization from the process of globalization. Though, the process, in a sense, began with the colonization of the Afro-Asian countries, the threat, for number of reasons, not to be analyzed here, was more acutely felt in the post-second world war period than before. During the colonization period too, number of protest movements against the Western cultural hegemonism were launched, but the urge for independence from the colonial masters predominated. It was felt that once the country was liberated, the colonial culture will also fade away and the native culture will become hegemonic once again.

However, this expectation was not fulfilled and the colonial culture continued to rule over the native culture. The ruling elite were generally immersed in the colonial culture and the governmental institutions also were shaped accordingly. The native institutions, language and culture were generally looked down upon and shunned by the ruling elite. The colonial language also enjoyed supremacy. French, in former French colonies and English in former British or American colonies became the languages of central administration.

However, the resentment did not build up soon after independence. It took several decades before the reaction set in. In the beginning the reaction was also cautious or in the form of debate. But later it acquired more strident tones and gradually it erupted in violence. The former colonial countries began to be liberated soon after the second world war. India was the first major country to become independent in 1947. Many other countries followed the suit. Many African countries got independence in early sixties. Algeria in western Africa was liberated in early sixties.

One more factor needs to be noted here and this is very crucial factor. All countries which were liberated from colonial clutches did not go democratic. India, the biggest among them, got independence through democratic struggle and therefore, found it easy to remain democratic even after independence. But many Afro-Asian countries which were directly or indirectly under colonial control, developed authoritarian power structures soon after their independence. Algeria and several other Afro-Asian countries are its example.

While the reaction against the colonial-western culture was more democratic in democratic countries, it tended to be violent in authoritarian countries. This was because the dictatorial rulers themselves were highly westernized and did not permit any opposition to western culture and administrative institutions. The opposition assumed violent form, particularly when the economic going was also not good. In democratic countries like India there was sufficient scope for democratic opposition and therefore, it hardly had any need for violent expression.

Second crucial factor, as hinted above, was economic in nature. Despite hegemony of western culture and institutions in post-independence period, much opposition did not develop as long as the economic going was good. However, when the economic condition deteriorated, poverty and unemployment increased and the ruling elite did not allow any democratic opposition. Thus violence broke out.

Also, much depended on native conditions and sociological institutions. The protesters exploited religious discourse, if no alternative social or political discourse was available. For example, in the Islamic countries like Algeria and Iran, neither there was democracy nor was there any alternative non-religious discourse native in nature available. The protesters, per force, had to adopt strongly religious discourse. Moreover, this religious discourse had great deal of mobilizing capacity and had very large social space. The opponents felt that the corrupt westernized elite is responsible for the deteriorating moral atmosphere and economic situation as they have no regard for religion and religious institutions. If they had enforced the religious teachings and *shari'ah* provisions strictly and rigorously, such deterioration would not have taken place. Thus, what we call Islamic fundamentalism is the product of given circumstances in certain Islamic countries. We will throw some more light on this little later.

Often the geographical boundaries of the liberated countries embraced several linguistic and cultural groups. The colonial powers went on uniting often different cultural and linguistic units for administrative purposes. Thus, many disparate units came under one colonial power. The ruling elites of the independent countries took over what was administrative rather than political unit and insisted on retaining it as it is and tried to create nation-state out of it. It created many complex problems and even led to violent movements. Thus these nation-states in the Third World countries came to be bewilderingly diverse. And diversity is both an opportunity as well as a challenge, a strength as well as weakness.

The Western countries, are often mono-cultural and mono-linguistic (with certain exceptions, of course), though increased migration from former colonized countries is fast changing the linguo-cultural scene in the metropolitan countries. The United States of America, in order to retain its cultural uniformity, had followed—with a sense of pride—what it called the melting-pot model. The various identities derived from European countries melted into one culturally uniform American identity. However, now that culturally diverse Afro-Asian groups are migrating to America, its melting-pot model has become irrelevant and now the Afro-Asian multi-cultural or mosaic model has acquired acceptability. Thus, now even Western countries are no more mono-cultural or mono-linguistic, though of course, their own culture remains predominant.

It was necessary to throw light on these aspects if we have to understand the impact of globalization on the Third World countries in general and the Islamic countries, in particular. As pointed out before, the process of western acculturation began with colonization itself, but the term globalization was never used. This term came to be used recently. There is good reason for this. Earlier, during the colonial days, the native country was culturally influenced by its own metropolitan country, say Britain, Germany, Holland, Italy or France. But now the cultural or political influences are not restricted to any one metropolitan country. The TV, the internet, the satellite, has demolished all cultural boundaries and brought the whole globe under its cultural network. And hence, the term globalization.

But, in a way, the term 'globalization' is certainly misleading. There is hardly true interaction between cultures of different countries which are part of this globe. It is Western, particularly, north American culture which is hegemonic and dominant. It has become, in a way, what is being termed as a global culture. All other cultures are termed as 'ethnic' which was termed, during the colonial days as 'native'. The term 'ethnic', like the term 'native', carries a sense of backwardness and something, though not contemptible, is not in keeping with the acceptable trend also. Thus, for all practical purposes, what is termed as 'globalization' is, in effect, westernization or, to be more precise, Americanization.

One more development took place in late eighties, i.e., total collapse of communist rule in the former Soviet Union. The world, which was bipolar, suddenly became unipolar and the American hegemony became supreme. This development was quite momentous in senses more than one. The term globalization is also post-Soviet phenomenon. It changed the very intellectual comprehension of world of politics, apart from the global power-equations. Some termed it as the 'end of history' while others termed the post-Soviet era as that of 'clash of civilizations'. It is interesting to note that both the articles the one on the end of history and the other on clash of civilizations were written by those who shape the American foreign policy.

Prof. Huntington's theory of clash of civilizations generated a great deal of debate, specially in the Islamic world. Prof. Huntington theorized that after the collapse of communist block, the forthcoming clash would be with the Islamic civilization. Though, on close scrutiny, Huntington's proposition is found to be quite facile and simplistic, it gained great deal of currency through the western dominated media. According to Huntington when the world was bipolar (divided between the USA and USSR) what was important was which side you are on, but now that the world was unipolar what is important is 'what you are' i.e., what is your identity—Western, Chinese, African or Islamic. According to him there is basic clash between these identities.

Earlier it was important to know what is your political alignment and now it is important to know which civilization you belong to. In other words, what is your identity. In fact in the Greek philosophy Socrates laid emphasis on knowing oneself. And in the eastern philosophies, the very basic emphasis has been on knowing oneself. In fact in the Sufi Islamic tradition too the basic emphasis is on knowing oneself ("one who could know oneself, would know the entire universe"). In Afro-Asian countries the emphasis has always been on self-identity.

What Prof. Huntington wrote was no new discovery. But since Huntington is a Western scholar, an expert on international law, he did not know the eastern thought intimately enough. For him to lay emphasis on self-identity is a post-Soviet phenomenon.

Also, for Prof. Huntington, the hegemonic civilization is the western civilization and perceives threat to this hegemonic civilization from the Islamic and Chinese civilizations. Any challenge to Western civilization is a threat and he terms it a 'clash'. What is not western is a threat. It is this arrogance of power which is highly problematic and evokes strong reaction from the Islamic world. The threat can go only when the western civilization and its hegemony is accepted and ones own civilizational identity is wiped out. Ones ethnicity is tolerable, but not ones civilization. The process of globalization can be complete only and only when Western civilization completely triumphs over all other civilizations. No civilization should challenge it. The Soviet block had posed a political threat to America. And at present it has been vanquished. Also, it was easier to vanquish a political foe, it is not so difficult to meet a military threat, but it is very difficult, almost impossible, to meet the civilizational challenge.

Thus, what the West terms as globalization is in effect total, or at least, near denial of civilizational and cultural diversity. Though, the western scholars are talking of pluralism in the post-modern world, but are not inclined to accept non-western cultures as their equals. Like pluralism the term globalization is also post-modern. Thus, what was accepted with one hand (pluralism) is being taken away with the other (i.e., through globalization). The West can hardly come to terms with the cultural and civilizational diversity.

This cultural homogenization as a result of globalization is creating strong reaction in many societies. The reactions are of course varied in terms of intensity and direction. More traditional and politically authoritarian a society is, greater is the intensity of reaction against global homogenization. Algeria, Egypt and Iran are obvious examples. We will deal with the situation in these countries briefly.

One should also remember that there are some factors which accelerate the process of this reaction: deterioration in economic condition and failure of the ruling elite to solve acute economic problems. Also, when the ruling elite charters the course of economic liberalization which itself is an economic dimension of globalization it further aggravates the problem. In fact the economic factor more often than not, turns out to be a key factor. The second important factor in this connection is consumerism and blind greed for accumulation by the ruling elite. It results in immiserization of masses on one hand and limitless accumulation of wealth in the hands of few all powerful multi-nationals, on the other.

If we examine the cases of Iran, Algeria and Egypt, among the Muslim countries, these factors turn out to be very crucial. Let us take the example of Iran first. Iran was politically an authoritarian society smarting under the rule of the Shah before the Islamic revolution of 1979.

The Shah was not allowing any democratic space for protest and ruthlessly suppressed those who opposed him. His economic policies were totally pro-West which resulted in hyper-inflation and increasing unemployment. His land-reform policy proved to be no less disastrous. The surplus land was turned over to the multi-national agri-business rather than to the small peasant. The peasantry thrown out from the land found itself in the slums of south Tehran in search of petty jobs. Over and above it, it also found itself afflicted by hyper-inflation. All these factors combined to arouse his wrath.

These factors by themselves would not have caused great social upheaval Iran went through had not the Shah pursued what he termed as 'white revolution'. The so-called white revolution was nothing, but unrestricted westernization imposed from above on basically a feudal traditional society. These policies created a westernized upper middle class which broke all traditions and ignored all traditional values. Usually the westernized elite indulges in consumerism and believes in hedonism. Their life-style is devoid of all values and is mere pursuit of this-worldly enjoyment.

Also, in a traditional society like Iran, the Shah took on a section of the clergy. The land reform deprived it of its income. All these factors combined into an explosive situation. The traditional merchant class also suffered in various ways, particularly because of the pro-western economic policies of the Shah. Shah's economic policies favoured the new economic elite depending on export-import related business. The bazaar merchants (the traditional mercantile class) became the support-base of the clergy led by Ayatollah Khomeini. Khomeini led stress on

Islamic values and made out a case that westernization has resulted in utter material corruption and destruction of traditional Iranian culture. It was western culture which had become hegemonic marginalizing the Iranian culture and values.

This had tremendous appeal for the Bazaar elements and the immiserised masses of South Tehran slums. The economic misery on one side and highly westernized life-style of the upper class elites, totally neglectful of Iranian cultural values on the other, was the ideal situation for the Islamic revolution whose dynamo was Bazaar elements and the poorer masses of Tehran slums.

The Islamic intellectuals like Ali Shari'ati and Ayatollah Taleqani also played very important role in arousing Islamic pride among the educated middle class Iranians. Ali Shari'ati was himself a highly educated intellectual. He was a product of Soborn in Paris. He reinterpreted Islam in keeping with the then prevailing Iranian situation. He inspired a large number of educated youth and his meetings in the Huseiniyeh mosque in Tehran were attended by thousands of people. He created a sense of Islamic pride in them and mentally prepared them for Islamic revolution.

Ayatollah Taleqani, unlike Ayatollah Khomeini, was not conservative. He had an open mind and was quite accommodative of modern developments. He emphasized the redistribution of wealth among the weaker sections of Iranian society and his Islamic discourse also made people proud of their Islamic identity. It was quite natural that when westernization led to de-emphasis on Islamic identity, the Islamic discourse of Ayatollahs as well as that of modern educated Islamic scholars like Ali Shari'ati restored pride in Islamic identity. It was result of this that many women whose mothers had taken to. miniskirts under the influence of Shah's white-revolution, took to Islamic *chador*. It is interesting to note that the *chador* itself was much more than an Islamic veil: it was, above all, a proclamation of ones pride in Islamic identity. But in the post-Islamic revolution period the *chador* became, an oppressive instrument in the hands of *pasdarans* (the Islamic guards). The significance of *chador* varied with the varying situation.

In this connection it is important to note that much depends on as to who monopolizes and manipulates the religious symbols. Unfortunately both Ali Shari'ati and Ayatollah Taleqani did not survive long. Ali Shari'ati was probably eliminated by the SAWAK, the Shah's notorious

secret intelligence service and Ayatollah Taleqani, though apparently
died a natural death, was also probably a victim of Ayatollah Khomeini's
displeasure. If Ayatollah Taleqani and Ali Shari'ati had lived longer and
been free to inspire the masses of Iran, the Islamic revolution could
have taken a different turn. However, it is just a conjecture. The history
takes its concrete course not just by 'ifs' and 'buts', but by the actors
and events which appear on its stage.

The case of Algeria is equally interesting, though somewhat different.
The military controlled ruling elite in Algeria were also under the influence
of the West. There too, no democratic space was available as Algeria
was ruled, since its liberation from France, by the military generals. The
socialist discourse too did not help as the economic situation remained
stagnant. Thirty years after the anti-colonial revolution, the Islamic
militancy broke out. The Islamic Front which had won the elections,
was not allowed, by the military dictatorship, to assume power. Most
of the militants came from lower middle or poorer classes. Their anger
and frustration against the system assumed violent form. The military
rule was essentially liberal secular rule, but it could not deliver Algeria
from economic mess. The rising unemployment and inflation ultimately
led to Islamic militancy. The frustrated youth think that the economic
and other ills can be removed if Islamic identity and *shari'ah* is truthfully
implemented. The failure on economic front is automatically ascribed by
them to adoption of Western secular policies and think that Islamization
would lead to their much sought after deliverance from all problems.
And to bring about Islamization they resort to indiscriminate violence
and go on killing innocent people.

Both Iranian and Algerian case studies show that the two factors
mentioned above, i.e., authoritarianism and failure on economic front
lead to explosive situation and the revolt against the system derives its
legitimation from Islamic sources. The American rulers often back up
dictatorial and authoritarian regimes in the Third World and force on
them economic policies which benefits American or western multi-
nationals and, the native ruling elite. It brings nothing, but misery for
the poorer masses and lower middle classes. Thus, religious
fundamentalism basically breeds among these sections of urban society.

The religious fundamentalism is basically an urban phenomenon.
Be it Iran, Algeria or Egypt, India or any other country for that matter,

fundamentalist extremism breaks out in urban areas. There are good reasons for that. The rural society in the third world countries is generally a traditional society, well rooted and integrated in traditional culture and religious values. The rural society hardly feels alienated from traditional values. Also, unlike urban society, life is simpler and away from unrestrained consumerism. The percentage of modern education is also not very high and hence, lower incidence of educated unemployment. The impact of globalization on rural areas is also comparatively much less.

Religious fundamentalism can and does breed in democratic societies also. Its intensity may differ and its impact more diffused as there is democratic space for protest. Fundamentalism has both religious as well as political dimension. The impact of globalization and westernization which results in bulldozing the local religious identities, evokes strong urge for re-emphasizing and reasserting religious values. It leads to religious revivalism. And, establishment of secular polity in a traditional society leads to an urge for reimposition of rule based on *shari'ah* or dharma shashtras. With that view political movement is launched by traditional religious elite. This is political dimension of fundamentalism. But in a democratic polity, protest movement has much greater possibility of democratic expression and hence, lesser tendency for becoming violent, though violence cannot be completely ruled out.

However, even if violence breaks out it can be handled by the democratic rulers given the will. Sometimes pressure from below may be immense and the democratically elected governments may loose the nerve. It was witnessed in India both during the Shah Bano Movement and during the Ramjanambhoomi Movement. In a multi-religious society the majority-minority syndrome may claim much fundamentalist space. This is precisely what happened during the Ramjanambhoomi Movement. The Ramjanambhoomi Movement had both religious as well as political dimensions. It did provoke a religious fervour among a large section of Hindus for building a Ram temple. As under the impact of modernization and westernization, the traditional values and identities were being undermined, the Ramjanambhoomi Movement could easily revive religious fervour.

However, it had strong political dimension also. The BJP tried to exploit this religious fervour among the Hindus to capture political power. The BJP targeted the biggest religious minority to consolidate the Hindu votes and thus, greatly increased its representation in the Parliament. But thanks to the resilience of our secular democratic polity, this religious fervour could not be politically exploited indefinitely. The Muslim masses too have developed a new awakening and no other religio-political movement on the scale of the Shah Bano Movement can be launched by the fundamentalist forces. This was possible only because of democratic space and political resilience.

CHAPTER 9
Islam and Other Religions

Islam is often thought to be an exclusivistic religion claiming authority over divine truth and considering all other religions inferior, if not false. It is also maintained that the semitic religions like Judaism, Christianity and Islam are based on 'one book, one prophet' and hence, tend to be authoritarian and intolerant. Though, usually all three semitic religions are targeted, Islam is thought to be the worst of the three. Judaism and Christianity are thought to be more liberal as they have been westernized. Islam essentially remains an Asian and hence, more sectarian and intolerant religion.

To say the least it is highly superficial view. First the very distinction between semitic and non-semitic religions is hardly a valid distinction. Religion in terms of beliefs, institutions, traditions, values and rituals is a common category. Semitic or non-semitic religion, all share these characteristics of a religion. The fact that some religions have one book and one prophet does not, if one takes realistic view of purples' beliefs and practices, make crucial difference. Religious beliefs, traditions and rituals whether based on one scripture or more exercise unique authority.

It is normally pointed out that Hinduism is far more liberal and tolerant as it is not based on one single book or authority. This is an erroneous view of tolerance or intolerance. It is important to note that tolerance or intolerance is a psychological and not a religious category. Faith, beliefs, traditions and rituals constitute religious category. It is any belief or tradition, derived from one book or several, one authority or more, which tends to exercise authority over human persons. As for tolerance and liberalism being psychological in nature, a person from the same religous tradition could be more tolerant and another quite intolerant. Thus, we find both tolerant and intolerant Muslims, Christians and Hindus. Both in Islam and Hinduism we find highly dogmatic and rigid sects, orthodox and reformed traditions. It is also observed that

some institutions are more authoritative and some practices more rigid
in one religious tradition and others in other religious traditions. For
example, the institution and practice of caste is much more rigid in
Hinduism than in any other religion. Also, in many respects Hinduism
is much more orthopraxic than orthodox religion. Hinduism may not be
theologically very rigid, but it is certainly more rigid than Islam in many
practices. Muslims tend to be quite rigid as far as shari'ah formulations
are concerned, though they tend to be more liberal in practice. They are
much less rigid in cultural practices.

There are numerous examples of this. A Muslim could marry in
medieval period across caste or religious barriers with much more ease
than a Hindu. A Muslim did not mind eating with people of any other
religion or caste, though a Hindu found it more embarrassing. The
Hindus, in short, were governed much more rigidly by caste institutions
than Muslims. Though, music has been traditionally banned by *Shari'ah*
law, hardly any Muslim—except a rigid coterie of 'ulama—ever refrained
from enjoying music. In fact Indian Muslims contributed richly to music.
The sufis openly defied the *fatwas* issued by theologians against *sama'*
(listening to music) and evolved the tradition of *qawwali* (devotional
music). Some sufis and dervishes even resorted to practice of dance
(dancing dervishes) which was considered much more strictly prohibited
by *shari'ah*.

However, Muslims have been quite rigid in terms of theology than
Hindus. Any deviation, for example, from the theological doctrine of
monotheism is considered unpardonable sin. Abdul Wahab of Najd
(now in Saudi Arabia) stretched monotheism to such lengths that even
calling anyone other than Allah (for example saying 'O! Muhammad')
was dubbed as *shirk* (associating partners with Allah which is denounced
by the Qur'an as major sin). But Muslims are divided not only in
numerous schools of *Shari'ah*, but also in numerous schools of
theological thought. The Mu'tazila and most of the Shi'ah schools—
Ithna 'Asha'iras and Isma'ilis included—consider it a *shirk* to believe
in divine attributes. They see God as devoid of all attributes whereas
the Asha'iras strongly believe in the attributes of God. Any such denial
for them would amount to *kufr*. The Isma'ilis, on the other extreme, not
only deny all attributes of Allah, but also believe that He is beyond all
comprehension and can only be referred to as *huwa* (that). Thus, the
Isma'ilis come much closer to the higher Hinduism's concept of God as

nirguna and *nirakar*. Also some sufis come close to what is expressed as *tat twam asi* (that you are that).

Thus, it will be seen that in every religious tradition apart from inter-religious differences, intra-religious differences also play an important role. Be it a religon based on a single scripture like Islam or Christianity, or a religion like Hinduism based on more than one authority, intra-religious differences persist and play, at times, quite crucial role. In Islam too history is replete with intra-religious intolerance rather than inter-religious ones. In the history of Islam more Muslims were dubbed as *kafirs* than non-Muslims. In Hinduism too there were conflicts of serious nature between the Shaivites and Vishnuvites as well as between different other sects. Many *bhakti* saints too faced great deal of persecution at the hands of mainstream or well-established traditions.

Before we proceed further I would also like to point out that tolerance and intolerance towards the 'other'—the religious or cultural or linguistic—depends on external factors, factors other than religious, cultural or linguistic. These other factors are either related to power or distribution of economic resources. The struggle for power between two religious groups or struggle to control resources often gets transformed into religious or sectarian struggle. The crusades are the best example of this.

The Muslims and Christians had coexisted almost harmoniously in Islamic regimes. But their relations deteriorated when the struggle to control political power and acquire supremacy over the other began between them. Gradually the threshold of tolerance was lowered. Earlier during the Prophet's time same thing happened between the Jews and the Muslims. The Prophet not only had no religious dispute with the Jews—he gave them full freedom to practice their religion and the Qur'an described both Abraham and Moses as the great prophets. Abraham was shown the highest regard by the Prophet describing him as *hanif*, i.e., one inclined towards true path. But still there was acute struggle and intolerance between the Jews and early Muslims and two major battles were fought amongst them. The struggle was not religious, but political in nature—to establish the political supremacy of one over the other. The Jews saw in Muslims a rising power in Madina soon destined to control the city—both politically as well as economically. Hence, religious conciliation and tolerance towards their religious doctrines by the Prophet and his followers did not make them less belligerent towards Muslims. But if such fear and suspicion does not exist and political power and economic resources are shared satisfactorily the two religious communities might exist quite harmoniously. During the Abbasid and the Fatimid periods, the Muslims, Jews and Christians coexisted fairly harmoniously. Imam Taymiyyas edicts of *kufr* against the Christians had more to do with crusades than with Islamic theology.

Similarly the Hindu-Muslim relations in India have gone through tortuous history depending on the power-relations between the two. Aurangzeb, despite his rigid orthodoxy had cordial relations with a large section of Rajputs who fought with him against Dara Shikoh. He had great confidence in Mirza Raja Jaisingh and gave him the highest *mansab* in his court. But he had highly hostile relations with Marathas, particularly those led by Shivaji, as unlike Rajputs, he could not enter into a power-sharing arrangements with them.

Thus, it will be seen that tolerance is not the function of religious faith, but that of social situation. In one situation two religious communities could coexist in near perfect harmony while in adverse social circumstances they could exhibit high degree of intolerance towards each other or even engage in bloody fight. If seen objectively and dispassionately no religious faith preaches that other religious traditions are false or based on untruth. No great religion of the world, be it Hinduism, Judaism, Buddhism, Christianity or Islam, has arisen in competition with the other. They were born in drastically different historical situations and geographical locales. They were more concerned with the immediate gravity of situation their founders faced than theological truths of other religions. And even when faced with other religions in the immediate vicinity like Islam faced Judaism and Christianity, they accepted their truth rather than have a sense of rivalry with them. Kabir and Nank too preached tolerance between all religious faiths and what they attacked was hypocrisy of their followers. These religions gave new vision and attacked the vested interests who had made pre-existing religions as handmaid of their interests. Thus, Islam did not attack the doctrines of Judaism or Christianity but the way vested interests had reduced them to serve their interests and made religion an amalgam of socially harmful and unjust traditions and superstitions.

The Qura'n's Attitude Towards Other Religions

First of all it is very important to note that the Qur'anic approach is not religion-specific, but conduct-specific. It comes out through various Qur'anic verses. It is this approach which determines the Qur'anic approach towards other religions. The fundamental Qur'anic category in this respect is *istibaq bi'l khayrat*, i.e., excelling each other in good deeds. Though, the Qur'an prescribes certain basic beliefs which form the fundamentals of Islam, but its attitude towards other religous beliefs and practices is far from hostile. Whatever the beliefs and practices, whatever the ways of worshiping God, one must perform good deeds. And good deeds are spelled out not in ritual, but in value-terms. One must be upright, truthful (*sadiqin*, 3:16) just (4:135 and 5:8), egalitarian (many Qur'anic verses and *hadith* refer to human equality) benevolent (2:112), charitable (4:114), compassionate (48:29), respecting human dignity (17:70) and pious (49:13). Thus, it is a human person who imbibes all these virtues and values who is at the centre of the Qur'anic religious discourse rather than his/her way of worship. Excellence in virtues (*istibaq bi'l khayrat*) is the most fundamental category in the Qur'anic ethics.

The Qur'an has emphasized this in numerous verses. It says, "Every community faces a direction of its own of which He is the focal point (i.e., has its own rites and ways of worshiping). Vie, therefore, with one another in doing good deeds." The Qur'an makes it more clear when it says, "True piety does not consist in turning your faces towards east or west—but truely pious is he who believes in God and the Last Day and the angels and revelation and prophets; and spends his substance—however much he himself may cherish it—upon his near of kin and the orphans and the needy and the wayfarer and beggars and for the freeing of human beings from bondage and is constant in prayer and renders the purifying dues; and (truely pious are) they who keep their promises whenever they promise and are patient in misfortune and hardship and in time of peril: it is they that have proved themselves true and it is they who are conscious of God." (2:177)

As will be seen this is very fundamental verse in the Qur'an as far as the Qur'anic approach to essence of religion is concerned. It will be seen that this verse is clearly conduct specific and not religion specific. What matters is the ethical conduct described in all its aspects in above verse rather than what religion one follows. Of course belief in God, his angels, prophets and the Day of Judgement is also important. But all religions prescribe belief in these matters. It is also important to note that this verse talks of belief in prophets, *not* in single prophet. Which means that all prophets were messengers of Allah. The central emphasis in this verse is on taking care of weaker sections of society (poor, orphans, needy) and liberation of slaves. Also fulfilling promises and remaining steadfast during adversities is emphasized. Thus, those who fulfill the conditions in the above verse should be considered truly religious persons, whatever their way of worshiping.

The Qur'anic approach to other religions is not at all hostile. All it condemns is *shirk* (associating partners with God) and worshiping idols *per se* as if they themselves are God. Even there it has quite liberal attitude as is evident from chapter 109 of the Qur'an. It says, "Say: 'O you who deny the truth (*kafirun*)! 'I do not worship that which you worship and neither do you worship that which I worship. And I will not worship that which you have (ever) worshipped and neither will you (ever) worship that which I worship. Unto you is your devotion, and unto me, mine.'" (109)

Even a glance at the above verses clearly shows that the Qur'an, though opposed to the kind of idol-worship practiced in pre-Islamic Arabia, tolerates it. It is thus, not true that Islam requires its followers to compel idol-worshipers to embrace Islam or choose death. "The sword in one hand and Qur'an in the other" is the greatest myth popularized by the hostile west. It is unfortunately believed by many in India too. It does not, however, stand any intellectual scrutiny. As for conversions they have hardly been through coercion in Islamic history. If one goes through the peace treaties mentioned by Baladhuri in his *Futuh al-Buldan* (Conquest of Countries) one will not find any treaty which mentions conversion to Islam as a condition for peace or stoppage of war. On the other hand, the conquerors were more concerned for worldly goods like Woodgrains, clothes and slaves.

Conversion can be put under three categories: (1) Conviction; (2) convenience and (3) coercion. The conversions under first and last categories were comparatively few while most of the conversions took place under second category. A thorough reading of source material will easily establish this. In fact people either because of caste oppression or oppression from their fellow-religionist landlords, embraced Islam which they found more liberative. In fact even *jizyah* which was negotiated rather than imposed, was much lighter than the oppressive taxes imposed by the Roman and Sassanid empires as mentioned by Baladhuri. As for coercion some conversions in this category did take place, but they were far and few in between. The Qur'an expressly says, "There is no compulsion in religion." (2:256) The Qur'an lays emphasis on wisdom and goodly exhortation for inviting people to accept Islam (see 16:125). As for some coercive conversions it was more of a political revenge by the ruler rather than a` zeal' to preach Islam. Such a zeal can never popularize a religion. It would create hatred rather than love for it. As for conviction such conversions were also very few. It is only those who are in search of some belief system which would satisfy them both intellectually and spiritually would convert to any religion. There are very few people who are in search of spiritually and intellectually satisfying belief system. The largest number of conversions usually come from the oppressed sections of society who want to escape the oppressive nature of the existing system.

Here it would be interesting to throw some light on the Qur'anic position of demolition of others places of worship. The Qur'an does not allow places of worships to be desecrated. It says, "And if Allah did not repel some people by others, monasteries and churches and synagogues and mosques in which Allah's name is much remembered, would have been pulled down." Here places of worship of all those religious communities who had their presence in Arabia of the Prophet's time, have been mentioned. The places of worship of those communities who did not live in the vicinity of the Prophet, though not mentioned in here, can also be included for extending protection.

Maulana Muhammad Ali says commenting on this verse, "The religious freedom which was established by Islam thirteen hundred years ago has not, yet, been surpassed by the most civilized and tolerant of nations. It deserves to be noted that the lives of Muslims are to be sacrificed not only to stop their own persecution by their opponents and to save their own mosques, but to save churches, synagogues and cloisters as well—in fact, to establish perfect religious freedom. The mosques, though they are the places where the name of Allah is remembered most of all, come in for their share of protection even after the churches and synagogues. Early Muslims closely followed these directions and every commander of an army had express orders to respect all houses of worship and even the cloisters of monks, along with their inmates." (See *Holy Qur'an*, Lahore, 1973, pp. 656). It will be perfectly legitimate keeping in view the verses of Chapter 109 of the Qur'an, to extend such protection to the temples too. If any ruler demolished temple, even for political reasons, it was against the express injunction of the holy Qur'an.

Qur'an's Approach Towards Pluralism

The Qur'an was revealed in religiously pluralist society and it accepted religious pluralism as a matter of fundamental principle. First of all it accepted the validity and truthfulness of religions preached by biblical prophets like Abraham, Moses and Christ. It lays emphasis on all prophets being messengers of Allah and it exhorts Muslims not to discriminate between one prophet and the other. And those who do are described as "truely disbelievers" (see 4:150-51). A true Muslim would accept and respect all prophets whatever religious tradition they belong to. Any discrimination is equated with *kufr* (disbelief).

Also, the Qur'an makes number of statements accepting plurality of religion. In one of the verses (5:48) it says, "For every one of you We appointed a law and a way. And if Allah had pleased He would have made you a single people, but that He might try you in what He gave you. So vie one with another in virtuous deeds." The Qur'an emphasizes three things in the above verse. One, that every nation or people has a law and a way of their own. The people follow this law and the way. While law refers to the legal requirements, 'way' refers to a spiritual path. The law and the way will naturally be conditioned by the requirements of the people, though the universal principles may be in common.

Two, that it is not Allah's desire to create one religious community through coercion. He, rather prefers plurality and throws it as a challenge to try whether believers in different laws and ways can coexist peacefully together. If he desired he could have made entire humanity a one (religious) community, but He did not choose to do so. Third, Qur'an lays stress on *istibaq bi'l khayrat* (vying one with the other in virtuous deeds). Thus, it is superiority of action which is emphasized over superiority of belief. It is sheer arrogance on our part that we stress and compete in superiority of our respective beliefs rather than superiority of our actions.

It is easier to stress superiority of belief through intellectual arguments, but very difficult to give proof of superiority of action. The later entails great deal of integrity of character and superiority of conduct. It requires lot of sacrifice of our own interests to be superior in action over others. To be truthful in action is the most challenging task. While superiority of belief is merely an intellectual exercise requiring no proof in action. Human conduct is a mixture of belief and interests with interests predominating. Hence, the Qur'an stresses excelling each other in action rather than in intellectual debates.

The verse 10-99 also lays emphasis on plurality. It says, "And if thy Lord had pleased, all those who are in the earth would have believed, all of them. Wilt thou then force men till they are believers." The verse 2:256 ("there is no compulsion in religion") is very similar to this one. The Prophet used to be anxious when Arabs spurned his faith. So it is again emphasized here that there cannot be any coercion in matters of belief. One can preach and explain principles of ones faith leaving it to the people to accept or reject.

The Qur'an divided humanity into three categories: Muslims, people of the Book (ahl al-Kitab), and non-believers. Among people of the Book were included all those who possessed one or the other scriptures. In immediate neighbourhood were the Jews and Christians who possessed scriptures The Torah and the Bible. The Qur'an tried to establish a dialogue with them. Thus, it says, "O' people of the Book, come to an equitable word between us and you, that we shall serve none, but Allah and that we shall not associate aught with Him and that some of us shall not take others for lords besides Allah. But if they turn away, then say: Bear witness, we are Muslims." (3:63). And in 29:46 Qur'an also laid down that, "Argue not with the people of the Book except by what is best, save such of them as act unjustly. And say: We believe in that which has been revealed to us and revealed to you and our God and your God is One and to Him we submit."

Thus, the Qur'an not only stresses on dialogue between Muslims and the people of the Book, but also lays down ground rules for dialogue which are quite fare. Thus, the Qur'an promotes dialogue of culture rather than culture of confrontation. It says firmly no to any kind of coercion in matters of religion. It is also interesting to know that,

though the Qur'an mentions only three religions as those of people of
the Book, the Prophet later included the Zoroastrians of Iran also among
them when he entered into a treaty with the Zoroastrians of Bahrain.
The third Caliph Usman included even the Berbers of West Africa
among the people of the Book. Some of the 'ulama (theologians)
accompanying Muhammad-bin-Qasim on his invasion of Sindh accepted
the Hindus belonging to this category citing Vedas as the Book they
possessed. Later in the 18th century a sufi of the Qadri Order Mazhar
Jan-i-Janan endorsed similar position declaring the Hindus as the people
of the Book citing Vedas as their revealed Books. Thus, the category
of *Ahl al-Kitab* was not rigid. It was inclusive and not exclusive.

As for the third category, i.e., unbelievers (*kafirs*—those who did
not possess any scripture) were of course to be guaranteed freedom of
belief, but to be subdivided into two categories: those who were
aggressive and were on war path with Muslims and persecuted them
(called *harbi kafirs*, i.e., warmongering *kafirs*) and those who coexisted
peacefully with Muslims called *ghayr harbi kafirs*. The Muslims have
to live in peace with *ghayr harbi kafirs* without quarrelling with them
about their beliefs. The Qur'an also made it clear in Chapter 109 referred
to above.

The Muslims came in conflict with unbelievers of Mecca not because
of their unbelief, but because their leaders persecuted Muslims for
believing in Allah and His Messenger Muhammad. The early history of
Islam in Mecca is full of cruel persecution of Muslims by the leaders
of unbelievers of Mecca. The verse 4:75 clearly refers to this situation
of extreme persecution and permits the persecuted Muslims to fight
against their persecutors. "And what reason" the verse says, "have you
not to fight in the way of Allah and of the weak among the men and
the women and the children, who say: Our Lord, take us out of this
town, whose people are oppressors and grant us from Thee a friend,
and grant us from Thee a helper."

Thus, it is clear that it was this persecution and not unbelief of the
people of Mecca which brought about conflict between Muslims and
the *kuffar* of Mecca. There is also a *hadith* of the Prophet which says
that one can coexist with unbelief, but not with persecution and injustice.
Thus, it will be seen that Islam believes in plurality of religion, culture,
race, and language. It celebrates diversity and plurality.

CHAPTER 10

The Concept of Islamic State

Islamic state is a most discussed subject both among supporters as well as among its opponents. Is there any such concept? Can we call any state an Islamic state? There are many claimants of course. Interestingly, among the claimants there are military dictators as well as monarchs. Can we legitimately call it an Islamic state? Is there any such criterion to judge the claim? If so, what is that criterion? Generally, some ritualistic aspects of Islam like prayer, fasting, *zakat* etc., are imposed in addition to the Islamic punishments to lay claim to the Islamic state. Will it be enough of a criterion?

First of all we should know whether there is any concept of Islamic state in the Qur'an or *hadith* literature. A thorough examination of the scripture and *hadith* literature shows that there is no such concept of Islamic state. In fact after the death of the holy Prophet the Muslims were not agreed even on the issue of his successor. The Muslims split on the question—a section maintaining that the Prophet never appointed any successor and another section maintaining that he did.

As far as the Qur'an is concerned there is, at best, a concept of a society rather than a state. The Qur'an lays emphasis on *'adl* and *ihsan* (justice and benevolence). A Qur'anic society must be based on these values. Also, the Qur'an strongly opposes *zulm* and *'udwan* (oppression and injustice). No society thus, based on *zulm* and *'udwan* can qualify for an Islamic society. The Qur'anic values are most fundamental. It is thus debatable whether a state, declaring itself to be an Islamic state, can be legitimately accepted as such without basing the civil society on these values. We will throw more light on this later.

First of all it is important to note that the pre-Islamic Arabic society had not known any state structure. It was predominantly a tribal society which did not know any distinction between a state and a civil society.

There was no written law, much less a constitution. There was no governing authority either hereditary or elected. There was a senate called *mala'*. It consisted of tribal chiefs of the tribes in the area. Any decision taken had to be unanimous and the tribal chiefs enforced the decision in their respective tribes. If a tribal chief dissented, the decision could not be implemented.

There was neither any taxation system nor any police or army. There was no concept of territorial governance or defence or policing. Each tribe followed its own customs and traditions. There were of course inter-tribal wars and all adult tribals took part in defending ones tribal interests. The only law prevalent was that of *qisas* (retaliation). The Qur'an put it succinctly as, "And there is life for you in retaliation, O men of understanding." (2:179) The whole tribal law and ethic in pre-Islamic Arabia was based on the law of retaliation.

The Islamic movement in Mecca inherited this situation. When the Prophet and his companions faced severe persecution in Mecca they migrated to Madina also known as *Yathrib*. Madina was also basically a tribal city governed by tribal laws. Like Mecca in Madina too, there was no state and only tribal customs and traditions prevailed. In fact Madina was worse in a way than Mecca. In Mecca inter-tribal wars were not much in evidence as it was turning into a commercial society and inter-tribal corporations for trade were coming into existence. However, Madina, being an oasis, was a semi-agricultural society and various tribes were at daggers drawn. It was to get rid of the inter-tribal warfare that the people of Madina invited the holy Prophet as an arbitrator.

The Prophet, a great spiritual and religious personality, commanded great respect and set out to establish a just society in Madina. First of all he drew up a pact between various tribal and religious groups known as *Mithaq-i-Madina* (the Medinese treaty) which guaranteed full autonomy to all tribes and religious groups like the Jews, the Muslims and other Pagan tribes. Thus, all religious groups were free to follow their own law and tradition and there was no coercion in such matters. The holy Qur'an also declared that, "there is no compulsion in the matter of religion (2:256)." The *Mithaq-i-Madina* was a sort of preliminary constitution of the 'state' of Madina which went beyond a tribal structure and transcended the tribal boundaries in matters of common governance. It also laid down that if Madina is attacked by an outside force all will defend it together. Thus, for the first time a concept of common territory so necessary for a state to operate, was evolved. Before this, as pointed out earlier, there was concept of tribal, but not of territorial boundaries.

The Prophet, in a way, took a revolutionary step, in dissolving tribal bonds and laying more emphasis on ideological boundaries and territorial boundaries. However, the Prophet's aim was not to build a political community, but to build a religious community instead. If Muslims evolved into a political community it was accidental rather than essential. Hence, the Qur'an lays more emphasis on values, ethic and morality than on any political doctrines. It is *din* which matters most than governance. Allah says in the Qur'an that *al-yauma akmaltu lakum dinakum* (I have perfected your *din* today, 5:3). Thus, what the Qur'an gives us is a perfect *din*, not a perfect political system. The political system had to evolve over a period of time and in keeping with the needs and requirements.

One of the basic duties of the Muslims is "enforcing what is good and combating what is evil" This clearly gives a moral and spiritual direction to an Islamic society. The later emphasis on integral association between religion and politics is, to the best of my knowledge, totally absent in the holy Qur'an. The Prophet was an enforcer of good *par excellence* and he devoted his life to eradicating evil from society. But he never aspired for political power. He was one of the great spiritual persons born on this earth. He strove to inculcate spiritual power among his companions. The following verse of the Qur'an enunciates the basic philosophy of the Muslim community. "You are the best *ummah* (nation, community) raised up for people: you enjoy good and forbid evil and you believe in Allah." (3:109)

Thus, it will be seen that the basic task of the Muslim *ummah* is to build a moral society based on good and negation of evil. The unity of Muslims is possible only if they remain basically a religious community engaged in building a just society which has no elements of *zulm* (oppression and injustice), though there may be different ways of approaching the truth. The holy Prophet is reported to have said that a society can persist with *kufr* (unbelief), but not with *zulm* (injustice). The Qur'an also describes Allah as *ahkam al-Hakimin* (best of the Judges, 95:8). These are all value-giving injunctions and hence, give a direction to the society.

Islam never required Muslims to evolve into a political community. Politics leads people basically to power-seeking projects and aspirations for power brings about division rather than unity. The Qur'an required Muslims to remain united and not entertain disputes weakening themselves. "And obey Allah and His Messenger," the Qur'an says, "and dispute not one with another, lest you get weak-hearted and your power depart and be steadfast. Surely Allah is with the steadfast." (8:46)

When some one aspires for political power they dispute with each other and thus, become weak which is what Muslims have been warned against. And in the history of Islam the dispute between Muslims arose on the question of political power. Who should wield political power and who should rule was the main question after the death of the holy Prophet. Thus, Muslims began to divide on the question of power.

Various disputes arose between different groups of Muslims, even leading to bloodshed during the thirty years of what is known in Islamic history as khilafat-i-Rashidah (period of the rightly guided rule). This thirty-year period was full of conflict and bloodshed. Three rightly guided Caliphs out of four were assassinated. Why the spirit of unity was lost? Why wars broke out between different groups and parties? It was mainly on account of fights between different aspirants for power and pelf. The first signs of these aspirations appeared immediately after the death of the holy Prophet.

The people of Mecca belonging to the tribe of Quraysh claimed their superiority over others and said that an imam can only be from the tribe of Quraysh as they first embraced Islam and they were most cultured and cultivated with adequate experience. The supporters of the Prophet from Madina, the Ansars, on the other, claimed that it is they who helped the Prophet when he was driven out of Mecca due to severe persecution by the people of Quraysh and hence, they better deserve to succeed the Prophet. The imam or caliph, they claimed should be from amongst the Ansars. The members of the family of the Prophet felt that 'Ali, the son-in-law of the Prophet and leader of the Hashimites, was better qualified to succeed the Prophet.'

Thus, these fissures appeared as different groups aspired for leadership and consequently for power associated with the 'nascent Muslim state. It is also necessary to stress here that a preliminary state structure came into existence because it was historical and not religious need. We would like to elaborate this a bit.

As every Muslim knows that the religious duties of Muslims are to pray, fast, pay the poor due (*zakat*), perform *haj*, and believe in *tawheed* (unity of Allah) and not associate aught with Him. This is necessary for spiritual control over oneself. A Muslim can perform these obligations wherever he/she lives. There is no need for an Islamic state for this. A Muslim living in a non-Muslim society can perform these obligations without let or hindrance. And even when there is Muslim rule no ruler can forcibly enforce these obligations on Muslims. Matters of *'ibadat* (acts of worship and spiritual exercises) cannot be coercively enforced by any authority. It is a matter between human beings and Allah.

However, it is a different matter as far as *mu'amalat* (relations between human beings) are concerned. A state has to govern these *mu'amalat* and ultimate aim of the state is to set up a society based on justice and benevolence (*'adl* and *ihsan* in the Qur'anic terms). *'Adl* and *'ihsan* are most fundamental human values and any state worth its salt has to strive to establish a society based on these values. But for this no particular form of state is needed. Even an honest monarch can do it. It is for this reason that the holy Qur'an praises prophet-rulers like Hazrat Da'ud and Hazrat Sulayman who were kings, but Allah's Prophet's too. Even Queen Bilquis is praised for her just governance in the Qur'an though she was not a prophet herself.

But the Qur'an is also aware that such just rulers are normally far and few in between. The governance has to be as democratic as possible so that all adults could participate in it. If governance is left to an individual, or a monarch, the power may corrupt him or her as everyone knows absolute power corrupts absolutely. It is for this reason that the Qur'an refers to democratic governance when it says: "And those who respond to their Lord and keep up prayer and whose affairs are (decided) by mutual consultation and who spend out of what We have given them (42:38)." Thus, the mutual affairs (those pertaining to governance) should be conducted only by mutual consultation which in contemporary political parlance will be construed as democratic governance. Since in those days there was no well defined practice of political democracy, the Qur'an refers to it as *'amruhum shura' baynahum* i.e., affairs to be conducted through mutual consultation which is very meaningful way of hinting at democracy. The Qur'an is thus, against totalitarian or

Here a problem may arise as far as the Shi'ah sects are concerned. They believe in the theory of *imamah* i.e., only an imam from the progeny of the Prophet's son-in-law and his daughter Fatima can inherit the Prophet. The Shi'ahs, in other words, reject the concept of *khilafah*, i.e., succession to the Prophet through election by the people. The right to succession is confined only to the members of the Prophet's family and it is available to no one else. It is no doubt the very basis of the Shi'ah tradition and faith.

But this hardly changes the ethos of governance. The state in Iran is today a democratically elected one. The President of Iran and the *Majlis* (Parliament) are elective in nature. In todays world there is no question of a ruler coming from the Prophet's family. It was a different matter when the controversy arose immediately after the death of the holy Prophet. A group of people then did feel that Hazrat Ali, the son-in law of the Prophet who was rigorously just, who had fought and won many an Islamic battle, who was one of the bravest and most honest persons should have succeeded the Prophet. He was qualified for good governance in ways more than one. Apart from being just, honest and brave, he was most learned as well. The holy Prophet had described him as gateway to the city of knowledge, Prophet being the city of knowledge himself. He was also greatly confident of his knowledge. He often used to say *saluni qabla tafquduni* (ask me before you loose me).

In such circumstances it is not surprising that many people felt that Ali was much more qualified to succeed the Prophet than any one else. His two sons Hasan and Husain were also eminently qualified as they too were inheritors of the virtues and qualities of the Prophet, they having been trained and brought up by the Prophet and Ali. No one else has such an excellent opportunity to have been so intimately connected to the Prophet and the whole Islamic atmosphere around him.

In fact the theory of imamah was based on this certainty of correct religious guidance and, a guarantee for good and just governance. It is this inner certitude which gave rise to the belief that the members of the Prophet's family are most suited to guide and govern. The Shi'ahs moreover believe that the imams were infallible and can do no wrong. But two things are again important to note here. The governance by imam also could not be absolute in personal terms, much less dictatorial or authoritarian. The imam will also have to consult the representatives of the people as per the Qur'anic injunction in 3:158 in which even the Prophet is required to consult them.

This verse 3:158 is a very important verse in laying down the guidance for governance. It is a divine statement against dictatorship or authoritarianism. The verse reads: "Thus, it is by Allah's mercy that thou art gentle on them. And hadst thou been rough, hard-hearted, they would certainly would have dispersed from around thee. So pardon them and ask protection for them, and consult them in (important matters)..." Thus, a ruler has to be gentle, not hard-hearted and rough and has to act in consultation with the representatives of the people. This verse has been addressed to the Prophet and no imam from his family can deviate from this divine injunction.

Thus, even an imam from the Prophet's family cannot be absolutist and has to base his rule on democratic principles. Thus, even the Shi'ah theory of imamah cannot lead to absolutist or purely personal rule. Also, an imam can be infallible in religious matters, in laying down religious rulings. But in all secular and worldly matters he will be bound by democratic structures of governance.

Secondly, the theory of imamah was much more relevant as far as the close relatives of the Prophet who lived either with him or very close to his period, was concerned. Today, more than fourteen hundred years after the death of the holy Prophet, no one can claim such physical closeness to the Prophet and its resultant benefits. And even within the first century of the Prophet's death there were many claimants for the office of Imam and the Shi'ahs were divided into number of sects and subsects what of today fourteen hundred years after the death of the Prophet who can determine the authenticity of the claimant to the office of the imamah? The twelve Shi'ahs and also the Isma'ili-Mustalian Shi'ahs believe in seclusion of their respective imams. No wonder than that Iran has adopted the elective principle of governance which is what is the ultimate aim of the Islamic scripture.

Also, once Islam spread to vast areas of the world outside the confines of Arabia new ethnic and racial groups were added to its fold. This proved both the strength as well as weakness of the Islamic society. Strength as far as rich diversity was concerned and weakness as far as complex problems and group conflicts it gave rise to. The group conflicts got greatly intensified even within the limited period of *Khilafat-i-Rashidah* which lasted for slightly less than thirty years.

During this period number of groups came into existence. The most powerful group was of the tribe of Quraysh who were *muhajirs* (immigrants) to Madina to which they migrated along with, or after the Prophet, to avoid persecution in Mecca. They claimed to be the *sabiqun al-awwalun*, i.e., those who responded to the call of Islam earlier than others and also belonged to the tribe of the Prophet. After the death of the Prophet they also came out with the doctrine that the *khilafat* be confined to the tribe of Quraysh. However, the Quraysh were divided into several clans of which the clans of Hashim (to which the Prophet himself belonged) and of Banu Umayyah were at loggerheads. Among the Qurayshites, the Hashimites and the Umayyads fought against each other for the leadership of the nascent Muslim state. Ali and his sons (particularly Hasan and Husain) who were claimants to the leadership all belonged to the clan of Banu Hashim.

Then there were *Ansars*, i.e., those who belonged to the tribes of Aws, Khazraj of Madina and who had helped the Prophet by swearing allegiance to the Prophet and helping him (hence, *Ansars* i.e., helpers) migrate to Madina and supporting him *vis-a-vis* his powerful opponents. The Ansars also claimed leadership of the state after the death of the Prophet on the basis that they had helped the Prophet and that without their help his mission would not have survived. But the Qurayshites strongly resisted their claim to the *khilafat*. Then the leaders of the Ansars proposed a compromise and said let one from the Quraysh and one from the Ansars share the leadership, but this was also turned down by the Qurayshites that it would lead to more conflict and confusion.

The third group was of those Muslims who embraced Islam from amongst the conquered non-Arab peoples of Iraqi or Persian or Egyptian or Syrian origins. The emphasis of Islam on justice and equality of all believers was great attraction for these non-Arab peoples. In course of a few years large number of non-Arabs, most of them belonging to weaker sections of society converted to Islam and demanded equal treatment. But despite strong emphasis of Islam on equality of all believers irrespective of their social status, nationality, colour or race, the ruling classes among Muslims were not prepared to accord equal treatment to them. Most of the Muslims were accepted Muslims only when they were made *mawla* (affiliate or associate) of a tribe. Kufa and Basra in Iraq, Egypt, Damascus, etc., became centres of these non-Arab Muslims. Many of these non-Arab people were those captured in various wars.

As for the first group, i.e., the Qurayshites, they wielded power with the second group of Ansars being their co-partners. These groups were contented to a great extent, though some subgroups were not. The Hashimites, for example, were a discontented group among the Qurayshites as the non-Hashimites had captured power. Similarly, among the Ansars who were initially the allies of the Quraysh, the younger generation among them felt neglected.

The fact that the second caliph was assassinated by a discontented non-Arab slave on the dispute about wages to be paid to him, showed the beginning of the dissidence in early Islamic society. It reached its peak during the period of third caliph Hazrat Usman when the non-Arab people from Egypt, Kufa and Basra surrounded his house and murdered him in presence of his wife when he was reciting the holy Qur'an. Dr. Taha Husain in his book *Al-fitnah al-Kubra* (The Great Insurrection) has dealt with this problem. This uprising against Hazrat Usman was result of deep discontent found among them as they felt completely neglected and found themselves discriminated against.

Islam had tried to usher in a just society based on compassion, sensitivity towards other fellow human beings, equality and human dignity. However, the well entrenched vested interests, though pay lip service to these values, in practice sabotage them in various ways and continue to impose their own hegemony. The weaker sections and the downtrodden attracted by the revolutionary thrust of Islam and its sensitivity towards them, felt disillusioned and revolted. This revolt brought about near anarchy in society and resulted in civil war in which thousands were killed.

There was, yet, another group of Bedouins who lived in desert and resented the hegemony of the urban elite. They considered the *khilafat* as an urban rule imposed on them. They were not accustomed to submission to any authority. Thus, in the Battle of Camel fought between the fourth Caliph Hazrat Ali and Amir Mu'awiyah, the Bedouins seceded from the army of Hazrat Ali and raised the slogan *al-hukmu lillah* (Rule of Allah). They adopted extreme postures and caused much bloodshed in the early history of Islam.

Ultimately the Umayyads captured power and *khilafah* was converted into monarchy. Maulana Abul A'ala Maududi has thrown detailed light on it in his book *Khilafat aur Mulukiyyat*. Thus, we see that the Islamic society went through great deal of turmoil and bloodshed and could not evolve a universally acceptable form of state. When the Abbasids overthrew Umayyads in the first half of the second century of Islam, there again was great deal of bloodshed. When the Abbasids captured power, some Umayyads fled to Spain and established their own rule there. Now there were two caliphs simultaneously in the Islamic world. Earlier the theory was that there could be only one caliph or imam at a time. Now that theory had to be revised in view of the empirical reality and two caliphs at a time were accepted. But still later at the end of 3rd century of Islam the Fatimid Imams established their rule in Egypt and now there were several rulers at a time in the Islamic world. The Abbasid caliphs were also reduced to nominal heads of the state as the Buwayhids and Saljuqs captured power and wielded real authority. They came to be known as Sultans, the real power behind the Abbasid caliphs. The Islamic political theory had to undergo change again. Now by and large non-Quraysh were wielding power and hence, the theory of Quraysh alone becoming caliph had to be abandoned. Earlier the *Kharijites* (Seceders) who were mainly Bedouins and hence, non-Qurayshites had rejected the theory that only a Quraysh could become the caliph.

Thus, we see that the political theory of Islam had to undergo frequent changes to accommodate the empirical reality. It is, therefore, not possible to talk of an 'Islamic State' with a sense of finality. It is extremely difficult task to evolve any *ijma'* (consensus of Muslims) on the issue. Today also there are several Muslim countries with as varied forms of state as monarchical to dictatorial or semi-dictatorial to democratic. All these states, however, call themselves as 'Islamic State'

The forms and structures of state are bound to vary from place to place and time to time. It would be very difficult, for example, to create a democratic state in a feudal society. Thus, the Qur'an does not give much importance to the form of state but greatly emphasizes the nature of society. While the state is contingent the society based on values like justice, equality, compassion and human dignity is a necessity in Islam. And needless to say in our time it is only a democratic state with widest possible power-sharing arrangement which can guarantee such a society. Also, as per the Qur'anic teachings the Islamic state should guarantee equal rights to all ethnic, racial, cultural, tribal, and religious groups. The Qur'an considers racial, national, tribal, and linguistic differences as signs of Allah and indicative of identity (see 30:22). It also accepts the right of other religious communities to follow their own religion and it also accords equal status to men and women (see 33:35 and 2:228). The Qur'an accepts plurality in society as will of Allah (5:48).

Thus, in view of all this an Islamic state should have following characteristics: (1) It should be absolutely non-discriminatory on the basis of race, colour, language and nationality; (2) it should guarantee gender equality; (3) it should guarantee equal rights to all religious groups and accept plurality of religion as legitimate and (4) lastly it should be democratic in nature whose basic premise will be human dignity (17:70). Only those states which fulfill these criteria can be construed to be Islamic in nature. Thus, an Islamic state is the very epitome of modern democratic pluralistic state.

CHAPTER 11

Islamic Ethic

Every religion lays great emphasis on ethical aspects of human conduct in its own unique way. Generally, there is great commonality between different religions as far as moral and ethical questions are concerned. In fact to mould a moral character is the most fundamental function of religion. All other functions are subsidiary to it. But it is also true that each religion has its own unique way of doing it and every religion puts differing emphasis on different aspects of human morality. Islam is also unique in this respect. It has its own ethical values and moral concepts, which are universal as well as specific to Islam. In this Chapter an attempt will be made to throw some light on Islamic ethic.

Islam has unique morality of its own. It puts great deal of emphasis, for example, on equality and justice and emphasizes dignity of all human beings. We will deal with these issues in the course of this study. However, there are also universal moral values, which Islam lays emphasis on. The Qur'an gives us the concept of what it calls *'amal salih* which, translated into English, would mean 'good deeds'. But this translation does not adequately convey the meaning. The key word here is *salih*. The root of the word is *slh* from which are derived many words with the meaning to be good, to repair, to mend, to improve, to be righteous, to be efficient, to be suitable, peace friendliness, reconciliation, etc.

Thus, it will be seen that *'amal salih* leads to a society which is reformed, good, efficient, suitable (to humanity), improved and above all which is peaceful and friendly to all human beings. The Qur'an uses the word *'amal salih'* repeatedly. For a moral conduct, according to the Qur'an, *amal salih* is very necessary. In the Chapter 103 the Qur'an says, "By the time! Surely man is in loss, except those who believe and do good work (*amal salih*) and exhort one another to truth and exhort one another to patience." Thus, the key ethical concepts here in this chapter are (1) *amal salih*; (2) to be truthful and (3) to observe patience. One can say that these are key elements of Islamic ethic. Man is surely in loss, but those who perform good deeds are truthful and patient would not be. Thus, for *amal salih* truth and patience are highly necessary. One can say that this is most comprehensive statement of the Qur'anic ethic.

Here an important question is why so much emphasis on 'patience'? Why truth and patience are made integral to each other? Because to be truthful is most arduous and challenging. One has to face great problems in order to be truthful. One will have to face opposition, even intrigues, from vested interests. It is, therefore, necessary, to be steadfast and patient and face all these challenges with fortitude and courage. All this requires great deal of patience. Hence, the Qur'an lays so much emphasis on being steadfast and patient to follow the path of truth. Only a man of great patience can be truthful.

Truth is a universal value in all religions. Some religions like Hinduism also maintain that truth (*Satyam*) is God. The Qur'an also elevates truth (*Haq*) to the status of being God. Allah has been described as *Haq* in the Qur'an. No human being can claim to be Truth in absolute sense. Mansur al-Hallaj, the famous Sufi saint who claimed to be *ana'l haq* (I am the Truth) was hanged because it meant claiming to be God. Thus, truth has great significance in the Islamic ethical system. Here it should be remembered that truth is not mere conformity with observable facts as in empirical sciences. Truth in moral sciences, especially in religion, has moral or ideological dimension also which is not necessarily verifiable. It is this aspect of moral or religious truth, which separates religion from science. However, it should also be born in mind that truth should not be contrary to observable facts also. All one can say is that truth, in moral and religious discourse, is not mere conformity with fact. It is more than mere conformity with fact.

In Islamic system of morality, as in some other religions too, it is establishment of a moral society that is very fundamental. The emphasis of Islamic teachings is not personal salvation, but establishment of a society that is just and free of *zulm* (oppression). Here we will like to deal with this aspect of Islamic ethic in greater detail, as it is most central to Islam. The Qur'an lays great emphasis on '*adl* (justice). It is the central value in the Islamic ethic. The Qur'an says, "Be just; it is closest to being pious." (5:8). Thus in Islam there is no concept of piety without being just. The opposite of '*adl*' is '*zulm*' (oppression). *Zulm* is derived from the root z.l.m. that has several shades of meaning to do wrong, injustice, darkness, iniquity, oppression etc. The Qur'an often uses it in the sense of wrong doing and oppression.

Islam basically lays emphasis on establishing a society free of all forms of oppression. The Prophet also says that a society can live with unbelief (*kufr*), but not with oppression (*zulm*). Thus, Islamic ethic conceives of a society which will be free of all forms of exploitation and oppression. Islam basically is a non-violent religion. It does not approve of violence at all. The most basic attribute of Allah is mercy and compassion of which we will talk little more later. But Islam approves of violence (in a highly controlled sense, of course) only to remove *zulm*, the structures of oppression. Thus, the Qur'an says, "And how could you refuse to fight in the cause of Allah and of the utterly helpless men and women and children who are crying, "O our Sustainer! Lead us forth (to freedom) out of this land whose people are oppressors, and raise for us, out of Thy grace, a protector, and raise for us, out of Thy grace, one who will bring us succour!." (4:75)

The Qur'an's emphasis is on fighting against injustice, against oppression. Everyone has right to live in peace in ones own country. If someone tries to throw them out just because they have their own inner conviction, they cannot be thrown out of their homeland. And if someone tries to do that, one has to stand up to that and fight against this injustice. Islam does not permit violence in matters of preaching of religion. It believes, as is obvious from the above verse also, in full freedom of conscience. In fact if this freedom is violated that Islam permits use of regulated force. As for preaching of religion it has to be done only through 'goodly exhortation and wisdom' (16:125). There is no question of use of violence for that purpose. If some one does that it is against the divine injunction. It is *zulm*.

There is much misunderstanding about inter-connection between Islam and violence which needs to be clarified here since we are dealing with the question of Islamic ethic here. Islam does not approve of violence except in certain extraordinary circumstances. The word Islam has been derived from the root s.l.m., which means to escape danger, to be free from fault, to deliver or hand over, to commit oneself to the will of God, to lay down arms, to establish peace. Thus, the best meaning of the word Islam will be to establish or promote peace in harmony with the will of Allah. Thus, a Muslim is not a true Muslim if he commits acts of violence either for spread of Islam or for purposes of achieving power be it in the name of Islam. His primary duty is to establish peace so that justice prevails and humanity prospers. The Prophet has also said that the best form of *jihad* is to say truth in the face of a tyrant ruler. Tyranny could be both physical and psychological.

The Qur'an says that no human life can be taken except in keeping with law. Thus, we find in the Qur'an, "whoever kills a person, unless it be for manslaughter or for mischief in the land, it is as though he had killed entire humanity. And whoever saves a life, it is as, though he had saved lives of all men." (5:32) The Qur'an, it will be seen is against violence against humanity. It could be resorted to only for a just cause that too after great deliberation and if all other doors are closed. It is true the Qur'an has permitted retaliatory violence (for *qisas*). But the Qur'anic statements should also be seen at various levels. At the level of the Arabian society, with its customs, norms and traditions, permitting *qisas* (retaliatory violence) was necessary. The Qur'an had to deal with a given society. But at the higher moral level retaliation is not a good moral practice. It may be necessary in a society which is not highly morally developed. But in a morally developed society the virtue of pardon is the highest virtue. There is great moral worth in the act of pardon. One of Allah's attributes is that He pardons. He is *Ghaffar* (forgiver). Forgiving is the great moral virtue. Retaliation may be human, but forgiving is divine. Retaliation amounts to giving vent to ones anger, but forgiving amounts to suppressing ones rage and suppressing ones anger or rage is described as great virtue by the Qur'an. Those who suppress their anger are called *kazim al-ghayz*. On moral level the Qur'an deals with this issue in the verse 3:133. The verse reads, "Those who spend in ease as well as in adversity and those who restrain (their) anger and pardon men. And Allah loves doers of good (to others)."

This verse (3:133) deals with the moral aspect whereas the verse dealing with the question of *qisas* deals with the prevailing practice. The Qur'an's intention is not to perpetuate the practice of retaliation, but to build a human character on the basis of restraining anger and forgiving. To absolutize the verse on retaliation and to maintain that it is the ultimate divine will is to do injury to the spirit of the Qur'an which is to cultivate higher morality among human beings. It is the verse 3:133 which represents this higher morality. This is further reinforced by Allah's own attributes of being Merciful and Compassionate on the one hand and repeated assertion by the Qur'an of the concept of *ihsan* (doing good to others). Thus, it will be seen that the Islamic scripture does not morally approve even retaliatory violence which has at least some justification.

Thus, the question of violence has to be dealt with great caution as far as the Islamic tradition is concerned. At the level of the value Qur'an upholds non-violence and exhorts Muslims to use wisdom and benevolence (*hikmah* and *ihsan*) while dealing with others. Whatever violence has taken place in the Islamic history it is Muslims and the then Arab society and their norms that could be held responsible than the teachings of the Qur'an. It is highly necessary to make this distinction in order to properly understand the essence of the Islamic ethic. Certain concessions to the situation should not be mixed up with the transcendental ethical norms given by the Qur'an. In this connection it should also be borne in mind that the Qur'an's repeated advocacy to fight (*qatilu*) is not to give permanence to violence or the glorify it, but in the situation the Qur'an was dealing with, there was absolutely no other alternative, but to fight. Inter-tribal wars went on for years. Violence, in other words, was very much in the air. Also, there were powerful vested interests who were out to destroy Islam in its infancy and to eliminate the Prophet physically. Any moral discourse would not have influenced such people. The only alternative was to first defeat or subdue such elements and then to build new moral human from out of the believers. It was very difficult task indeed.

If there has been bloodshed in the history of Islam, the problem lies with the type of the society rather than the quality of the religious teachings. Most of us read in religion what suits our interests. In other words we often instrumentalize religion for our own purposes. There is abundant proof in history if we care to examine it carefully. Buddhism, Jainism and Christianity laid great deal of stress on compassion, non-violence and love and yet, these religions put together could not build a society based on these values. Society still is full of violence, conflict and clash of interests. However, there is one more aspect we have to deal with to clear Islam of the charge that it promotes violence. It can be said that the Buddhist, Jain or the Christian scriptures do not permit or talk of violence whereas the Islamic scripture does. But here one has to keep in mind the historical and social situation those scriptures were dealing with and the Islamic scripture was called upon to deal with.

Here one has to refer to the Meccan context also. In Meccan verses there is absolutely no mention of meeting violence with violence. Therefore, some of the religious thinkers like Mehmoud Mohammad Taha of Sudan have laid emphasis on the Meccan Islam. The Muslims were a persecuted minority in Mecca and they bore with great patience all the persecution let loose on them. Islam in Mecca was a great spiritual force. Those who lay emphasis on Meccan Islam would argue that had Muslims not migrated to Madina, Islam would have remained a passive spiritual force like Buddhism or Christianity. There is great deal of truth in this argument. But there are some problems, if not flaws, in it. Firstly, even in Meccan stage Islam was not a religion of individual salvation. Right from beginning Islam laid great emphasis on building community. The concept of *ummah* was a collective concept. The concept of the community was always at the heart of the Islamic movement. In tribal society in which Islam arose in Mecca, individual is always subordinate to the collectivity. If Islam had laid emphasis on individual spiritual salvation the Meccan tribal lords would have hardly bothered to oppose it.

However, Islam had a social agenda. It aimed at reforming not only the individual, but also the whole society. It knew that the roots of exploitation and oppression lay in social structure, not only in individual avarice. So it aimed at transforming the society along with the individual. If the Meccan verses are examined carefully the transformatory agenda of Islam becomes very clear. It forcefully attacks accumulation of wealth and exhorts the believers to spend their wealth on the poor, needy, orphans, and widows. The rich of Mecca were neglecting them. This was the Islamic agenda even at the Meccan stage was to set up a society which was based on socio-economic justice. Look at this powerful denunciation of accumulation of wealth in one of the Meccan chapters (104):

    (1) Woe to every slanderer, defamer!

    (2) Who amasses wealth and counts it

(3) He thinks that his wealth will make him abide.

(4) Nay, he will certainly be hurled into the crushing disaster;

(5) And what will make thee realise what the crushing disaster is?

(6) It is the Fire kindled by Allah,

(7) Which rises over the hearts.

(8) Surely it is closed on them,

(9) In extended columns.

More such chapters and verses could be cited from the Meccan verses. Thus, it becomes clear that Islam was attacking the very roots of social and economic exploitation and trying to lay foundation for a just society. The Meccan lords were, therefore, determined to throw out such a movement lock, stock and barrel. They, therefore, severely persecuted Muslims and forced them to migrate. When the Prophet migrated to Madina he seriously busied himself in laying the foundation of a just society. In doing so he became threat not only to the Jews of Madina whom he had given full religious freedom in his covenant with them (known as *Mithaq-e-Madina*), but also continued to remain a threat for the Meccan vested interests. The Meccan vested interests were determined to thwart any attempt to set up a just society even in Madina as successful experiment in Madina could pose serious challenge to their own interests. They were lording over an exploitative system. Thus, they went in full force and attacked Madina. The Prophet was again faced with a violent situation and had to defend himself and urge his followers to fight for the defence of Madina and Islam. The Jews and hypocrites betrayed him and thus, he had to face internal strife also. He had to mobilize forces to fight the Jews with whom he had no religious quarrels. The Jews, who otherwise free to practice their own religion, felt threatened that they could no longer dominate the Madinese market. The migrants from Mecca too were expert traders and were now posing challenge to the dominance of the Jews.

The Prophet of Islam had hardly any choice. In an attempt to set up a society based on high ethical standards, integrity of character and spiritual values he had to take on most powerful vested interests out to rack his movement. Thus, violence appears in the history of Islam not out of choice, but out of compulsion. It is certainly not prescriptive violence, but imposed one. Now as for the instances of Meccan model of Islam we do come across them in history, particularly in Sufi Islam.

Sufi Islam is essentially build around the theory of individual salvation. A Sufi saint is engaged more in individual character building and spiritual practices and hence, his whole emphasis on 'ibadat (prayers). The Prophet of Islam, it is interesting to note, was a perfect synthesis of a sufi and an activist engaged in building a just society. That is why the sufis consider the holy Prophet as their master from whom they derive their spiritual practices. But in later history of Islam we find either the sufis or the activists or the 'ulama (theologians) who theorized on the basis of the Qur'an and available reports of the Prophet's sayings and practices. The problem with the 'ulama was that they froze Islam in its first century and lost track of its fundamental vision. Thus, they could not keep pace with the changing society or new challenges emerging from different historical situations. The Prophet combined in himself both the Meccan and the Madinese Islam and thus, he became a perfect model to follow. However, for those who came after him the Meccan Islam lost all relevance and they became more involved with building up a political community. The overemphasis in history of Islam on building up a political community created several problems and Islam became politicized rather than spiritualized. Hence, its critics usually maintain that Islam is integrally associated with power.

However, it would be a serious mistake to associate Islam with power. Islam, like any other religion, has strong spiritual and ethical base. Its basic emphasis on ethical foundations of individual action cannot be ignored. The 'ibadat (which include praying, fasting, giving alms and performing hajj—pilgrimage—) are very central to Islam. It is these 'ibadat which, according to the Qur'an, lead to inner peace (sakinat al-qalb). Thus, the Qur'an says, "He it is who sent down inner peace into the hearts of the believers that they might add faith to their faith." (48:4). Inner peace and spiritual solace are the very foundation stones of an ethical conduct.

Here we would like to point out that compassion like in Buddhism, is very central to Islam also. The key word for this is rehmah. This word has been derived from its root r.h.m. which in its root meaning means womb of the mother. And one of the ethical concept of Islam is sila-i-rahmi, i.e., maintaining close relationship with those connected with ones mother's womb, i.e., close relatives. Since mother nurtures and sustains life, she is more compassionate than man. Thus, compassion and mother's womb are derived from the same root in Arabic. God is most compassionate (*arham al-rahimin*) as he is the creator and sustainer of all life. His mercy and compassion envelop everything in this universe (7:156). Thus, a Muslim who worships Allah has to display compassion by all his actions. True worship does not mean merely physically bowing down before Allah. It means bowing down to His attributes and to imbibe these attributes in ones life. Thus, a true Muslim is compassionate to all forms of life and he is committed to remove suffering from this earth. In other words a Muslim is quite sensitive to sufferings of all living beings and he should never be a cause of suffering of others. The Prophet is reported to have said that a good Muslim is one at whose hands others are safe.

The Islamic prayers (*'ibadat*) sensitise Muslims to others suffering. The *salat* makes him sensitive to equality of all human beings since all Muslims, irrespective of their social status have to stand in one line to pray; fasting during the month of *Ramadan* makes him sensitive to others hunger and thirst and *zakah* makes him conscious of others financial needs. And we need these prime virtues in human beings to make them righteous and conscious of their duties to other human beings. The Qur'an also lays great stress on spiritual freedom and accepts different ways of worship. Spiritual freedom is the very basis of a free human person responsible to himself as well as to whole humanity.

CHAPTER 12

Islam, Women and Gender Justice

It is generally thought that Islam treats women unfairly and gender justice is not possible within Islamic law known as the 'Shari'ah law'. This assertion is partly true and partly false. True as far as the existing *shari'ah* laws are concerned. False, as the existing laws were codified during second and third centuries of Islam when general perspective of women's rights was very different from today's perspective. The Qur'anic verses which are quite fundamental to the Islamic law, were interpreted so as to be in conformity with the views about gender rights prevailing then.

It is important to note that scriptural injunctions are always mediated through prevailing social ethos. Also and it is more fundamental to framing of laws based on scriptures, scriptures both reflect the given situation and also transcend it. There cannot be any scripture—revealed or otherwise—which is unidimensional, i.e., it reflects only given situation. Every scripture tries to go beyond what is given and it faces stiff opposition from those who loose out if the transcendental perspectives are spelled out and enforced. The scriptures condemn prevailing social malaise and provide a new vision. Those who benefit from the new vision embrace the new faith. Those who loose, oppose it tooth and nail. But, the vested interests and those who want to perpetuate the old order, have their own strategies. Soon they find the ways and means to hijack new religion to their own benefit. This is done in a number of ways: (1) They capture political power and religion becomes a part of political establishment and looses its initial revolutionary thrust as it is appropriated by the ruling classes; (2) they convert religion into an establishment and a power-structure develops around it. Religion is then used more for distribution of favours than for spiritual enrichment; and (3) intellectual resources are used to restore *status quo ante* and this is done chiefly by interpreting the scriptures in a way which will rob it of its transcendental thrust. Thus, a theology is developed which is supportive of status quo. One must distinguish between what scriptural pronouncements are and what theology is woven around it. Scriptural pronouncements are divinely inspired and hence, transcendental and theological formulations are humane and hence, often contradict divine intentions. Scriptural pronouncements are an option for the weaker sections whereas theological formulations are weapons in the hands of powerful interests. It is therefore, necessary that theological formulations be continuously challenged by scriptural pronouncements. One must strive to build up creative tension between theological and scriptural. While scripture remains immutable with its transcendental spirit, theology must change facing new challenges and newly emergent situations.

Those who oppose any change in theological formulations and *shari'ah* laws are those who loose their dominant position and the priesthood who monopolize theology and religion for them is instrumental in promoting their interests rather than spiritual source of inner enrichment. The priesthood, monopolizing theology, project it as divine and immutable. The run of the mill faithfuls' understanding of religion is mediated through the priesthood and hence, they are made to believe that theology as formulated by them or their predecessors is divine and hence, immutable. Any change will amount to changing the divine will.

In Islam, it is common belief that the *shari'ah* is divine and hence, immutable. Whenever, any measures for gender justice are proposed one meets with this stock argument. It is important to note that *shari'ah*, though undoubtedly based on the holy Qur'an, is a human endeavour to understand the divine will. The priesthood, i.e., the community of 'ulama projects it as a divine end itself and hence, refuse to admit any change. 'The Shari'ah is divine' has become a commonly accepted position. Thus, what was thought of women's rights during the early period of Islamic history has come to be the final and immutable. Even to think of it is interfering with the divine and hence, an unpardonable sin.

As pointed out above, there is big gap between the scriptural, i.e., the Qur'anic pronouncements and *shari'ah* formulations. While the Qur'anic pronouncements are purely transcendental in spirit, the *shari'ah* formulations have been influenced by human situation as well as human thinking on all related issues. Women were in subordinate position in the patriarchal societies and this subordinate relationship came to be reflected in the *shari'ah* laws relating to her rights. The transcendental divine spirit was conveniently ignored and the prevailing situation was rationalized through contextual Qur'anic pronouncements. As pointed out above, there is always a creative tension between what is and what ought to be in scriptures. However, this tension is often resolved in favour of the prevalent rather than the emergent and prevalent is eternalized by rationalizing certain divine pronouncements.

On the Methodology of Creating Islamic Legal Structure

If we want to effect necessary changes in the *shari'ah* laws, it is important to understand the methodology of creating of Islamic legal structure. The Islamic legal corpus is known as 'Shari'ah'. As *shari'ah* is, after all, a human approach to divine will as reflected through the scripture the holy Qur'an, it is not uniform, but has several variants. In the Sunni Islam itself there are four different schools of jurisprudence, i.e., Hanafi, Shafi'i, Hanbali' and Maliki. Besides these schools there is what is known as the Zahiri School. Also, there are several schools in the Shi'ah Islam as well. The Ja'fari or the Ithna 'Ashari School, the Isma'ili and the Zaidi School.

The Sunni Islam bases *shari'ah*—besides the Qur'an—on *sunna* (the sayings and doings of the holy Prophet), *qiyas* (analogy) and finally *ijma'* (consensus). However, except the Qur'an, the remaining three sources *sunna, qiyas* and *ijma'* are controversial. Some *ahadith* (sayings of the Prophet) are acceptable by some while they are rejected by others. Some *ahadith* are considered weak (*da'if*) and some of doubtful origin and some outright forgeries. Also, *qiyas*, analogical reasoning varies from jurist to jurist. There is controversy about *ijma'* as well. The crucial question is whose *ijma'*? Of the jurists and the 'ulama or of the entire community? Also, has *ijma'* ever been possible? Have all 'ulama, let alone the entire community, ever developed consensus on any issue? There are hardly any instances of this nature in the history of Islamic jurisprudence. Thus, it will be seen that except the Qur'an which is divine and there are no textual differences about it, the three other fundamental sources *sunna, qiyas* and *ijma'* are human and hence, controversial. It is also important to point out here that about the Prophet's pronouncements—*ahadith*—there is controversy whether they be considered as divine or human. The *Ahl-e-Hadith* (the followers of *hadith*) consider *hadith* as divine like the Qur'an while many others do not give it that status and consider it as human and hence, not eternal.

The Shi'i jurisprudence (*shari'ah*) is based on the Qur'an and the pronouncements of the Prophet as reported by Imams (the male descendants of the Prophet's daughter Hazrat Fatima and her husband 'Ali). The Qur'an as interpreted by these Imams is considered as the only right interpretation, every other interpretation is considered as mere conjecture or opinion (*ra'i*). And *tafsir bi'r ra'i* (Qur'anic interpretation or exegesis through human opinion) is rejected outright in the Shi'ah Islam. But there is controversy in the Shi'ah Islam as to who is rightfully appointed Imam. The Ithna 'Asharis (twelvers), the Isma'ilis (also referred to as seveners), Zaidis, the Qaramitas and the Alavids, all mutually differ on this issue. All these sects have Imams of their own and consider others as not rightfully appointed and hence, have no legitimacy. Also, the juridical pronouncements of these Imams differ from each other even on the matters of principles.

Thus, had it been immutable the *shari'ah* would not have differed from one school to the other and from sect to sect. The Qur'an, being divine, does not differ and is immutable. It admits of no change. However, its interpretation differs from sect to sect and from one school to the other. Thus, the Qur'an is divine and its interpretations are humane and what is humane admits of change. The *shari'ah*, being based on human interpretations of divine word, can and does admit change. What was thought to be just in respect of women's rights in medieval ages, is no longer so. The idea of justice also changes with changing consciousness and what is just in one age may not necessarily be just in the other. We will throw more light on this aspect little later. It is in fact very important aspect as far as the Qur'anic concept of law is concerned.

One of the important sources of the *shari'ah* law is *hadith* or *sunna*. As pointed out above, this too is not above controversy. There are two types of controversies about this seminal source of Islamic law: (1) whether *hadith* is divine or human and (2) whether it is authentic, weak or forged. The Qur'an is unanimously accepted as divine and there is no controversy about it. Also, its contents are accepted with unanimity and without any controversy. No one maintains that this or that verse of the Qur'an is unauthentic, or added later, or of doubtful origin. But it is not so as far as *hadith* literature is concerned. There are several *ahadith* which are controversial. Either they are considered of doubtful origin or weak or outright forgery. It is said that Imam Abu Hanifa, the founder of the Hanafi School of Law, accepted only 17 *ahadith* as true and authentic and yet, he used many more while giving his juridical opinions.

There are Muslims who maintain that *ahadith* are divine like the Qur'an. They believe that the Qur'anic verse, "Nor does he speak out of desire. It is naught, but revelation that is revealed" (53:3-4) applies to the Prophet's all pronouncements including his *ahadith*. These Muslims believe that *ahadith* too, are divine and hence, above any human controversy. Thus, this source of *shari'ah* also becomes equally divine for them. However, there is no unanimity about it. Not only that *ahadith* is not believed to be divine by large sections of Muslims, it is not above controversy as to its origin. Imam Bukhari, one of the greatest collectors of *ahadith*, is said to have collected more than six hundred thousand *ahadith* of which he accepted only four thousand and rejected others as of doubtful origin or outright forgeries. This clearly shows how some interested people were producing *hadith* literature to serve their own ends. Unfortunately, many of these *ahadith* went into juridical formulations in general, and about women, in particular. These formulations reflect the prejudices and dominant thinking of the time rather than the Qur'anic principles. These formulations, therefore, cannot be treated above change.

Also, there is yet, another problem about *hadith* literature. And this problem remains, even if *hadith* literature is treated as divine and immutable. The Qur'an which is unanimously held to be divine by all Muslims contain many pronouncements which are directly related to the then prevailing Arabian social structure. These pronouncements also reflect the social norms or social problems as they existed then. These pronouncements cannot be of universal application in other societies and cultures. We would like to cite examples. There was a practice called *zihar* among Arabs. It is mentioned in 33:4 and 58:2-3. It was a practice to declare their wives like their mothers and abandon them. Thus, in verse 33:4 the Qur'an says, "Allah has not made for any man two hearts within him; nor has He made your wives whom you desert by *Zihar*, your mothers..." Edward William Lane defines *Zihar* in his Arabic-English Lexicon as husband telling his wife *thou art to me as the back of my mother*. In verse second of Chapter 58 the Qur'an says, "Those of you who put away their wives by calling them their mothers—they are not their mothers. None are their mothers save those who give them birth and they utter indeed a hateful word and a lie..." And in verse third of the same chapter it is said, "And those who put away their wives by calling them their mothers, then go back on that which they said, must free a captive before they touch one another. To this you are exhorted..."

From above two verses we come to know that Arabs used to desert their wives calling them like the back of their mothers and some used to go back on that vow and would like to touch their wives again. The Qur'an prescribed that they must free a captive (a slave) before breaking their vow. Now this practice was unique to the Arabian society of that time. We do not find such practices in other societies. Also, today there is no institution of slavery. It has already been abolished. If an Arabs today pronounces *zihar* on his wife and wants to take back his vow, there are no slaves available to free. Thus, such verses in the Qur'an should be treated as contextual, i.e., revealed in the context of that society and are no more valid as social practices have changed. But in *shari'ah* as formulated in the second and third century *Hijrah* (Islamic Calendar) these practices prevailed and hence, elaborate laws were made by the jurists based on Qur'an or *hadith*. However, they are totally irrelevant today. Thus, the proposition that *shari'ah* laws are immutable is not maintainable.

The Qur'anic verses thus, should be divided into two categories namely (1) contextual and (2) normative. The normative pronouncements of the Qur'an are eternal and while re-thinking issues in Islamic *shari'ah*, particularly pertaining to women's rights the normative pronouncements will have precedence over the contextual. But during the early centuries contextual often had precedence over normative and it was quite 'normal' then. And hence, these formulations became widely acceptable in that society. These laws were thought to be normative then and hence, struck deeper roots in society as well as in hearts and minds of the people as well and came to acquire status of immutability with the passage of time.

Thus, even if *hadith* is accepted as divine its contextuality will have to be kept in mind. It is also said and rightly so, that the Prophet explained the Qur'anic verses through his words and deeds and who knew the meaning and import of the Qur'anic verses better than the Prophet. Quite true. But the question of contextuality remains. The holy Prophet, while dealing with the given society, could not have gone beyond its context in explaining and practising the Qur'anic pronouncements. Again it can best be illustrated with an example of women's status in that society. While explaining the cause of revelation of the Qur'anic verse 4:34, all classical commentators like Tabari, Fakhruddin Razi and others maintain that the Prophet allowed a woman's (daughter of his companion) right to retaliate against her husband who had unjustly slapped her but, in view of the prevailing social ethos it laid to unrest among the men and Qur'an reversed the Prophet's decision. This once again shows that the question of contextuality is very important and highly relevant in all judicial pronouncements be they those of the Prophet or other Islamic jurists.

Another example in this respect is that of *milk-e-yamin* (legitimising sexual relations with a slave girl). There is near unanimity among the Islamic jurists that it is permissible to have sexual relations with slave girls and that the Prophet himself had such relations with a Coptic Christian slave girl. The modernists and some other commentators of course challenge this formulation and maintain that the Prophet had married her. But Maulana Maududi, one of the contemporary Islamic thinkers and founder of the Jam'at-e-Islami, maintains in his commentary on the Qur'an (*Tafhim al Qur'an*) that the Prophet had relations with the slave girl without marrying her. Most of the eminent medieval jurists concur with this. But if this view that sexual relations with a slave girl is permissible and is accepted the contemporary society would not approve of it. Thus, the Prophet's *sunna* cannot be seen out of its social context.

There were four great jurists in Sunni Islam who founded four different schools of jurisprudence. All four differ from each other on many issues. Much has been written on causes of these differences. But the modern scholars maintain that one important reason was their differing social situations. Imam Hanbal and Imam Malik lived in Madina and thus, were quite close to social ethos of that society in which the

Prophet himself lived. They were closer in their juridical formulations to what the Prophet said and did in that society. Imam Shafi'i and Imam Abu Hanifa, on the other, lived in Egypt and Iraq respectively, which were confluences of many cultures and thus, were unorthodox in their methodology in arriving at juridical opinions. While Imam Malik and Hanbal mainly relied on *hadith*, Imam Sahfi'i and Abu Hanifa used *qiyas* and *ijma'* more liberally, apart from *hadith*. Thus, while the former two Imam's formulations were closer to Arab practices in Mecca and Madina, the latter two Imam's formulations had been largely influenced by other practices as well. This clearly shows that *shari'ah* is influenced by human situations and can incorporate situational changes. The Arab *'adat* (the Arab customary law) also became integral part of the *shari'ah* law. Thus, the then prevailing opinions about women in the Arab society greatly influenced the *shari'ah* laws pertaining to women. The Arab *'adat* cannot certainly be considered divine injunctions and hence, not immutable. In fact the Arab *'adat* had great relevance as long as Islam was confined to the Arabian society. But once it spread out to far off areas, the need to incorporate other practices also became equally important. And now the changed consciousness about women's rights can also not be ignored.

There is, yet, another problem about the *hadith* literature which is, as pointed out above, an important ingredient of *shari'ah*. The *ahadith* were generally reported by the Prophet's companions. In this respect even the most authentically reported *ahadith* present different kinds of problems. Firstly, most of the *ahadith* reported by the companions were not the exact words of the Prophet, but the overall meaning of what he said. There are hardly few *ahadith* which can be said to be the exact words of the Prophet. Secondly, the *ahadith* literature also incorporates the reports about what the companions saw the Prophet doing. Thus, the prophetic sunna includes both what the Prophet said as well as reports about what he did in different situations.

Now among the Prophet's companions there were all kinds of people. There were companions who had sharp memory and good understanding and comprehension of the problems. There were companions who had very poor understanding of the complex issues and also were companions who had poor memory. And there were companions who spent several years with the Prophet and there were companions who spent only a few hours with him and even those who saw and heard him from a distance. All that these companions reported having heard from the Prophet became part of *hadith* corpus which then was used for formulating *shari'ah* laws.

Not only that. Yet, there is another problem. The *ahadith* have been reported by people who heard it from the companions of the companions (*tab'i tabi'in*) of the Prophet. Thus, there is whole chain of narrators known as *rijal* (the narrating men or women). The collectors of *ahadith* did try to develop the science of *rijal* (*'ilm al-rijal*) criteria to judge the honesty and integrity of the narrators. But this criterion judged the honesty and integrity of the narrator rather than his or her understanding, comprehension or intelligence. Moreover, there were often missing links. And also the cases wherein much was not known about one or more of the narrators in the chain. Many narrators were of totally different cultural backgrounds as some narrators being Arabs and others belonged to non-Arab cultures not properly acquainted with the Arab affairs. Also, many narrators had their own biases for or against women (also about other matters) and these biases definitely affected their narrative or reports.

It was for this reason that the Prophet had strictly prohibited his followers from compiling his sayings. He knew very well that his sayings may not be reported faithfully to future generations for various reasons. Also, he was fully aware of the fact that the future generations will insist on strictly following what reaches them as the sayings of Allah's Messenger, though they may be facing different circumstances. Even the first Caliph Hazrat Abu Bakr did not permit compilation of *ahadith* for similar reasons. Still people did compile these *ahadith,* though much later. And by the time they were compiled spurious ones had mixed up with authentic ones.

Thus, it will be seen that *hadith* literature, even if entirely authentic, presents several problems. Hence, it cannot be considered as highly reliable source of Islamic legislation. But the Islamic *juris corpus* is as much based on the problematic *hadith* literature as on the holy Qur'an. Still the 'ulama project it as unquestionable divine and hence, immutable. They refuse to admit any change even, though sweeping changes are taking place in the social, cultural, economic and political circumstances. The doctrine of *taqlid* (mechanical imitation) is emphasized by the contemporary jurists in the world of Islam. They maintain that rethinking about the formulations of the great Imams is not permissible. In fact these formulations are treated as divine. Also, most of the 'ulama do not even permit taking more favourable provisions for women from other schools of law. They insist that any one school should be followed in its entirety. Some 'ulama of course permit such an approach. But they are fewer in numbers. Now more and more 'ulama are coming around to permitting this approach which has given some relief to women. The Ottoman rulers had adopted this approach in nineteenth century itself. But still it is not widely accepted. *Taqlid* is the generally established rule. It is causing great deal of hardships to Muslim women everywhere.

The holy Prophet had anticipated the problems which will arise in future. He took care to leave some guidance in this respect. Firstly, he encouraged what is known as *ijtihad* (exerting oneself to solve newly arising problems if no precise guidance was available in the Qur'an and Prophet's *sunnah*). The *hadith* regarding Ma'adh bin Jabal is well-known about this. When the Prophet appointed Ma'adh as governor of Yemen, he asked him how would he govern. According to the Qur'an, Ma'adh replied. And if it is not in the Qur'an? the Prophet asked him. According to the Prophet's *sunna*, replied Ma'adh. And if he does not find anything of the sort in the *sunnah* also?, the Prophet inquired. Then I will exert myself to solve the problem (*Ana ajtahedu*). The Prophet patted his back in approval. Also, the Prophet is reported to have said that even if one makes mistake in doing *ijtihad* he/she will earn one merit and if one does not err he/she will earn two merits. The Prophet did this to encourage Muslims to solve problems which were likely to arise in future.

From this many modernists argue that one must resort to *ijtihad* to solve new problems and issues including women's issues. However, the orthodox 'ulama argue that the gates of *ijtihad* were closed long ago and also that now there are no qualified persons to do *ijtihad*. They feel the great imams and some of their followers had the requisite qualification and none today has such impressive merits. Some 'ulama do feel the need for *ijtihad*, but they too stop short of resorting to it for fear of consequences. Some who did face the wrath of the fellow jurists and even ostracised. The debate is raging in the Islamic world for and against *ijtihad*. And when it comes to women's issues and rights, the resistance to change and rethink is much greater in the male-dominated Islamic world.

Dr. Muhammad Iqbal, a noted Urdu poet and thinker from India (d.1938) was greatly in favour of *ijtihad*. He wrote in his *Reconstruction of Religious Thought in Islam*. "The ultimate spiritual basis of all life, as conceived by Islam, is eternal and reveals itself in variety and change. A society based on such a conception of reality must reconcile, in its life, the categories of permanence and change. But eternal principles when they are understood to exclude all possibilities of change which, according to the Qur'an, is one of the greatest 'signs' of God, tend to immobilize what is essentially mobile in its nature." (p.147-48).

Iqbal states in the above book very boldly, "The only alternative open to us, then, is to tear off from Islam the hard crust which has immobilized an essentially dynamic outlook on life and to rediscover the original verities of freedom, equality and solidarity with a view to rebuild our moral, social and political ideas out of their original simplicity and universality." (p-156). Iqbal thus, maintains that *ijtihad* is necessary to rebuild the law of *shari`ah* in the light of modern thought and experience.

Ijtihad, I would like to emphasize here, is even more necessary today in respect of *shari`ah* laws pertaining to women. It is highly regrettable that the *shari`ah* law is almost inoperative in many other respects (like property and contract laws, criminal laws, financial transactions, etc.,) but when it comes to women's issues, the *shari`ah* laws are sought to be strictly applied. In several Muslim majority and minority countries modern secular laws are applied in respect of all other things except laws pertaining to marriage, divorce, maintenance, inheritance, etc., i.e., in the sphere of what is called personal laws. The greatest resistance, in the name of *shari`ah*, is manifested by men when it comes to according better status to women. In this respect the *shari`ah* becomes sacred and immutable and arouses great passions. The Islamic world, if it has to understand the dynamic spirit of Qur'an and enact it in real life, will have to enact changes in the *shari`ah* laws and accord women an equal status. In fact time has to come to put the Qur'anic vision of sexual equality in practice.

As pointed out earlier there are verses in the Qur'an which have contextual significance. These verses formed the legal foundations of Islamic law in that age. But these were not the verses having impress of permanence and principles. There are certainly the verses which lay down norms and principles. Today the Islamic legislation should be based on these verses. Before we examine these verses, we would like to set out certain values which are fundamental to the Islamic teachings. Any legislation which ignores these fundamental values could be anything, but not Islamic. So, it is necessary to understand that the classical jurists though did not ignore these fundamental values, but the application of these values was constrained by the social ethos of the age. The Prophet's traditions also had to take these constraints into account.

The most fundamental values in Islam, as expounded by the Qur'an are justice, benevolence and compassion. The Qur'anic terminology for these values is *'adl, ihsan* and *rahmah.* The Qur'an talks of these values in imperative category. The Qur'anic verse 16:90 testifies to this: And surely Allah enjoins justice and benevolence (to others). Thus, it will be seen that justice is very central to the Islamic value system— as central as love to the Christian ethics. No legislation in Islam which ignores this value can be valid.

It is this concern for justice which makes the Qur'an show deep concern for the weaker sections of society. Thus, the verse 28:5 expresses this concern for them and says: "And We desire to bestow a favour upon those who were deemed weak in the land, and to make them the leaders and to make them the heirs." The Qur'an desires to bestow the mantle of leadership of this earth upon the weak. The Islamic jurisprudence has to imbibe this spirit towards the weaker sections of society. And women certainly belong to this category as far as the patriarchal society is concerned.

It is important to note that the values like justice and compassion cannot be applied independent of the age. In the medieval period the understanding of the concept of justice was very different from what it is today. Our era is a democratic era and justice in our era cannot be deemed to have been done if equality of all humans irrespective of sex, race and creed, is not ensured. Discrimination between one and other human being on any ground, including the sexual one, will be taken as injustice. But in medieval ages these discriminations were thought to be quite natural and non-violative of the concept of justice. Even slavery was thought to be natural and in keeping with the principles of justice.

In fact if a slave ran away from the master it was thought to be an unjust act. Today, let alone slavery, even bonded labour or child labour is considered as grossly violative of justice. Thus, the concept of justice greatly varies in a democratic era from that of feudal one. And yet, justice as a value remains important in both the ages. The expression of the concept of justice in a particular era is not fundamental, but justice *per se* is. However, in religious traditions, including in those of Islam, give more importance to the expression of justice in a particular age then to the notion of justice itself. It is because of this that the expression of justice in the *hadith* literature is more important than the notion of justice as fundamental value in the Qur'an. What was thought to be just during the classical period of Islam is thought to be just even today. And not only that the orthodox think the expression of the notion of justice today is violative of divine will. It is this attitude which impedes change in Islamic legislation so as to accord women equality with men.

However, one finds in the Qur'an full support for sexual equality in several verses. The Qur'an was certainly mindful of what was just in that era when it was revealed and what ought to be just in the transcendental sense. When the Prophet permitted a Muslim wife retaliation against her husband as a measure of justice, the Qur'an overruled him and permitted a measure of conditional male domination, though conditionality of justice was stipulated (see the verse 4:34). It would have been thought to be unjust if the Qur'an had permitted wife to retaliate against her husband and it would not have found acceptability in that society.

However, the Qur'an also did not intend to eternalise the then acceptable notion of justice. The dynamics of 'is' and 'ought' or interaction between history and eternity informs the whole spirit of Qur'an. Unfortunately, the orthodox miss this very spirit while reading the Qur'an form their own perspective. The verse 33:35 is much more fundamental in this respect as it clearly accords women equality with men in all respects. While 4:34 is informed by the spirit of that era, the verse 33:34 deals with the eternal dimension. The orthodox, however, do not wish to go beyond the divine injunction expressed in 4:34. They have frozen their minds in the classical age of Islam. What was temporal has become permanent for them and what is permanent is just brushed aside as of no consequence.

The Qur'an must be reread and reinterpreted in today's context as the classical jurists read and interpreted it in their own context. No reformation is possible without such rereading and reinterpreting the Qur'anic verses. The real intention of the Qur'an—that of sexual equality—comes through several verses. Those verses need to be reemphasised. The verse 2:228 ("And women have rights similar to those against them in a just manner") is quite definitive in this respect. It hardly needs any comment. Maulana Muhammad Ali, a noted Pakistani commentator says commenting on the above verse, "The rights of women against their husbands are here stated to be similar to those which the husbands have against their wives. The statement must, no doubt, have caused a stir in a society which never recognized any rights for the woman. The change in this respect was really was a revolutionising one, for the Arabs hitherto regarded women as mere chattels. Women were given a position equal in all respects to that of men, for they were declared to have rights similar to those which were exercised against them. This declaration brought about a revolution not only in Arabia, but in the whole world, for the equality of rights of women with those of men was never previously recognized by any nation or any reformer. The woman could no longer be discarded at the will of her 'lord', but she could either claim equality as a wife or demand a divorce." (Maulana Muhammad Ali, 1973, p-97).

However, much of this spirit of justice and equality was lost when the Islamic doctors legislated under the influence of their own social ethos. The Qur'anic categorical imperatives were ignored, as pointed out before, in favour of those verses which were of the nature of concession to the age. There are many instances of this. The polygamy, for example, firstly, it was a permissive measure in some circumstances (large number of war widows and orphans to be taken care of as many men perished fighting in the battle of Uhud) with great emphasis on justice to all the wives (their number not exceeding four). It was great advance over the pre-Islamic practice of marrying unlimited number and without any obligation towards the wives.

Secondly, the verse on polygamy (4:3) is followed by the verse 4:1 which emphasizes sexual equality in the words that... "Lord Who created you from a single being (*min nafsin wahidatin*) and created its mate of

the same (kind) and spread from these two many men and women..."
and the verse 4:2 which talks of justice for orphans and widows. Then
polygamy is permitted provided one marries with widows and orphans
(and not any women) and there also justice with all wives is a must
failing which one must marry only one. No one before had insisted on
such conditionalities for plurality of wives. Thirdly, the verse 4:129
states that even if you desire you cannot do justice between wives and
ends by saying that do not leave the one with total disinclination and
incline towards the other leaving the first in suspense. If the verses 4:3
and 4:129 are read together polygamy is as good as not permissible. But
the jurists, in order to avoid implications of reading the two verses
together invented various explanations and took resort of *hadith* to
keep possibility of polygamy open. And much worse, in practising it,
conditionality for justice was hardly enforced. In today's conditions
polygamy should be done away with in order to implement the Qur'anic
conditionality. Abolition of polygamy will serve the end of justice far
better than its practice today. The arguments that men are more sexual
or that in case there are more women than men, it will be better to permit
polygamous marriages to avoid immoral relations etc. are all attempts at
human rationalization than divine intention. These arguments do not
hold much water as there may be excess of women over men in one
country and excess of men over women in another. And prostitution
and immoral sex thrived even when men could marry any number of
wives and also keep slave girls without limit.

Also, normatively speaking the Qur'an has conceded all rights to
women which were available earlier only to men. She could exercise her
right to divorce her husband as men could divorce her at will. The
Prophet permitted a woman called Jamila to divorce her husband—
against his will and without consulting him—just because she did not
approve of his looks. While the verse 2:229 permits her to liberate
herself from an unsatisfactory marriage by suitable compensation to
husband (returning the dower amount) the verse 4:35 gives her right to
appoint an arbiter of her own to settle the marital dispute or agree to
divorce. Also, the Qur'an requires of men to keep their wives in goodly
manner and to leave them, if necessary, in a benevolent manner. And
the verse 4:19 lays down that women could not be inherited or taken
as wives against their will. Men are also exhorted in this verse not to

take a portion of what they have given to their wives and to treat them kindly. It was also emphasized in 9:71 that believing men and believing women are each others friends and they (both men and women) enjoin good and forbid evil. Thus, both enjoy equal obligations and from this verse jurists like Abu Hanifa have concluded that a woman can become *Qazi* judge as it is her obligation also to enjoin good and forbid evil.

It is argued from the verse 4:11 that a daughter inherits half that of son and hence, man is superior. Some modernists also argue on the basis of this verse that it is injustice to a daughter as she has been given half that of son and hence, it is bias against female sex. It is simply not true. From one perspective one can say it was a cautious reform in favour of daughters. In pre-Islamic society daughters did not inherit at all and now they were given right to inherit half that of son. From another perspective it could be argued that it was not bias against daughter that they were given half that of son, but daughters were duly compensated by *mehr* (dower amount at the time of marriage) whereas, sons had to loose out by paying dower to their wives. And the wives do not have to spend anything by way of maintenance as it is enjoined upon the husbands to maintain their wives. Also, a woman inherited as wife and mother too. Moreover, she did not contribute to family wealth in those days by way of earning, but now she does and her portion could be increased in view of the changed conditions. Thus, the Qur'an has done no injustice to her in matters of inheritance also.

Another question is of *hijab* (veil). There is no injunction in the Qur'an that she veil her face. The verse 24:31 only lays down that women should not display their adornment and fineries publicly and that they should cover their breasts (tribal women in those days used to leave their breasts uncovered) and that they should not strike her feet with anklets in public so as to draw attention to their adornments. In this verse both men and women have been asked to lower their gaze (4:30-31) and to restrain their sexual passions. As for what constitutes adornment and what should be displayed and what should be not, there are sharp differences of opinion. These differences are human and every commentator has his own views. But Tabari, the noted classical commentator has summarized the views of many eminent jurists in his *Jami' al-Bayan*. According to him adornment means: (1) adornment of dress or the clothes that a woman wears; in other words, she is not required to cover the clothes she wears; (2) it means the adornment which the woman is not required to cover, such as collyrium, rings, bracelets and her face; (3) the exception (*illa ma zahara minha*) relates to a woman's clothing and her face.

These were opinions of the theologians of those days. Today the sensibilities in this respect are very different and the scope of the exception can be made much wider subject to—and that is real intention behind it—to restrain sexual passion and protect ones chastity. To prevent extra-marital sex is the responsibility of both men and women and not of women alone, as per the Qur'an. Also, both should avoid wearing sexually stimulating dress. They should wear dignified dress. Covering of face by women is not required in the Qur'an at all. It was cultural practice of some post-Islamic societies. The Qur'an also does not require women to be confined to homes. On the contrary they could earn and what they earned was theirs alone as per verse 4:32 (and for women is the benefit of what they earn). The cultural practices like confining women to home were sought to be legitimized later by inventing suitable *ahadith* or by far fetched interpretations of the Qur'an.

In conclusion it should be said that if one goes by those verses of the Qur'an which belong to the normative category or which are of the nature of laying down principles and givers of value, men and women should enjoy equal rights in every respect. It would be necessary to reread and reinterpret many verses which were used for centuries to subjugate women in Muslim societies. This subjugation was more cultural and patriarchal than Islamic or Qur'anic. The whole *corpus juris* of Islam relating to women needs to be seriously re-thought on the basis of Qur'an.

CHAPTER 13

Islam and Pluralism

Today's world is fast becoming pluralist with variety of religions, languages and cultures in one country particularly due to fast developing processes of modernization, liberalization and globalization. Also, feudal socio-economic and socio-political structures have either crumbled or crumbling very fast in the Third World also of course with certain exceptions. In the past there was no concept of civil society at all and the state was all powerful. The subjects people did not enjoy any rights, they had to discharge only duties towards the state. The modern democratic state, has to concede well defined rights to the citizens. The civil society has its own autonomy in a democratic set up and the notion of human rights has acquired great significance.

The notion of human rights is quite fundamental to a society which is pluralistic. All religious, linguistic and cultural groups should enjoy well defined rights and should not live at the mercy of the state or the majority community. Thus, it will be seen that the notion of civil society is very fundamental to the modern pluralist society. It is unfortunate that the Islamic world is, yet, to cope up with the notion of civil society. Most of the Islamic countries do not have full-fledged democracy and there is no respect for human rights in these countries. In fact most of the rulers condemn human rights as a western notion and some, even 'un-Islamic'.

Here it is important to examine, from theological perspective, what is the attitude of Islam towards pluralism? Does Islam approve of pluralism or promotes a monolithic society? Also, when we talk of pluralism, are we referring to political pluralism or religious and cultural pluralism? As far as this study goes we are referring to religious and cultural pluralism, though political pluralism has its own importance, it is very seminal for religious and cultural pluralism.

If one goes by the Qur'anic pronouncements Islam not only accepts the legitimacy of religious pluralism, but considers it quite central to its system of beliefs. There are very clear statements to this effect. First we will refer to the verse 5:48 in this respect. The verse goes as follows: "Unto every one of you We have appointed a (different) law and way of life. And if Allah had so willed, He could surely have made you all one single community: but (He willed it otherwise) in order to test you by means of what He has given you. Vie, then, with one another in doing good works! Unto Allah you all must return; and then He will make you truly understand all that on which you were wont to differ."

This is very seminal statement in favour of religious and legal pluralism which Muslims, specially the Muslim regimes, have not considered seriously. Many classical as well as modern commentators have commented on this significant verse. The most significant and operative part of this verse is, "Unto every one of you have." We appointed a (different) law and way of life." The term 'every one of you' obviously denotes different communities. Every community—obviously religious or religio-cultural community—has its own law (*shir'atan*) and its own way of life (*minhaj*) and it attains its spiritual growth in keeping with this law and way of life of its own. The term *shir'ah* or *shari'ah* signifies, literally, "the way to a watering place" (from which men and animals derive the element indispensable to their life) and in the Qur'an to denote a system of law necessary for a community's social and spiritual welfare. The term *minhaj* on the other hand, denotes an 'open road' that is a way of life. (see Muhammad Asad, *The Message of the Qur'an*, Gibraltar, 1980, p. 153).

Thus, it will be seen that the prophets of Allah sent to different communities (*ummah*) gave laws and indicated way of life to their people in keeping with their genius and that which could ensure their spiritual and material growth. This is further emphasized in the next part of the verse, i.e., "And if Allah had so willed, He could surely have made you all one single community." It was not difficult for Allah to make entire mankind one community. But Allah graced us with pluralism as it adds richness and variety to life. Each community has its own unique way of life, its own customs and tradition, its own law. But these laws or way of life should be such as to ensure growth and enriching of life, howsoever different and unique they might be. Allah does not want to impose one law on all and creates communities rather than community.

Allah has created different communities on purpose: to try and test human beings in what has been given to them (i.e., different scriptures, laws and ways of life). And that test is to live in peace and harmony with each other which is the will of Allah. The differences of laws and ways of life should not become cause of disharmony and differences. What is desirable for human beings is to live with these differences and vie with one another in good deeds.

In the last part of the verse Allah says that unto Him all will return and it is He who "will make you truly understand all that on which you were wont to differ." Thus it is not for human beings to decide for themselves who is right and who is wrong. It will lead to disturbances and breach of peace. Thus, it should be left to Allah to decide when they return unto Him. The human beings should only vie one with the other in good deeds. It is the best way to do away with inter-religious and inter-cultural conflict and to promote acceptance of the 'religious and cultural other' with dignity and grace.

This verse has also another important dimension. It leads to what some scholars like Shah Waliyullah and Maulana Abul Kalam Azad from India have described as the concept of *wahdat-e-din*, i.e., unity of religion. The earlier part of this verse (5:48) says, "And We have revealed to thee the Book with the truth, verifying that which is before it of the Book and a guardian (*muhayman*) over it." This is also very significant pronouncement and most modern in its approach. The Qur'an has thus, come to vouchsafe for what was revealed earlier to different communities through their prophets. The shari'ah, the law and the way of life may be different as we have discussed above, but the essence of all religions—*Din*—is the same. All religions are based on the revelation from Allah. The Qur'an has come to be guardian of earlier truth revealed through other scriptures.

This is inclusive approach and is very vital for acceptance of the 'religious other'. The laws, the ways of life, may differ and yet *Din*, the divine essence, the divine truth, is the same. It is reflected in all religions, in all spiritual traditions and we humans have no right to reject the 'other' as illegitimate, much less, false. Thus it is our human ego which rejects the religious other and not the falsity of other faith traditions.

The Qur'an has named several prophets and the list of prophets in the Qur'an is illustrative, not exhaustive. Thus, more faith traditions could be included in the list of those mentioned by the Qur'anic commentators. The sufi saints from India were inclined to include Indian religions also.

The Qur'anic pluralism finds different expressions in different places. The Qur'an does not maintain that there could be only one way of prayer to Allah. There could be more than one. Thus, the Qur'an says: "For each community there is direction in which it turns, so vie with one another in good works (2:148)." All commentators from companions of the Prophet down to others interpret this as a reference to the various religious communities and their different modes of 'turning towards God' in worship. Ibn Kathir, in his commentary on this verse, stresses its inner resemblance's to the phrase occurring in 5:48 (discussed above) "Unto every one of you have We appointed a (different) law and way of life".

This verse clearly refers to different directions, which different religious communities have adopted, whereto they turn for prayer. All of them, however, submit to God and pray to Him. The Qur'an conveys that the direction of the prayer, whatever its symbolic value for a religious community, does not represent the essence of the prayer or faith. This is further corroborated by the Qur'an in the verse 2:177.

This verse also makes a very significant statement: "It is not righteousness that you turn your faces towards the East and the West, but righteousness is the one who believes in Allah and the Last Day and the angels and the Book and the prophets and gives away wealth out of love for Him to the near of kin and the orphans and the needy and the wayfarer and to those who ask and to set slaves free and keeps up prayer and pays the poor rate; and the performers of their promise when they make a promise and the patient in distress and affliction and in the time of conflict; and these are they who keep their duty."

Thus, the above verse proves beyond any doubt that the real aim of the Qur'an is to produce an ideal human person who is virtuous, sensitive to others suffering and hence, spends of his wealth on the needy, on setting slaves free, taking care of orphans, is true to his word and is patient in times of distress and conflict. And only such persons are truly *muttaqun*, i.e., God conscious and keepers of their duty to Allah. This verse too, needless to say, lends great support to the basic premise of religious pluralism by de-emphasizing a particular way of prayer and extolling the importance of human conduct and sensitivity to others suffering and ones own steadfastness in the face of calamities and afflictions.

The Qur'an does not take narrow sectarian view as many theologians tend to do. It possesses very broad humanitarian view and lays emphasis not on dogmas, but on good deeds. And it strongly condemns evil deeds which harms the society and humanity at large. In this respect also it makes no distinction between Muslims and non-Muslims. Thus, the Qur'an says in 4:123: "It will not be in accordance with your vain desires nor the vain desires of the people of the Book. Whoever does evil, will be requited for it and will not find for himself besides Allah a friend or a helper." Thus, no one, Muslim or the people of the Book, can claim any exception from this iron law of Allah; one who does good will be rewarded and one who does evil will be punished. Elsewhere the Qur'an states, "So he who does an atom's weight of good will see it and he who does an atom's weight of evil will see it (99:7)."

The Qur'an is very particular about freedom of conscience and freedom of conscience is key to pluralism. The Qur'an clearly states that there is no compulsion in religion (2:256) and maintains that all children of Adam are honourable (17:70). It does admit of inter-religious dialogue, but with decorum: "And argue not with the People of the Book except by what is best, save such of them, as act unjustly." And Say: "We believe in that which has been revealed to us and revealed to you, and our God and your God is One, and to Him we submit (29:46)."

The Qur'an lays great stress on unity of humankind. It says in 2:213, "Mankind is a single nation. So Allah raised prophets as bearers of good news and as warners and He revealed with them the Book with truth, that it might judge between people concerning that in which they differed. And none, but the very people who were given it differed about it after clear arguments had come to them, envying one another. So Allah has guided by His will those who believe in the truth about which they differed."

This whole verse is suffused with the spirit of pluralism and freedom of belief and conscience. According to this verse the whole mankind is one, but different prophets in their given situations come with revealed scriptures to guide them or warn them and thus, depending on their specific situation, different ways of life emerge. But then people start differing from each other and envying one another instead of respecting each others specificity and thus people get divided. That is not the purpose of divine guidance. Allah guides those who believe in the truth about which they differed.

The theme of oneness of humankind is repeated in the Qur'an in different ways. We are told that all human beings have been "created of a single soul" (4:1); again that they are all descended from the same parents (49:13); still again that they are as it were dwellers in one home, having the same earth as a resting place and the same heaven as a canopy.

Apart from wholeness of humankind the Qur'an also lays stress on racial, linguistic and national identities. These identities are projected as signs of God. "And of His signs," the Qur'an says, "And of His signs is the creation of the heavens and the earth and the diversity of your tongues and colours. Surely there are signs in this for the learned (30:22)." Thus, diversity is projected by the Qur'an as sign of God and hence, to be respected. Different identities are for recognition and hence necessary. In the verse 49:13 it is said, "O mankind, surely We have created you from a male and a female, and made you nations and tribes that you may know each other" Thus, national and tribal or for that matter other identities are necessary for knowing each other and it should not lead to any conflict. Thus, different identities are product of national and tribal diversities and play a useful social role. And thus, the Qur'an clearly accepts the legitimacy of diversity.

It also makes it clear quite forcefully that all places of worship should be respected and protected. The Qur'an states, "And if Allah did not repeal some people by others, cloisters, and churches, and synagogues, and mosques in which Allah's name is much remembered, would have been pulled down (22:40)." It is significant that Qur'an maintains that be it church or synagogue or mosque, Allah's name is much remembered in these places. No single religious place is being privileged in this respect. Thus, here too religious pluralism is stressed.

The Prophet of Islam when he migrated from Mecca to Medina found himself in a pluralist situation. There was religious as well as tribal diversity. He not only accepted this diversity, but legitimized it by drawing up an agreement with different religious and tribal groups and accorded them, through this agreement, a dignified existence and rights of their own was established. This agreement is known in history of Islam as *Misaq-i-Madina*.

It begins thus:

In the name of God, the Merciful, the Compassionate!

This is writing of Muhammad the Prophet between the believers and Muslims of Quraysh and Yathrib (Madina) and those who follow them and are attached to them and who crusade along with them. They are a single community distinct from other people".

This agreement can be called the Constitution of Madina and it was definitely a milestone which sought to lay the foundation of a new political and religious culture. What is significant to note in this agreement is that all together—Muslims of Quraysh from Mecca, Muslims of Madina belonging to the tribes of Aws and Khazraj and Jews belonging to different tribes—together constituted a single community—an Ummah. The agreement was also quite democratic in spirit. The holy Prophet did not claim to be the ruler of this community. The emigrants (*Muhajirs*) were, in fact, treated as a clan, and the Prophet was their chief and there were eight other clans with their chiefs. If the Constitution is a good evidence at this point, he was only marked off from other clan chiefs on two counts: firstly that for the group of believers, i.e., Muslims he was a prophet and whatever was revealed to him was binding on the believers; secondly, the Constitution states that 'whatever there is anything about which you differ, it is to be referred to God and to Muhammad'. The idea seems that the holy Prophet should act as arbitrator between rival factions and maintain peace in Madina. The Qur'an also describes as one of the functions of the Prophet as an arbiter. It says: "And for every nation there is a messenger. So when their messenger comes, the matter is decided between them with justice and they are not wronged (10:48)."

It is interesting to note that the eminent Muslim theologians of India represented by Jami'at ul-'Ulama-i-Hind had cited this Constitution of Madina drawn up by the holy Prophet in support of their acceptance of composite nationalism. They opposed separate nationalism based on religion advocated by the Muslim League. They argued, citing the Constitution of Madina, that the Prophet had accepted different religious and tribal groups as part of a single community—*ummah wahidah* . The Medinese society was, thus, a democratic civil society which had tribal, religious and racial diversity.

The modern democratic civil society cannot become a strong stable and prosperous conflict free society unless religious diversity or pluralism is accepted as legitimate way of life. It is unfortunate that most of the Muslim countries do not adhere to this spirit of pluralism and diversity in the Qur'an and *sunnah*. The extremists and fundamentalists among the Muslims in these countries attack the spirit of pluralism and want to create a monolithic society.

Many socio-political doctrines which we consider as 'pure Islamic' and worthy of emulation today developed during medieval age when *mulukiyat* (personal and monarchical power structure) had become all pervasive and the Qur'anic values and Islamic spirit were hardly practiced. There was of course no question of any concept of civil society because the ruler was all powerful and followed his own personal whims or went by compulsions of power rather than the injunctions of the Qur'an. Also the arrogance of power and all pervasive authoritarian atmosphere also influenced formulation of Islamic political doctrines. These medieval doctrines can hardly have any validity today.

It is for the Islamic political theorists of today to develop new political theories which are in keeping with the Qur'anic injunctions and *sunnah* on one hand and takes the realities of modern world, on the other. There need not be any sharp contradiction between the two. The concept of civil society which respects autonomy of a citizen and his/her religious, cultural and political rights does not, as shown above, in any way, contradictory to the Qur'anic injunctions. Human rights respect the dignity and freedom of conscience of every individual. The Qur'an clearly states that all children of Adam have been honoured (17:70). This of course includes right to live with dignity and to promote ones own religious, cultural and linguistic or ethnic interests.

In this 21st century we must not carry the imitative (*taqlidi*) mind set, but with a creative and critical mind set which, while adhering to the Qur'anic values, enables us to live freer life and life of full dignity while, at the same time, accepting the dignity of the other. The Qur'an, accepted, fourteen hundred years ago, the Christian other and the Jewish other with full dignity and respect for their beliefs. It was later accepted the Zoroastrians and even Berbers. Many 'ulama and the Sufi saints, extended it to the Hindus also.

It is interesting to note that the words *kafir* and *mushrik* have definite historical connotation and should be used with great caution and restraint. Unfortunately many Muslims use these terms very loosely and describe every other religious follower as *kafir* or *mushrik*. These being terms of contempt are resented by others. Only those who refuse to accept truth in any form and negate good (*ma'ruf*) completely and advocate *munkar* (evil) would qualify as *kafirs* and those who refuse oneness of God and associate partners with Him will qualify as *mushrik*. And, it is also important to note, even *kafirs* and *mushriks* would have civil rights as long as they do not cause any disturbances in society and maintain peace. The Qur'an has given the *kafirs* also the right to worship in their own way and have their own beliefs. The freedom of conscience cannot be taken away form any human person, whatever his or her beliefs. Thus it will be seen that Islam does not come in the way of promoting a pluralist civil society ensuring dignity and freedom of conscience to all.

But it has, yet, to be realized in all Muslim countries. In many Muslim countries like Turkey and Iraq, let alone non-Muslims, even Muslims of other nationalities and ethnic origin like the Kurds are severely persecuted. It is in clear violation of the Qur'anic injunctions, as pointed out above. An Islamic civil society should treat all with equal degree of dignity and accord them equal citizenship rights.

CHAPTER 14

Ikhwanus Safa—A Rational and Liberal Approach to Islam

Rasa'il-e-Ikhwanus Safa (Epistles of Brethren of Purity) have been considered an encyclopaedic work of 3rd or 4th century of Islam. This work consists of 52 epistles (*Rasa'il*), though there is controversy about the exact number. Some scholars claim they are 50, in number while others maintain 51 and yet, others 52 or 53. However, more authentic number is 52nd and the 53rd *risala* is known as *Jami'*, i.e., the summation of the earlier *rasa'il*. There is great deal of controversy about every aspect of this path breaking encyclopaedic work. Who wrote these epistles and when? There are no easy answers forthcoming as far as scholarly controversies are concerned. Also what was the *madhhab* (i.e., sect) of the compilers of these epistles? Were they Sunnis or Shi'as? Or if Sunnis were they M'utazilas or Sufis or others? Or if Shi'ahs were they Ithna 'Asharis (twelvers) or Isma'ilis? Were these epistles written by a single individual or by a group of people?

Some scholars claim that there was a debating society in Basra which met once every week and debated issues of which notes were taken and these notes were later compiled in the form of these epistles. There is no doubt that whosoever they were they were very liberal in their approach and well informed about various sciences including the Greek sciences of their time. There is an attempt to examine various issues, particularly Islamic, in the light of these sciences. Thus, the liberal approach is obvious.

We would like to examine, though briefly, some of these controversies. The Isma'ilis (who are so named as they followed Isma'il, the elder son of Imam Ja'far al-Sadiq, as their Imam after Imam Sadiq's death) claim that the *rasa'il* were compiled by their 9th Imam Ahmad al-Mastur or some maintain by earlier Imam Abdullah al-Mastur and these epistles were kept in the mosques of Baghdad during the Abbasid period (at the end of 3rd century *hijri*). The reason for compilation of these *rasa'il* is said to be that the Abbasids were transferring the Greek works on various sciences and philosophy into Arabic thereby creating doubts in the minds of believers and the compiler(s) of *Ikhwanus Safa* met this challenge through this compilation.

One finds references to this work in the Isma'ili sources. Prof. Abbas Hamdani has shown the Isma'ili authorship of these *rasa'il* in his study "An Early Fatimid Source on the Time and Authorship of the *Rasa'il Ikhwanus Safa*" published in *Arabica* in 1979. Abbas Hamdani says, "The great encyclopaedic work of medieval Islam, *Rasa'il Ikhwanus Safa* has been described as Mu'tazilite, Sunni, Sufi, Shi'ite, Isma'ili or Qarmatian. Its Fatimid character (the Isma'ili Imams referred to themselves as Fatimi Imams) is now no longer in dispute...Various dates have been suggested for its appearances ranging from 350/961 to 557/1162. The most tenacious theory about the authorship of the *Rasa'il* and its time of composition is the one derived from Abu Hayyan al-Tawhidi (320-414/932-1023) who supposedly provides a contemporary evidence. I have, however, refuted this theory in a recent article..." Abbas Hamdani quotes the famous Fatimi *da'i* (missionary or summoner) Sayyidna J'afar bin Mansur al-Yaman who says in his work—the biography of his father Ibn Hawshab (*Sira Ibn Hawshab*)—that Abdallah, the son of Imam Muhammad bin Isma'il, went into seclusion and faced many hardships, his *hudud*—the hierarchy of the Fatimi D'awah officials—carried on the mission during his absence until his son Ahmad who also remained in concealment took over and he issued the *Rasa'il*. Da'i Ja'far is supposed to have lived between 270/883 to 360/970 and died at the advanced age of 80-90 in Maghrib, i.e., North western Africa. *The Rasa'il*, if they are of Fatimid origin—and there is every reason to believe they are, were compiled around the end of third century *higra*, i.e., during the life time of his father Ibn Hawshab. This further strengthens the Fatimid claim that the *Rasa'il* (epistles) were compiled during the time of Imam Ahmad al-Mastur.

However, there are some references in the *Rasa'il* which indicate their Sunni origin. At one place there is a praiseworthy reference to al-Siddiq, al-Farouq and Dhu'l Nurayn, i.e., Abu Bakr, 'Umar and 'Uthman. A later Isma'ili writer tries to explain it away. But then there is also insistence in the *Rasa'il* on the esoteric interpretation of the Qur'an (i.e., its *ta'wil*) which is a Shi'i, particularly the Isma'ili concept. At another place a *hadith* is related from Hazrat 'Ayisha' (I, 358) which no Shi'i would ever do, unless the introduction of 'Ayisha's name is an editorial interpolation. Also, at two places (III, 489 and IV, 408) there are references to *al- khulafa al-rashidun,* i.e., the first four Caliphs which again is a Sunni belief.

But also here are references to the sufis and praise for sufism. In fact one of the sections is devoted to love, i.e., *fi mahiyyat al-ishq* (III, 269-286). Also there is one section on *wajd* (an inner spiritual sufi experience) (I, 240). Both these sections are full of sufi terminology. In fact an ideal person is described as *al-sufi al-sira* (i.e., possessing the sufi character) (see II, 376). Sayyid Husayn Nasr would, however, consider this to be a Shi'i Sufi instead of a Sunni Sufi tendency, agreeing with A.L. Tibawi who says, "The Ikhwan al-Safa' may be taken as symbolizing the Shi'a attempt, while al-Ghazali represents the Sunni attempt at a synthesis. Susanne Diwald on the other hand would consider the *Rasa'il* just Sufi, not Shi'i, thus implying its Sunni character.

Philip K. Hitti syas about *Brethren of Purity* in his well-known work *History of Arabs*: "About middle of the fourth century (*ca.* 970) there flourished in al-Basrah an interesting eclectic school of popular philosophy, with leanings toward Pythagorean speculations, known as Ikhwan al-Safa' (the brethren of sincerity). The appellation is presumably taken from the story of the ring-dove in *Kalilah wa-Dimnah* in which it is related that a group of animals by acting as faithful friends (*ikhwan al-safa*) to one another to escape the snares of the hunter."

However, Hitti also accepts the Isma'ili origin of the *Rasa'il* when he observes, "The Ikhwan, who had a branch in Baghdad, formed not only a philosophical, but also a religio-political association with ultra-Shi'ite, probably Isma'ilite, views and were opposed to the existing political order, which they evidently aimed to overthrow by undermining the popular intellectual system and religious beliefs. Hence, arises the obscurity surrounding their activities and membership. A collection of their epistles, *Rasa'il*, arranged in encyclopaedic fashion survives, bearing some obscure names as collaborators." (*History of Arabs*, London, 1988, p. 372-73).

He further observes, "The epistles number fifty-two and treat of mathematics, astronomy, geography, music, ethics, philosophy, embodying the sum-total of knowledge that a cultured man of that age was supposed to acquire. The first fifty-one epistles lead up to the last, which is summation of all sciences. The language of the epistles shows that Arabic had by that time, become an adequate instrument for expressing scientific thought in all its various aspects. Al-Ghazali was influenced by the Ikhwan's writings and Rashid al-Din Sinan ibn-Sulayman, the Chief of the Assassins in Syria, used them diligently" (P. 373).

But it is difficult to agree with Hitti, when he says that Abu Hayyan al-Tawhidi (1023), the famous Mu'tazilite who with al-Rawindi and al Ma'arri (1057), formed the trinity of arch heretics in Islam, was a pupil if not an active member of the fraternity. In fact the historians and scholars have often relied on Abu Hayyan al-Tawhidi's version of the origin of *Ikhwan al-Safa Rasa'il* which is difficult to stand critical scrutiny. If the *Rasa'il* are of the Isma'ili origin which Hitti himself thinks probably is, Mu'tazili association with it is unlikely. The Isma'ilis and Mu'tazilis, though both liberal and rational in their approach, had very different views on theological and philosophical matters. On most of these matters they totally disagreed with each other.

Husayn Marwah, a noted Marxist philosopher from the Arab world has also written extensively in his *Al-Naz'at al-Maddiyah f'il Falsafat al-'Arabiyah al-Islamiyyah* (Beirut, 1981) on *Ikhwan al-Safa Rasa'il*. Al-Marwah quotes Jamal al-Din Qifti from his *Akhbar al-'Ulama' fi Akhbar al-Hukama'* that the group of *Ikhwan al-Safa* compiled the *Rasa'il* containing wisdom of knowledge, but they concealed their names and people differed about their names and origin and everyone said what they thought according to their guess. some maintain that this group belonged to the Imams from the progeny of Ali ibn Abi Talib. But they differed about the name of the Imam and some maintain that these *Rasa'il* are the compilation of some M'utazilites.

Thus, it will be seen that al-Qifti also admits that it might have been compiled by an Imam from the progeny of Ali ibn Abi Talib. No historian or scholar, it seems, can ignore the claim of Isma'ili Imam to compilation of this great work, though no one seems to be sure about it. If it had been the work of Mu'tazilites there is no reason why they should have concealed the name of the compiler. Mu'tazilites were not an underground organization. Number of their works were being circulated around that time with the names of their authors. The Isma'ilis, on the other hand, had set up an underground organization as they were fighting against the Abbasid empire and were aspiring to establish their own rule. Thus, the Isma'ili Imams were in concealment and had perfected an underground organization. Thus, they had every reason to conceal the name of the author(s) of the *Rasa'il*. Thus, it looks quite probable that the *Rasa'il* in all probability were authored by an Isma'ili Imam.

There is also the question of the period when the *Rasa'il* were written or compiled. The noted scholar Abbas Hamdani who has authored several research studies on *Ikhwanus Safa* says: "The questions relating to the identity of the authors of the *Rasa'il* and their *madhhab* are largely dependent on the question of the date of the composition of the *Rasa'il*. A later chronology may suggest a composition of the encyclopedia over a long period, by several authors living at different times and several revisions and rearrangements of the component tracts. It can also accommodate the internal allusions of a much later period. An earlier chronology would pre-suppose a shorter period of composition, the minimum of rearrangements and revision and a committee of authors writing at the same time under a coordinator or an editor and working on a planned sequence of composition. Internal references to a later period would have to be proved as interpolations".

Abbas Hamdani then comes to the conclusion about the year of publication of the *Rasa'il* and says, "To my mind, the dividing line between these two chronologies is represented by the year 297/909, that is, he establishment of the Fatimid caliphate. In fact, in much of the scholarly argument about the dating of the *Rasa'il*, this has proved to be the battle line. Having taken their stand on the date of the composition of the *Rasa'il*, scholars have argued whether its authors were Sunnis or Shi'is; if Sunnis, whether they were Mu'tazili or Sufi; if Shi'is, whether they were Zaydi, Ithna 'Ashari, Fatimid or Qaramatian. The later chronology is the easier and safer of the two and is generally accepted. I have, however, preferred the earlier and the more difficult and have argued the case for it in articles." (*Journal of Semitic Studies*, Spring 1984, p. 98)

There is lot of internal evidence which shows the Shi'i inclination of the author(s). We find in (IV, 460) the Prophet's saying, "I am the city of knowledge and 'Ali is its gate". So also is emphasized the love (*walaya*) of the Prophet's household (*ahl al-Bayt*) (IV, 375). Also, it is said that the Prophet is reported to have said to 'Ali, "I and you are the parents (*abawa*) of this community (*umma*)" (I,385). We also notice "*salawat*" for 'Ali (II, 59 and III,211). Generally this benedictory expression is reserved by Sunnis only for the Prophet. The *Rasa'il* also refer to the progeny of the Prophet as he 'rightly-guided Imams' (*al-a'immat al-Hudat*) (II, 377). We also find emphasis on imamah and also that imamat of prophesy belong to the prophet's family as opposed to the imamat of domination which might belong to others.

We find further proofs of shades of Shi'is in the *Rasa'il*. They describe the four festivals of the philosophic year (IV, 267-272), the third of which is the '*Id Ghadir al-Khumm*, the day on which the Prophet designated, according to the Shi'a tradition, Ali as his successor, but, the *Rasa'il* maintain, the 'joy (of the occasion) was marred because it was mixed with the breaking of (the covenant) and treachery' (IV,268). The last festival, '*Id al-musiba* (the day of calamity) is one described as the day of the Prophet's death and also as the day of the battle of Kerbala (10th of Muharram when Imam Husayn was martyred) which is also described as the day of 'disgrace of Islam' (IV, 269). This is all unmistakably Shi'ite.

There are also references in III, 511-514 to the esoteric meaning of the Qur'an, i.e., *ta'wil* which is also a distinct Shi'ite belief. The manifest meaning of the Qur'an (*zahir*) is described as the lower level of knowledge and it is meant for '*awamm* (i.e., the common people) who prefer *taqlid* (i.e., blind imitation) and the higher form of knowledge is *batin* (esoteric, concealed) which is meant for the elite (*khwass*). This is distinctly Shi'ite position. Thus, we find in the 3rd section, page 379 that "Among people there are groups of intellectuals who would not be satisfied with *taqlid*, but would demand proofs and the uncovering of truths (*haqa'iq*) and the seeking of '*illah* (i.e., purpose or the reason of the religious law)".

Again the important question is to what sect of Shi'a the compilers or authors of *Ikhwanus Safa Rasa'il* belong. Obviously, they could not be Zaidis as the Zaidi theology does not accord what is generally maintained in the *Rasa'il*. Now let us examine the possibility of the authors being the Ithna 'Asharis. There is clear statement in the *Rasa'il* which rules out this possibility also. For example, we find in III, 523 that "So also is considered (erroneous a group) that believes that the great and guiding awaited Imam is hidden and does not appear because of the fear of the opponents. Know that the holder of such opinion remains all his life expectant of the Imam's appearance, wishful of his coming, eager for his advent. He, then, wastes his life and dies in despair and sorrow, not having seen his Imam, nor having known his person".

The Ithna 'Asharis believe till today that Imam Mahdi is, yet, to appear whereas the Isma'ilis or Fatimids believe that Imam Mahdi (Abdullah al-Mahdi) appeared in the West (North Africa) in early 9th century and founded the Fatimid empire. The above passage does not accord with the Ithna 'Ashari belief about the hidden Imam. Thus, if we eliminate the Zaidis and Ithna Asharis, the only conclusion is that the *Brethren of Purity* belonged to the Isma'ilis.

The liberal attitude of the Brethren is obvious from various passages of the *Rasa'il*. There is also emphasis on the youth rather than the old. Thus, we find in one of the epistles, "Do not occupy yourself with reforming of old men who have kept since their childhood false ideas, bad habits and evil qualities, for they will weary you and will not be changed. If they do change, it would be very little and of no avail. Your concern is with young men of sound heart who incline towards letters, begin to study the sciences, seek the path of truth and the other world, believe in the day of reckoning, make use of the religious codes of the Prophets, study the secrets of their books, renounce passion and polemic and are not fanatical in matters of doctrine" (IV, 161-168).

As pointed out earlier the *Ikhwan* had very liberal outlook. It is borne out by the following passage also. "Know that," the Brethren state, "the truth is found in every religion (*din*) and is current in every tongue. What you should do, however, is to take best and to transfer yourself to it. Do not ever occupy yourself with imputing defects to the religions of people; rather try to see whether your religion is free from them (III, 501)."

Also, "Acquire knowledge, any type of knowledge, philosophical, legal, mathematical, scientific or divine. All that is nourishment for the soul and life for it in this world and the hereafter" (III, 538).

There is a long epistle (no. 22) on animals and birds (II, 178-377) which is of great interest. In fact it is an allegory in which man's qualities are compared to those of animals, birds and the *jinn* (a hidden being referred to in the Qur'an). Representatives of different species and nationalities speak in a conference of creation. At the end an ideal individual addresses the assembly. The description of this ideal individual clearly indicates the liberalism and openness of the brethren.

This individual is described as, "excellent, intelligent and possessing insight, (as if) he is Persian in origin, Arab in faith, a *hanif* (inclined towards straight path) in religion, an Iraqi in manners, a Hebrew in tradition, a Christian in conduct, a Syrian in devotion, a Greek in knowledge, an Indian in vision, a mystic (*sufi*) in his way of life (*sira*), an angel in his morals, a divine (*rabbani*) in opinion, godly (*ilahi*) in Gnosticism (*ma'arif*) and of everlasting qualities" (III, 376).

This is the proof of commendable liberalism of the *Ikhwan* which we find post-modernist in character today. In the above passage there is respect for all religions and plurality of culture is accepted. This was written in the 9th century AD when such liberalism could not be thought of. Such liberalism is rare, even in modern society. Narrow sectarianism often prevails and more often than not politics is also based on such sectarianism. This is what we witness in most of the countries today. The *Ikhwanus Safa* could be described as the manifesto of the Isma'ili movement.

It is important to note here that the Isma'ili movement at that time was a revolutionary movement and was subversive of the establishment, particularly of the Abbasid empire. It was also trying to attract the support of various sections of society, the nobles, the learned, the peasants and the merchants. Thus, we find a passage in the epistle which says, "Know O brother, may God aid you and us with His Spirit, that we have brethren and friends among the noble and gracious people, spread out in different places; among them is a group of the sons of kings, *amirs*, *wazirs*, secretaries, and governors; among them are sons of notables, the *dihqans* (rich peasants), small holders and merchants; and among them is a group of the sons of 'ulama, men of letters (*udaba'*), jurists and religious men; and among them is a group of the sons of craftsmen, local headmen and leaders of crafts and professions. We have delegated to each group of them a brother from our brethren, whose knowledge and insight we approve, to represent us in their service by counselling them with fellow-feeling (*rifq*), kindness and affection" (IV, 188).

This clearly shows that the Brethren were leaders of a revolutionary movement who established cells among different sections of society who could coalesce together to overthrow the coercive and exploitative establishment. It is also important to note in the above passage that the Brethren appointed one brother to be associated with one or the other group described above so as to lead them. Such a brother had to be properly chosen for his qualities, experience and knowledge. The revolutionaries carefully chose their group leaders. They were supposed not only to prepare these groups for revolutionary change, but also play part in it.

A study of these *Rasa'il* clearly shows that the author(s) had grasp over all available knowledge of their times. As pointed out above they have written epistles on mathematics, philosophy, politics, religion (including comparative religion), music, ethics, morality, astronomy, physics and other sciences. No one could be more informed in contemporary knowledge then the Brethren of Purity.

Husayn Marwah, the noted contemporary Arab philosopher, referred to above, quotes observations of a 4th century hijra scholar Zaid bin Rifa'ah who was supposed to have met the Brethren of Purity and served them for long, about these epistles. Ibn Rifa'ah says that the authors of the epistles had wide knowledge of prose and poetry, expertize in mathematics, communication, history, religions and vision of comparative religion.

The Brethren of Purity, as we have seen, were revolutionaries and wanted to overthrow the Abbasid regime which they considered oppressive and exploitative. They describe the Abbasids as oppressors and usurpers of the rights of *du'afa'* and '*masakin* (i.e., weaker sections). They maintain that the Abbasid do not deserve to be *khalifah*. Those who defy the Divine Will to Adam are what the *Ikhwan* describe as "*khalifat al-iblis* (i.e., the deputy of Satan). The Abbasids were *khalifahs* as people accepted them to be *khalifahs*, not because they deserve to be so. The Abbasids, the Brethren maintain, killed the friends and children of prophets. (II, 303)

It is interesting to note that the *Ikhwan al-Safa* predict the downfall of the Abbasids on the basis of astronomical calculations. They calculate the coming together and parting of certain stars and this period which according to astronomical calculation is two hundred and forty years and hence, they predict that the Abbasid downfall will occur in 240 years from the beginning of their rule. And to whom this rule will be transferred from the Abbasids? We find answer in the *Rasa'il* themselves again on the basis of astronomical calculations. They say this will happen when the *dawr al-falki* (i.e., one revolution of skies) takes place and enters the House of Scorpio which takes, according to the Brethren, 330 years and four months. At that time the power will pass onto the hands of the Brethren and the period of their rule will be 159 years. (See *al-Risalah Jami'ah*, II, p. 129-130). According to the Brethren these changes (in political power) keep on taking place and it is transferred from one group to another.

The rule of *Ikhwan al-Safa* is described as *dawlah ahl al-khayr* i.e., the regime of people of good-will. This regime began with the people of knowledge and wisdom (*'ulama wa hukama*) and meritorious people of goodness who evolve consensus and agree on one creed and religion (I, p. 131). And those who will establish this regime of goodness and benevolence are knowledgeable about the religious matters, have intimate knowledge of the mysteries of prophets and well disciplined in the philosophical matters. (IV, p. 198). The Brethren also declare that their religion, opinion and knowledge is inclusive of all religions and knowledge. (IV, p. 5). The Brethren also advise the people not to pick holes in others religion but to see whether such defects are not there in ones own religion. (IV, p. 37-38)

The Brethren also invite the people to be critical of all religions, including the one they have inherited, without exception. But it should be attempted with due caution. The Shari'ah, according to them, have two aspects *zahir* and *batin*, i.e., exoteric and esoteric, manifest and hidden. What is manifest is for common people through which they find cure for their diseased souls and those who are people of strong intellect feed themselves on deeper wisdom and philosophy, on the esoteric aspects. (IV, p. 46). For *'ibadat* (worship) also the Brethren say they are of two types: one the Shari'i normative mode of worship and the other is what the Brethren call— *'ibadat al-falsafiyah al-ilahiyyah* (i.e., philosophical divine worship) (IV, p. 301 and what follows). Those who follow the Shar'i worship obey all the exoteric laws of Shari'ah and all the rules laid down by it. But those who are disposed towards philosophical worship are what the Holy Qur'an calls are *al-Rasikhun fi'l 'ilm* (i.e., great pillars of divine knowledge). They know the real meaning of the Qur'anic verses and its esoteric essence. They possess the *'ilm al-batin*.

Thus, it will be seen that the Brethren of Purity, though they emphasized the importance of Shari'ah for common people and thought it necessary for them to abide by its rule, they accorded higher position to those *al-rasikhun fi'l 'ilm* who were immersed in higher philosophical knowledge and knowledge of ultimate reality—*'ilm al-haqiqah*. Again, according to the *Ikhwan al-Safa* the lower souls cannot extricate themselves from the materialistic world and remain sunk in the sea of this world. It is knowledge, philosophy and wisdom (*hikmah*) which liberates human soul and accords it higher position in the divine hierarchy.

It would thus, be no exaggeration to say that the Brethren of Purity summed up all available knowledge of their time in their epistles and left a deep and permanent imprint on the world of learning. The Abbasids tried to popularize the Greek knowledge through translations into Arabic. All they did was to make Greek knowledge available in Arabic to Muslim intellectuals (a great achievement by itself, no doubt), but what *Ikhwanus Safa* did was to synthesize the Greek knowledge with Islamic one and this synthesis was very creative synthesis indeed. The Brethren upheld Islamic knowledge as well as the Greek one. A much greater achievement for the world of Islam.

CHAPTER 15

Muhammad (PBUH) as Liberator

Why liberation and from what? are important questions to be answered before we get on about Muhammad (PBUH), the Prophet, (Peace Be Upon Him) and his liberation movement.

For any liberation movement the existing social situation like, social, political, religious, cultural or economic, is extremely important. Any liberation movement actually takes off from this situations. It is therefore, necessary to talk of the socio-cultural and politico-economic situation existing before the Prophet Muhammad (PBUH) appears on the social scene of Mecca. Then and only then we can understand the significance of Muhammad (PBUH) as liberator. First, let us take the social scene on the eve of Prophet's appearance on the social scene of Mecca. Illiteracy was widespread. It is thought by the noted historian Tabari and others that there were hardly 17 persons who were literate at the time. The Arabs, in fact, considered it is merely waste of time to learn to read and write and even took pride in their being 'illiterate', they were extremely fond of poetry which was something to be recited and heard, not written, no other genre had developed, except poetry in Arabic literature of the time. It was said of Arabic language that it was sacred to the ears, not to the eyes. Written prose was almost unknown and Arabic was mere a spoken language. Due to this in Arab the period before Islam was called a period of *Jahilliah* (ignorance). It was not mere illiteracy which mattered most. The social outlook also was very narrow. In fact they hardly ever saw anything beyond their own tribe. Their code of conduct too was limited to unwritten tribal customs and there was no written laws. At the sametime the Arabs took great pride in their ancestry. If the tribal pride was hurt then it would result in prolonged bloodshed, at times lasting over generations.

The religious scene was even worse. Each tribe had its own idol. Historians tell us there were more than 360 idols in K'aba, the holy abode of God. Tribal gods brought about even sharper divisions. There was no concept of humanity beyond ones tribe. The whole existence of an Arab was circumscribed by tribal limits. Superstitions were a great religious force. These superstitions have been referred to in the Quran and condemned. There was no attempt whatsoever to widen the frontier of knowledge. Their whole life was governed by superstition.

The position of women was very unenviable. Though there was no practice of veil like feudal society, they were socially and economically unfree. They could not play independent role in social, economic or political affairs. Their marital status was even worse. They had to live, at times, with more than a dozen co-wives. And, sometime they were also considered a burden and in many cases an attempt was made to bury them alive to which the Quran also refers in a verses, (81: 8-9).

Economic scene was no less depressing. The social woes of the weaker sections were indescribable. Tribal structure was collapsing (in economic sense) and a commercial oligarchy was coming into being. This oligarchy was motivated by material greed and was blatantly disregarding even tribal obligations. As a result the orphans, the widows and the needy (miskin) greatly suffered. Also, there was innumerable slaves and slave girls. They were forced to work without any reward. The slave girls were compelled to cohabit with there masters. These slaves existed on the periphery of the society and had no human dignity.

Also, among the free there were many who had been completely marginalized. They were forced to provide cheap labour. The commercial caravans passed through Mecca. The camels carrying commercial goods had to be loaded and unloaded. This cheap labour was provided by the poor and the needy, those existing on the margin of the society. Neither they could protest or unionized. Such a concept did not exist at that time. The artisans too were condemned to struggle for bare existence. They included tanners, smiths, carpenters and others. However, the neo-rich, led life of luxury.

Politically the situation was less dismal. Arabs were fiercely independent people and jealously guarded their independence. No attempt to subjugate them ever succeeded, whether at the hands of Romans or the Sassanids. They thus, lived independently in Arabian peninsula. However, as pointed out earlier, there was no unity among the Arabs as they belonged to various tribes fighting fiercely against each other. Moreover, there was no concept of unity beyond ones own tribe. Such a unity was considered blasphemous, to say the least. Only few tribes in Mecca tried to form inter-tribal corporations for commercial purposes and the commercial caravans were often owned by individuals belonging to different tribes.

Muhammad (PBUH) appears on the social scene on Mecca in such despicable conditions. He had no schooling as neither it was encouraged (as pointed out earlier) nor it had any functional value (except for commercial contracts, a need which was newly emergent and was met with the help of a few literates in Mecca). He was orphaned at an early age, led life of penury and was steeled through struggles of life. He married a rich widow at the age of 25 and began to lead a life of a recluse in the cave of Hira where he spent time brooding over the social, religious, political and economic situation around him. He than literally burst over the Meccan scene at the age of 40 to liberate his people as well as the whole humanity.

Liberate from what? Whom? and Why? Liberation from ignorance, superstition, oppression, slavery and injustice. Liberation to give dignity and freedom of thought and action. These are the noble ideals which not only provide inspiration to live, but also encourage creativity and purposeful action. Also, Muhammad worked for the liberation of the oppressed, poor needy and the ignorant. He was, in this project of liberation, not only a teacher and philosopher, but also an activist participant and fighter. Under his inspiration the Arabs not only liberated themselves, but also sought to liberate others by shattering the two greatest oppressive empires of the world then, i.e., the Roman and the Sassanid. Their stormy victories were ensured as they were seen by the oppressed of these mighty empires as liberators.

II

We would now discuss the liberative elements and liberative aspects of Muhammad (PBUH) the Prophet's teachings and actions.

For any liberative praxis knowledge is a must. In fact it is knowledge which provides perspective for liberation and for liberative actions. It is thus, not for nothing that the very first revelation (see Chapter 96 The Clot) came with the word *iqra* 'recite'. The following verses in the chapter also lay stress on acquiring *ilm* (knowledge). The verses run as follows: "Read in the name of thy Lord who creates (the implications being one should study and acquire knowledge of creation) man from a clot, Read, thy Lord is most Bountiful One who has taught (man) the use of pen, taught man what he did not know".

It is important to note here that there was no concept even of pen among the Arabs, literacy being very rare. Here the Quran stresses the use of pen as it is through pen that knowledge is transmitted from one place to another and from one generation to the other, thus, revelation to the Prophet began with stress on knowledge and its transmission to others. Elsewhere the Qur'an also likens knowledge to *nur* (light). Thus, Allah led the Arabs (as they were the immediate people around the Prophet then) from darkness of ignorance to the light of knowledge. One can understand what liberative effect this acquisition of knowledge must have had on the minds of the Arabs. The Prophet further reinforced this by his making acquisition of knowledge obligatory (*faridat*) for both men as well as women. The Prophet also induced his followers to acquire knowledge, even if it be in China (Sin).

Undoubtedly these exhortations by the Prophet had great liberative effect on the Arabs and his other followers. The Arabs who had nothing, but abhorrence for knowledge became masters of learning within a century. During the Abbasid period the Arabs and the other Muslims acquired the treasure of the Greek knowledge so much so that they were referred to as its foster father. Not only this they produced great philosophers like Avicena and Avveros and several other philosophers, masters of medicine, chemists, geographers, physicists and mathematicians to whom even the west is indebted. The Muslims could have hardly achieved this excellence in knowledge, but for the exhortations of the Qur'an and the Prophet. Thus, the Arabs were liberated from ignorance.

Social Liberation

Liberation from ignorance had deeper consequences in other areas. The Arabs, as pointed out earlier, were greatly constrained by tribal outlook. This outlook was completely shattered by the Qur'anic teaching that entire human kind has originated from the same man and women and no one has any distinction over the other on the basis of tribe, nation, race or colour. These divisions only serve the purpose of identification. The most honoured is one who is most just and most pious. The Qur'anic verse runs thus, "O humankind! We have created you all out of a male and a female and have made you into nations and tribes, so that you might recognise one another, verily, the noblest of you in the sight of God is one who is most righteous (and just)."

This was most revolutionary concept not only for the Arabs but for entire human race. The barriers of colour and race are powerful even today so much that the UNO had to stress equality of all irrespective of caste, creed and colour in its charter of human rights which is considered most liberative and rightly so. But the Qur'anic charter anticipated this by several centuries. The Prophet demonstrated this by elevating an emancipated Negro slave Bilal to the status of his *muazzin* (caller to the prayer), an honour coveted by many free men among the Arabs. It is after him that some black Muslims in the United States have formed a Bilalian Society. By elevating a freed Negro slave to this status the Prophet clearly demonstrated human dignity is above colour as well as social status.

The Prophet also fought against superstitions and supernatural beliefs. He refused to perform miracle. He projected himself not as a supernatural being, but as a human like any one else. The Qur'an was very categorical about it. The Qur'an ridicules any demand for miracles. In Chapter 17 there are several verses to this effect (see verses from 90 to 95). The unbelievers demanded miracles like causing a spring to gush forth from earth, or to create garden of palms and grapes among which riverse to flow forth abundantly, or cause heaven to come down upon us in pieces or bring Allah and the angels face to face or you create for yourself a house of gold or to ascend into heaven and so on. Allah wants people to accept the guidance as it comes to them through the Prophet. Had there been angels living on earth we would have sent down an angel for guidance. Among human beings only a human being would be sent as Prophet. Thus, the Qur'an rejected the demand of unbelievers to perform miracles. The only miracle was the Qur'an itself.

The Qur'an's style was simple, fluent and powerful. It was the first example of a powerful purposeful prose. It's diction was urban and classical. It's style and power simply astounded the Arabs who were so proud of their inimitable style and diction. They could not rival its style despite repeated challenge. Still they continue to deny the truth of its message.

A revolutionary, radical and liberative movement stresses reason as reason teaches one to question and critically examine. The Qur'an revealed to Muhammad (PBUH) lays stress on reason, not on mystery or miracles. The Qur'an repeatedly calls upon the people to think and addresses them *as u' l ' il albab* which means reason. *Lubb* in Arabic means an essence of a thing and reason is considered as essence of humanity and thus, by inference *lubb* is used for reason, its plural being *albab*.

Also, those who follow ancestral tradition and do not change are called *a'ma* (blind) and those who think as *bas ir* (i.e., one who can see). It goes on to say, "Say (O Muhammad (PBUH)): I say you, I have with me neither the treasures of Allah, nor do I know the unseen, nor do I say to you that I am an angel; I follow only that which is revealed to me. Say: Are the blind and the seeing alike? Do you not them reflect." (6:50)

In this verse once again Muhammad (PBUH) is asked to deny all supernatural powers and preference is given to one who sees and reflects. Thus, appeal is to reason, not to tradition. In another verse the Qur'an says, "Does one of you like to have a garden of palms and vines with streams flowing in it—he has therein all kinds of fruits—and old age has over taken him and he has weak offspring; when (lo!) a whirlwind with fire in it smites it so it becomes blasted. Thus, Allah makes the signs clear to you that you may think." (2: 266)

Here a very earthly example has been given which is often experienced and there is nothing supernatural or superstitious about it and then thee Qur'an invites us to think and reflect on it. Nowhere the Qur'an requires us to accept anything blindly, signs are made clear and then we are urged upon to think over it. Islam was a revolutionary movement which wanted to liberate people from shackles of tradition and irrational conventions perpetrated through ages. Hence, it invites its addresees again and again to reflect and think, not to follow blindly. It had liberative effect on thousands of the Prophet's followers.

Muhammad (PBUH) was basically engaged in liberating the weaker sections of the society, both those who were sexually and economically weaker. Women, as pointed out earlier, suffered great disabilities in Arabia in particular and the whole world in general. Muhammad (PBUH), announced through the Qur'an a charter of rights for women. Qur'an for the first time gave them rights, never conceded them before in any legal code. Women's individual existence as a legal entity was accepted without any qualification for the first time. As far as the Qur'an was concerned she could contract marriage (without any marriage guardian), could divorce her husband without any condition, inherit her father, mother and other relatives, could own property in her own absolute right (neither her father nor her brother or husband could temper with it or deprive her of it), could have custody of her children (upto certain age after which children would exercise their option) and could take her own free decisions.

It is also laid down in the Qur'an that her male relatives cannot coerce her in anyway, even in matters of marriage. No legal charter before Islam gave these rights to women. In Europe women could not even own property in their own right, even upto late nineteenth century. In fact the Qur'an announced in clear words that in her rights and obligations she is equal to man (see the Qur'an 2: 228). It was nothing short of revolution for her. For the first time in history she was given legal status equal to that of man and she was liberated from the clutches of male domination.

The only stigma she can be said to have suffered was permission given to man to marry more than one wife (upto four). This no doubt detracts from her status of equality with man. However, one has to take a historical view of the matter. The Arabs married any number of wives; Islam restricted it to four. Earlier multiple marriages were just for the sake of pleasures and without any reason. Islam put strict conditions. The marriages were not to be allowed just for pleasure. It was permitted strictly in case of orphans and widows, to take care of such unprotected women (both the Qur'anic verses on polygamy are with reference to the orphans and widows and their properties. Also, the Qur'an lays down a strict condition of equal treatment in all matters including in the matter of love. Thus, the Qur'an says, "And if you fear that you cannot do justice to orphans, marry such women as seem good to you, two, or three, or four, but if you fear that you will not do justice, then (marry) only one or that which your right hands posses." (4:3)

Thus, it would be seen that it is not a general license to marry more than one wife for pleasure. Also, at that time it was historical necessity, but now it is no more necessary. As it militates against more cardinal principle of justice, there would be nothing un-Islamic to either ban it or severely restrict it and permit only in exceptional cases. Many Islamic countries have done it. Also there is no concept of *purdah* (veil) in Qur'an. Qur'an had only prescribed pulling down a bit the head gear in order to discriminate free women from slave girls as unbelievers used to tease Muslim women and when caught used to get away by saying "we thought she was a slave girl." The Qur'an nowhere requires women to cover their faces or hide themselves.

These mild disabilities on women should also be seen in sociological context. If the society, or sociological context changes these disabilities should no longer be imposed. It is important to note that the Qur'an first accepts the concepts of freedom and individual dignity of women and then, in view of the historical and sociological context proceeds to impose these mild disabilities referred to above. Basic principle of freedom and individual dignity is more important then the sociological disabilities. The earlier concept would have precedence over the later as it is fundamental, not contingent.

Economic Justice

The Qur'an lays great emphasis on distributive justice. It is totally against accumulation and hoarding of wealth. It condemns accumulated wealth as strongly as possible. It also exhorts the people to spend to take care of orphans, widows, needy and the poor.

It does not want the wealth to circulate only among the rich (59:7). It also, warns the people that wealth should not be counted again and again nor one should think it can give eternal life. One who accumulates and counts again and again will certainly be hurled into crushing disaster and what is this crushing disaster? It is hell fire, which rises over the heart (see chapter 104). Again in Chapter 9, verse 34 it gives severe warning to those who accumulate wealth and do not spend it in the way of Allah. The Qur'an also exhorts the believers to spend whatever is surplus (after fulfilling basic needs) (2:219).

The practice of usury in Mecca was back-breaking and a great many people were in debt. The Qur'an strongly denounced usury and warned those who perpetrates it to be prepared for a war with Allah and His Messenger (see verses 275 to 278 in Chapter 2 and verse 39 of chapter 30). Many scholars strongly feel that *riba* means not only usury, but exploitation in general and include exploitative profit.

The Prophet also disapproved of share-cropping (*mukhabira, muhaqila*) which again is an exploitative practice. He also banned speculation in every form to prevent exploitation of the poor at the hands of the rich and powerful. For example, he banned buying of unripened standing crop as it often results in exploitation of the needy peasant. He approved of only legitimate margin of profit (as a reward for ones work and entrepreneurship) and strongly disapproves of hoarding, black-marketing, etc., he not only permits hungry to snatch food from one who has excess of it, but also declares him a martyr if he dies in the process of procuring it.

The Qur'an also, strongly denounces *zulm* (injustice, oppression) and permits the oppressed to fight against oppression. It says, "And what reason have you not to fight in the way of Allah and of the weak among the men and the women and the children, who say: Our Lord, take us out of this town, whose people are oppressors, and grant us from Thee a friend, and grant us from Thee a helper." (4:75). Thus, one who fights for the weak is the helper and friend of the Lord. the Quran not only includes believers to fight for the weak and oppressed, but promises that the oppressed would lead and inherit this earth (28:5).

Thus, it would be seen that the Qur'an is a charter of liberation for the oppressed. Islam exercises its option for the poor and the oppressed and has no kind words for *mutrifun* (i.e., those live in luxury). When we wish to destroy a town, the Quran says, we induce its rich to transgress all limits and we destroy that town with utter destruction (17:16). Thus, it is clear that when the rich become insensitive to the sufferings of the poor and needy the whole social structure becomes topsy-turvy and is ultimately destroyed at the hands of the revolutionary.

Attitude Towards Other Religions

Openness, tolerance and respect for other religions is another important liberative element. The Qur'an makes it clear there is no compulsion in religion (2:256) and that for you is your religion, for me is my religion (109:6). Qur'an also exhorts Muslims not to abuse those who call upon besides Allah lest they abuse Allah through ignorance (6:109). Also, Qur'an teaches that a believer should show equal respect to all the prophets) They all believe in Allah and His angels, His books and His messengers. We make no distinctions (4:150-51).

That is why a Muslim shows equal respect to all the Prophets right upto Muhammad whether named or not in the Qur'an. The Qur'an also declares unequivocally that paradise is not the monopoly of any religious group. whosoever submits himself entirely to Allah and he is a doer of good (*muhsin*), he has his reward from his Lord (2:112).

Thus, the Qur'an did not condemn any religion as false, but stressed that the priests have corrupted the teachings for their own interest. All the prophets had brought Allah's message. Qur'an never preached disrespect, let alone hatred or violence against any religion.

However, within three decades after the death of the Prophet, Islam lost its liberative and democratic character and became a part of monarchical establishment under the Umayyads. Prophet had gathered the poor, the oppressed and the slaves around him and never hesitated to suffer alongwith them. Now the Umayyad emperors gathered powerful tyrants and oppressors around them and ruthlessly suppressed all those who challenged their oppressive rule. Number of slaves multiplied, women subjugated and confined to *harems*, female slaves sexually abused, non-Arabs discriminated against and liberative teachings of Islam replaced by fatalistic outlook. Dogma of *Jabr* (determinism, fatalism) was actively propagated and that of *qadr* (freedom to act) was suppressed. After development of monarchy feudal values became supreme. Power hierarchy developed, socio-political equality was lost and equality confined only to the lines of prayers in the mosque, women came to be completely subjugated and their social status was very much eroded and Arab domination established firmly.

It was steep decline down and Islam lost all its liberative thrust (except in dissident movements and rebellions) and could never recapture its earlier spirit when Muhammad PBUH preached and practiced.

CHAPTER 16

The Concept of Ijtihad in Islam

Change is inevitable in human life and society. Dr. Iqbal, the noted poet also says "it is only revolution which is permanent and everything else keeps on changing." In the even of constant change can religion and religious law remain unchanged? again the important question is what is permanent in religion? Is there any component which changes? Does divine mean something static? Then what is he meaning of the Qur'anic verse "..every day He manifests Himself in, yet, another (wondrous) way" (29:55). Does this not mean that Allah and His creative powers manifest themselves in ever new and wondrous ways? Can then we reject change as blasphemous? Which change is blasphemous and which one legitimate? Does the holy Qur'an reject the concept of change altogether? Does it not invite the unbelievers repeatedly to abandon their ancestors ways, reflect over changes around them and respond to the Prophet's call? These are very important questions which need to be answered with great deal of deep reflection.

It is true that many orthodox souls are horrified by the very mention of 'change'. They find great consolation in following what they have inherited. What is 'given' is a proud heritage for them and what is evolving and changing is not only unacceptable, but 'blasphemous'. In fact most of the 'ulama today set great store by *'taqlid'*. In fact *taqlid* has been elevated to the status of principle today, though no such principle exists in Islamic jurisprudence.

What is to be noted is that there is no concept of priesthood in Islam unlike Christianity or Hinduism. Every believer is obliged (*mukallaf*) to perform all the functions obligatory in Islam. There was no tribe of 'ulama during the lifetime of the holy Prophet (PBUH). The companions of the Prophet, whenever faced any problem, requested the Prophet to guide them. The Prophet, either waited for revelation—and often he did so—or guided the companions out of his prophetic wisdom.

After the death of the holy Prophet when new problems arose, the Caliph would hold assembly of the companions and place the problem before it and it would be resolved either in the light of Qur'an and *sunnah* or in the absence of it through collective wisdom. The best example is of punishment for drinking. When nothing was found in the holy Qur'an and the Prophet's *sunnah*, Hazrat Ali's suggestion that eighty lashes be given as a punishment for drinking and was accepted on the grounds that after drinking a person tends to make false accusation and the punishment for false accusation in the Qur'an was eighty lashes. Thus, many other similar problems arose from time to time and the assembly of the Prophet's companion would resolve them eitherly one way or the other. Thus, the process of legislation continued even after the death of the Prophet.

The Prophet himself had encouraged the faculty of thinking and reasoning among his followers. He himself was acutely aware of the developing situations possibility of problems arising in future and hence, approved of Ma'adh bin Jabal, his companion whom he had appointed as *'Amil* (Governor) of the Yemen, exerting himself intellectually (this is what *ijtihad* means—to strive, to make efforts to solve a problem) to find a solution of the problem he did not find either in the holy Qur'an or in Prophet's *sunnah*.

In fact the Muslims continued to face new problems many of which had not been mentioned in the two principal sources of Islam. New problems arose for variety of reasons mainly on account of geographical spread of Islam and the *'adat* (traditions and customary laws) of new people embracing Islam. The two principal sources were not enough to resolve these new problems. New concepts, therefore, had to be devised to meet the new eventualities. Thus the institutions of *qiyas* and *ijma'* (analogy and consensus) had to be used. Thus for *shari'ah* these four sources, Qur'an, *sunnah*, *qiyas* and *ijma'* became widely acceptable for the Islamic legislators. However, the additional two sources, i.e., *qiyas* and *ijma'* were not acceptable to the Shi'ah Muslims. They were limited to Sunni Islam.

In Shi'ah Islam the *ahl al-bayt* (the people of the Prophet's family), particularly the Imams, are considered the absolute authority in not only interpreting the Qur'an but also in pronouncements over new problems. But, even Shi'ahs faced problems after the last imam (12th in the case of Ithna 'Ashari Shi'ahs and 21st imam in case of Isma'ili-Musta'lian Shi'ahs) went into seclusion. Their place was taken by *mujtahids* in case of Ithna 'Asharis and by *Da'is* in case of Isma'ili-Musta'lians. And in case of Isma'ili-Nizaris the problem did not arise at all as one of their imams suspended the application of Shari'ah itself.

In early Islam, first two centuries after the demise of the holy Prophet (PBUH), many qualified people those who had adequate knowledge of Qur'an and *sunnah* among the Sunni Muslims continued to solve various problems—apart from ones which had already been settled—in all sincerity and according to their legislative acumen. They were known as *fuqaha'* (those who developed deep understanding of religion and the principles of religion and their application). The Qur'an uses the word *fiqh* and its derivatives in many places like 78:4, 44:17, 122:9 etc. Thus, the process of grasping and developing deep understanding is very central to the whole process of compilation of *shari'ah*.

Among the common Muslims there is general belief that the *shari'ah* is divine and hence immutable. And it is on this basis that they oppose any re-thinking of issues in *shari'ah*. It is not correct view of *shari'ah* nor this is what is maintained by the competent authorities like, ulama, etc. In fact what is known as *shari'ah* did not descend ready-made. It evolved over a period of time and the jurists differed from each other on several issues. That is why there are several schools (*madhahib*) of *shari'ah* (five in the Sunni Islam—if we include the Zahiri School also) and three in the Shi'ah Islam, i.e., Ithna 'Ashari, Zaidi and Isma'ili). Thus, it is very clear that the *shari'ah* is as much a result of human endeavour as of divine revelations. It is differences of human thinking and approach which is reflected in different schools of *shari'ah*. In fact in early period of Islam there were more than 100 *madhahib* (schools) of which only few survived.

Needless to say these were result of *ijtihad*. Many eminent and learned Muslims made an honest and sincere efforts to solve the problems confronted by them in their lifetime in the light of Qur'an and *sunnah,* even though they differed from each other. Even the Shi'ahs who mainly depend on the authority of Imams from the Prophet's family for Shar'i pronouncements, developed differences (even in matters of principles) as they differed on the question of who the properly appointed Imam was and these Imams also differed from each other on many issues pertaining to *shari'ah*. Thus, the Ithna 'Ashari Imams and the Isma'ili Imams—though all of them from the Prophet's family—differed from each other, for example on the question of *muta'* marriage (a time bound temporary marriage). While the Ithna 'Ashari Imams allowed it the Isma'ili Imams considered it, like the Sunni *Fuqaha'* as strictly forbidden. Many more examples could be cited to illustrate the differences.

It is also important to bear in mind that there are two aspects of religion, transcendental and transient and which are applicable to all religions of the world. The transcendental is immutable, whereas the transient—as the word itself indicates is subject to change depending on the contingencies of the situation. What we understand by *shari'ah* is composed of both the elements, transcendent and transient or, in other words, the divine and human. The Qur'an also incorporates both the elements. For example, the institution of slavery is transient one, whereas the concept of human dignity, equality and fraternity is transcendent one.

The *shari'ah* had permitted slavery as a transient principle, a contingent institution and persisted all through medieval ages. However, it was abolished in our times without injuring any divine principle. Here it is important to understand that principles of *shari'ah*—what is called *usul al-fiqh* is fundamental to *shari'ah* and hence, are immutable, whereas their application in the given human circumstances is contingent and subject to change. There have always been and will always be differences of opinion about the ways of applicability of a principle and hence, different schools of thought.

Thus, it will be seen that the concept of *ijtihad* is extremely important, if the *shari'ah* is to keep pace with developing society. In fact it was the result of human *ijtihad* that the *shari'ah* was compiled as inherited by us. Even *qiyas* and *ijma'* were human institutions devised to meet emerging situations not faced by Muslims in Madina during the Prophet's lifetime. The doors of *ijtihad* remained open for a few centuries specially upto the fall of Baghdad in early 13th century. In fact the decline of the Abbasid empire even earlier made the 'ulama and fuqaha' quite apprehensive and they began to conserve what was inherited by them. It was Imam Ghazali who, by compiling his *Magnum opus Ihya al-'Ulum* (Revivification of Knowledge) led the process of closing the gates of fresh thinking. It was the period of decline and intense insecurity and what Imam Ghazali did was quite in the interest of Muslim society.

It is true that the 'ulama, after the fall of Baghdad, felt acutely insecure and closed the gates of *ijtihad*, but this may not fully explain the causes of abandoning the concept of *ijtihad* in Islam. *Ijtihad*, as pointed out above, has been very central to the very process of compilation of Shari'ah rules. One may also point out that after the disappearance of the Abbasid empire and fall of Baghdad, other Muslim empires like the Turkish empire, Safavid empire in Iran and the Mughal empire in India came into existence and these empires were quite powerful ones. Why then the process of *ijtihad* did not revive? Firstly, all these empires did not have the legitimacy which the Abbasid empire had—the Abbasid empire being conceived as the 'core Islamic empire' and the other later empires being thought as the outer peripheral empires.

Also, the Abbasid empire being the most powerful and the first one was conceived as—what the noted historian Toyenbee calls the 'Universal empire' of Islam. The most talented jurists—some of them under direct patronage of the Abbasid caliphs—engaged themselves responding to new juridical needs which arose in a place like Baghdad which was, at that time, a confluence of several cultures. These jurists used their talents to interpret the Qur'an and sunnah in response to these needs and compiled the laws of Shari'ah. *Ijtihad* became highly useful institution for these jurists who had to exercise their intellectual faculties to comprehend new situations and find solutions to them—what the holy Prophet had advised Ma'adh bin Jabal to do.

However, once elaborate rules were evolved by the classical jurists those who succeeded them did not question these formulations. They acquired universal character and came to be widely accepted. Moreover, during the medieval ages situation remained more or less stagnant and the jurists belonging to the subsequent generations did not feel it necessary to question the classical Shari'ah formulations. The subsequent empires which came into existence in Turkey, Iran or India also were feudal empires wherein much social change was not occurring. What was formulated by the classical jurists could serve the needs of the people in these empires also. Thus, the classical Shari'ah continued to be enforced.

However, a qualitative change took place in Islamic societies from

19th century onwards. Though until then these societies were feudal in structure, but encounter with colonialism brought about certain basic changes which made people think about many issues. Also, the Muslim jurists and intellectuals were faced with the criticism and western scholars and orientalists had to defend themselves. Their own legal and juridical categories were found problematic in meeting with the western criticism. Certain practices like slavery, concubinage, polygamy, etc., came under attack. Some 'ulama withdrew into their shells and simply denounced orientalists and western scholars as enemies of Islam and unworthy of being taken note of while others, specially modernists among Muslims answered the orientalist criticisms with creative thinking.

Mohammad 'Abduh of Egypt was disciple of al-Afghani and despite his orthodox training, he spent several years in France as a political exile. He was a great 'alim and rose to be the Grand Mufti of al-Azhar, the premier institution of Islam. He was a great *mujtahid* and utilised his profound knowledge of Islam to rethink many issues confronting the society. He issued many *fatwas*' among them was the one legitimizing interest on postal savings. He also criticized the practice of polygamy which was rampant in Egypt in his time. He laid stress on dignity of womanhood and was in favour of entrusting them higher status. He also emphasized the necessity for their education.

In India too some Muslim intellectuals, though not the traditional, 'ulama, responded to the new developing situation creatively and persuasively, not simply dismissing the western colonial criticism as mere hostile propaganda. I must emphasize here that the orientalists were not motivated by best of intentions in mounting criticism of oriental societies they encountered and their attacks on Islam were often hostile. But to dismiss their criticism as mere hostility towards Islam and keeping quiet about the issues raised by them or simply withdrawing into the shells would not have been the right response. It was necessary to take their criticism seriously and apply ones knowledge and intellectual faculties in creatively responding to the criticism.

Some intellectuals like Sir Syed Ahmed Khan, Syed Amir Ali, Maulvi Chiragh Ali and others rose to the occasion and responded to these orientalist attacks seriously and creatively. Sir Syed Ahmad Khan wrote a voluminous reply to Sir William Muir's *Life of Muhammad*. Justice Amir Ali wrote his classical book *The Spirit of Islam*. Similarly Maulavi

Chiragh Ali wrote books on slavery, jihad, personal law, etc. His book *A Critical Exposition of the Popular "Jihad"* is an important work in this genre. Later on Maulana Saeed Ahmad Akbarabadi, though a product of Darul 'Uloom Deoband, was a critical thinker and approved of the need for *ijtihad* in our times.

It is important to note that *ijtihad* is an accepted concept in Islam. No one, not even most orthodox *'alim* can deny its legitimacy. Apart from the tradition pertaining to Ma'adh bin Jabal referred to above, there is also another *hadith* of the Prophet approving of *ijtihad* which says that if one does *ijtihad* and makes a mistake he will have one reward and if he does it correctly he will get double reward. This tradition clearly brings out the significance of *ijtihad* in Islam. It must be borne in mind that Islam itself came into existence in a Meccan society which was undergoing basic socio-economic changes. The pre-Islamic or *jahiliyah* laws not only were becoming obsolete, but downright obstacles for further moral, spiritual and material growth of society. Islam and its laws thus, were not the product of a stagnant society, but a society which felt need for transcendence. Islam catered to the spiritual moral and material needs of this newly emerging society. It gave new principles and laws acutely needed by the people. The Islamic response to the changing needs of the Meccan society was not only material, but also moral and spiritual. Since Islam came into existence in a changing society it emphasized the need for dynamism and the principle of *ijtihad* embodied its spirit of dynamism.

It was the later generation of 'ulama who while accepting the principle of *ijtihad* in theory de-emphasized it in practice. They evolved the concept of *taqlid* (unthinking imitation) in its place, though they cannot quote any hadith from the Prophet in its favour. *Taqlid*, in a stagnant Islamic societies, thus became a widely accepted principle, as pointed out above. However, today all Islamic societies are experiencing fundamental social changes and rethinking on many issues has become very vital.

The conservative 'Ulama point out that, though *ijtihad* is an accepted principle in Islam there are no qualified people to indulge in it. They feel—and rightly so—that one intending to resort to *ijtihad* should have thorough knowledge of Qur'an and *sunnah* and also of what is known as *usul al-fiqh*, i.e., principles of jurisprudence. They feel no one, including themselves, have these qualifications. However, this is not true. There are many among the 'ulams, as well as the modern scholars of Islam, who are qualified to do *ijtihad*. It is fear of consequences or conservatism, rather than lack of qualification, which deters them from undertaking *ijtihad*. Also, there is internal struggles for controlling institutions which becomes an impediment. If one *'alim* shows inclination to accept the need for *ijtihad*, his rivals denounce him as 'heretic' and seize control of the institution from him. A member of the Muslim personal law board confessed privately that it is fear of rivals rather than lack of perception for certain badly needed changes in matters like triple divorce in one sitting which is the main impediment.

Also, one has to bear in mind that at least in India—and in several other Islamic countries too—the people who choose career as 'ulama come from poorer and backward classes who have no other choice. The children from middle and upper classes opt for professional education like engineering, medical or management courses. However, the parents from poorer classes send their children to religious institutions as not only education in those institutions are free, but also they get free board and lodge. These children grow up with backward outlook and also have deficient knowledge about other developments in the world. Moreover, religion becomes a power in their hands with which they rule millions of backward, poor and illiterate masses and also, in many cases, believing educated people who do not care to study religion by themselves. These sociological aspects of religious community has to be borne in mind while trying to understand its belief system.

In a fast changing world recourse to *ijtihad* is a must and Islam is among those religions which approves of healthy change and allows its believers to not only grapple with the changes taking place around them, but also to strive to reapply Islamic principles of jurisprudence. As far as *ijtihad* is concerned it should be made absolutely clear that no one can change principles and values. These are most fundamental to religious teachings. *Ijtihad* could be done only in reapplication of these values and principles in changed circumstances.

It would be in order to explain what I mean by reapplication of principles and values. For example, justice in Qur'an is a most fundamental value. It is so fundamental that while permitting slavery in a given circumstances, it is required, in the Islamic shari'ah, that the slaves should be fed what master feeds upon himself and should be clothed in what master himself dresses in. This was rightly thought to be a just behaviour in those circumstances. Now, in the changed circumstances, the principle of justice—i.e., its reapplication requires that slavery be abolished. If slavery is continued in today's circumstances it would be grave violation of principle of justice. Also, the transcendental aspect of religion has no place for slavery, it was permitted only as a transient measure. It is regrettable that our 'ulama never issued any *fatwa* for abolition of slavery before the West did it on grounds of human rights. In fact the Muslim 'ulama should have done it, much before the West abolished it, had they understood the real spirit of Islamic justice.

Similarly, today when women's rights are being universally accepted and the concept of sexual equality has come to stay, our ulama refuse to rethink women's issues in Islam. They still continue to insist on those *shari'ah* measures which were evolved by the classical jurists in radically different circumstances. They fail to appreciate that it is Qur'anic principles which are immutable and not their application by the jurists (*fuqaha'*) in their own circumstances. Again, like slavery, polygamy was a transient measure approved by Qur'an in the then given circumstances. Also, polygamy, it should be borne in mind, was not at all indicative of subservience of women to men nor was it divine intention to reduce them to the status of second sex. This thinking came to be prevalent in view of patriarchal structure of society. The holy Qur'an, if studied carefully and impartially, made several statements according equal status to men and women (see, for example, verses 2:228 and 33:35). However, during medieval ages, when women were thought to. be secondary to men, these verses were ignored and verses like 4:34 were repeatedly quoted to prove man's superiority over woman though the above verse was not value based like the two other verses (i.e. 2:228 and 33:35) which were value-based.

Today there is urgent need that the value based verses according equality to both sexes be highlighted and all women issues throughly rethought in the light of these two verses and other verses—giving slight edge to man over woman—be de-emphasized as transient verses valid only in certain circumstances. In the same spirit polygamy should be strictly regulated, at the most bigamy being permitted in certain exceptional circumstances by the court. In no case it should be decision of an individual. In fact the Qur'an had permitted polygamy only after the battle of Uhud wherein large number of Muslim men were killed, to take care of widows and orphans. And equal justice with all wives was strictly stipulated. Today such circumstances do not exist and hence polygamy should be nearly abolished (allowing bigamy, as pointed out, in exceptional circumstances). Muhammad Abduhu rightly maintained that it would be unjust to take another wife in presence of one and hence, he recommended its abolition.

Triple divorce in one sitting is highly problematic and is based, not on Qur'anic injunction, but on *hadith* of *Rukana* which is quite controversial in which Prophet permitted triple divorce. On the other hand we have *hadith* widely accepted in which Prophet condemned triple divorce and he described it as 'playing with the divine law in his (Prophet's) own lifetime and he ordered the person to take back his wife. This *hadith* has been reported by Ibn Dawood. It is also accepted that triple divorce was not practiced during the Prophet's time and during the time of the first Caliph. The second Caliph allowed it under some circumstances to check its abuse. The Qur'an does not mention this form of triple divorce in one sitting at all. It requires that both man and woman appoint their arbitrators who will finally decide whether divorce should take place or not (see 4:35). Qur'an also requires two witnesses for divorce see 65:2. But we ignore all these injunctions of the Qur'an and base the practice of divorce on *hadith* which is, at best, quite controversial. Thus, there is a strong case for abolition of triple divorce which is highly unjust to women and violative of fundamental principle of Islam which is justice.

Similarly we should not treat a woman as half witness. It amounts to grossly misunderstanding the real spirit of the Qur'anic verse 2:228. It is far from Qur'anic intention to reduce women to half witnesses. The second woman was required to remind, if the first woman forgets and not to treat the first woman as half witness. Moreover, this was also stipulated only in financial matters wherein women, in those days, were rather inexperienced. In all other matters she was treated as full witness including in cases of murder (in case of assassination of the third caliph Uthman, his wife Na'ila was the sole witness and no one questioned her testimony). Thus, it was not at all the Qur'anic intention to treat woman as half witness and now women are experts in all fields as they head

many financial institutions. Thus, even in financial matters she should
be treated as full witness in her own right. Moreover, the divine
pronouncement in the verse 2:282 is not a value-pronouncement, but a
recommendatory one. After all it is not obligatory on Muslims to reduce
all financial transactions to writing. Many deals take place on mutual
trust. Thus, one must distinguish between recommendatory and value-
pronouncements while evolving a rule or a law.

Another important, but controversial matter is pertaining to bank
interest. Does bank interest amount to *riba'* strongly condemned in the
Qur'anic verses 2:275-278 and 3:130? Most of the 'ulama treat the bank
interest also as *riba'* and several books have been written on this
subject. However, there are others— modern Islamic scholars who have
studied in depth both Qur'anic injunctions and modern economy and
feel that banking interest should not be treated as *riba'* and that
interest-free financial institutions should be established to help weaker
sections of society for housing and consumption loans, but commercial
banking could be based on interest. If banking interest is treated as
prohibited what about paper currency? Paper currency also amounts to
deferred payment (a promised payment by the Reserve Bank) and could
be included in the deferred payment category (*nasia'*) which 'ulama
treat as strictly prohibited. Also, stock exchange operations amount to
speculation and should be treated as *haram* (prohibited), but one does
not see these operations condemned by the 'ulama as they condemn
banking operations. The Qur'an has condemned *riba'* as highly
exploitative and unjust and hence its strong condemnation. But 'ulama
treat interest as prohibited on non-risk factor which is not mentioned
in the Qur'an. If banking interest is condemned only on absence of risk
what about practice of renting? It also does not involve any risk and
will stand condemned. Thus, it is highly necessary to rethink on banking
interest keeping in view the Qur'anic spirit and values. In fact the
Qur'an is strongly opposed to exploitation of one human person by
another. Thus, what needs to be decided is whether banking interest
amounts to such exploitation? One should not introduce extraneous
elements like risk etc. in arriving at proper conclusion.

It is also necessary to evolve proper approach as regards the
punishments for crimes like theft, adultery, etc. It is true the Qura'n
mentions cutting off hands of thieves (see 5:38), but the fundamental
question is what is intended: prevention of theft or punishment.

Obviously prevention of theft. Can it not be prevented by other means. Punishments are instruments of prevention of crime and not goal by themselves. Also, punishments are often specific to society and the holy Qur'an also prescribed, as an effective measure what was specific to that society, but also added in the following verse that "But whoever repents after his wrongdoing and reforms, Allah will turn to him (mercifully). Surely Allah is Forgiving, Merciful" (5:39). Thus, this verse makes it quite clear that real intention is to reform and emphasis is laid on Allah's forgiveness and mercifulness. In usual cases reformatory measures should be adopted and the maximum punishment could be given only in case of hardened criminals. It would not be in the real Spirit of Qur'an to cut off hands for any and every theft as is being done by some Islamic countries.

Similarly Qur'an no where mentions punishment for adultery as stoning to death. It prescribes only 100 lashes in 24:2. Stoning to death was in fact a Jewish practice which found way in the Islamic law later. There is no proof that the Prophet inflicted stoning to death on any adulterous Muslim after revelation of this verse. In fact half the punishment for slave girl for adultery in 4:25 also makes it clear that the Qur'an no where intends to prescribe stoning to death as punishment for adultery (how can one otherwise halve the punishment of stoning to death?).

There are several other new issues like transplantation of organs, cloning, euthanasia, etc., which have come up in our times. The Fiqh Academy in India has been doing good work in this direction. It has approved of transplantation of organs to save human life provided it is not of pig. Cloning of course has not been accepted even by medical profession. It has been condemned widely as unethical practice and pregnant with dangerous possibilities. Cloning has been restricted so far to animals only.

However, it is unfortunate that some Muslim jurists are still opposing eye donation. There should not be any objection if a dying or a dead person's eye is used to give sight to a living blind person. There is no mention of such a problem in the Qur'an or *hadith* literature as such a problem never arose then. The Prophet has been described in Qur'an as "Mercy of the worlds" and can one imagine such a compassionate person would have prohibited human beings from restoring sight to a blind person through donation of one's eyes?

CHAPTER 17

Sir Syed and His Commentary on Qur'an

Sir Syed is usually known for his advocacy of modern education for Muslims in the nineteenth century. Very few people know about his profound knowledge of Islam and of *tafsir* (commentary on holy Qur'an) and *hadith*, besides other Islamic sciences. He began as an orthodox (belonging to the School of Shah Waliyullah), but soon renounced his orthodoxy in favour of rational approach to Islam. When he began writing on Islam from rational perspective many of his orthodox colleagues denounced his views. As Sir Syed had to give priority to his educational project he agreed not to express his views on Islam through his writings.

Sir Syed Ahmad Khan also undertook to write a commentary on Qur'an from rationalist angle but could not complete it. His rationalist point of view being outrageous to the orthodoxys so his commentary on the Qur'an not only remained incomplete, but did not become popular among the people. It was suppressed and did not come out in more editions as it ought to have.Only recently Khuda Bakhsh Library published its new edition in two volumes. This essay on Sir Syed's *tafsir* is based on this Khuda Bakhsh Library edition.

In the beginning of his *tafsir* he wrote an essay on *Tahrir fi' Usul al-Tafsir* (a note on principles of *tafsir*) in which he laid down fifteen principles for writing commentary on the Qur'an. He wrote in this note that after the mutiny of 1857, he worried about the religious and worldly reforms among the Muslims and after lot of reflection he concluded that it was not possible to bring about reforms among them without disseminating the modern sciences which are matter of pride for other communities, in the language which was prevalent among the Muslims.

Many Christians, Hindus or Muslims, according to Sir Syed, gave up their traditional beliefs when they found them contrary to the discoveries of modern science. And as far as Muslims were concerned, it was not a new experience, according to Sir Syed. The Muslims had faced similar situation when confronted with the Greek philosophy and sciences in the history of early Islam. However, the 'ulama of that period met the challenge and invented *'ilm al kalam* (science of dialectics) and they defended religion by using this intellectual weapon. They did three things: either they showed that the religious teachings are in conformity with the principles of Greek philosophy; or they proved arguments of Greek sciences false or created doubts about them. But there is added difficulty in our own time, Sir Syed argues and maintains that even many suppositions of Greek classical sciences and philosophy on the basis of which the 'ulama had founded some religious problems have been proved wrong. The arguments of modern sciences, Sir Syed says, are not merely speculative or products of deductive logic but are based on empirical observations.

Sir Syed then says that he began to popularize English language and modern sciences among the Muslims, and began to think whether these are against Islamic religious teachings as many people think. Then he started to read different commentaries on the Qur'an and found them, except what pertained to Arabic literature, full of absurdities (*fuzul*) and based on weak traditions (*riwayat-e-za'if*) which were derived from Jewish sources. Then he undertook to reflect on the principles on which the traditional commentaries were based and whether these principles of classical commentaries were based on the Qur'an or some other sources which cannot be challenged. There also he drew blank. He could not discover anything which could solve the difficulties being faced. Then Sir Syed himself began to reflect on the contents of the Qur'an to discover some fundamental principles and he understood the Qur'an to the best of his capacity and discovered that the principles which he could deduct from the holy Book do not conflict with modern sciences and 'if you ask me I am (Sir Syed) highly grateful to the great Qur'an and then Sir Syed began to write a commentary on Qur'an.

Thus, Sir Syed goes on to elaborate the principles on which he bases his commentary in his introductory part *Tahrir fi' Usul al-Tafsir*. For students, researchers and others it would be quite fruitful to go through this introductory essay. As it is well-known Sir Syed was not a believer in miracles (*m'ujizat*). Thus, he mentions this in his ninth principle. He says that there is nothing in the Qur'an which is against the law of nature and again he quotes the excerpt from Shah Waliyullah's *Al-Tafhimat al-Ilahiyah* to that effect (Sir Syed quotes Shah Waliyullah quite frequently as he belonged to the Waliyullahi School, though he was not a mere imitator). Shah Waliyullah denies existence of miracles. But then Sir Syed raises the question whether this denial is only in respect of the Prophet of Islam or denial of all miracles. He again quotes from *Tafhimat* of Shah Waliyullah (p-53) and shows that Shah Waliyullah considers all miracles as happenings according to the law of nature and thinks for every effect there is a cause. Thus, the law of causality is not thrown away. Sir Syed says that Shah Waliyullah does not accept anything what is called 'supernatural' or beyond the law of causality. Shah Waliyullah says openly that nothing can be proved to exist what can be called 'supernatural' (*ma fauq al-fitrat*).

Some people might argue, Sir Syed says, that there is mention of miracles in the Qur'an or what is supernatural. They may cite the Qur'anic verses to this effect. But the Syed maintains that one will have to look into other meanings of such words which are according to the usage, idiomatic expressions or allegories of the Arabic language. If there is no such other meanings then we will accept the contention of miracles in the Qur'an. However, if someone argues that for hundreds of years the companions of the Prophet or companions of the companions or 'ulama and *Mujtahidin* have understood the meaning of the words which favours miracles then Sir Syed is not prepared to accept such an argument. The argument that Allah is Almighty and can do whatever He wishes is not a valid argument in favour of miracles because Allah honours the law laid down by Him that you will not find any change in *Sunnati Allah* (33:62).

According to Sir Syed nothing has been mentioned in the Qur'an in contravention to the law of nature laid down by Allah Himself. Even the description of paradise and hell is not contrary to the law of nature. Of course these concepts seem to be beyond human imagination as no eye has seen them or no ear has heard about them or no heart has experienced them, but they have been described by Allah in a way which can be understood by human beings. Thus, these descriptions of *jannat* and *jahannam* (paradise and hell) are allegorical and symbolic. No such phenomenon is in fact outside the laws of nature as laid down by Allah.

Sir Syed also believes and as he lays down in his principle number twelve that there is nothing like *nasikh-o-mansukh* (the verses in the Qur'an which cancel other verses and the verses which have been cancelled). Most of the commentators have believed that some verses have cancelled some other verses in the Holy Qur'an though there has never been a unanimity over which verse has cancelled which verse. There is not even a hint in the Qur'an about it. And as for the verse 2:106 (Whatever message We abrogate or cause to be forgotten, We bring one better than it or one like it), Sir Syed argues, does not indicate cancellation of verses, but refers instead to the Shari'ah which existed before Islam which were replaced by the verses of the Qur'an. There is no question, in Sir Syed's mind, about any verse of Qur'an having been cancelled by any subsequent verse. There are serious implications of this on many aspects of Shari'ah laws. Shah Waliyullah also argues against cancellations of verses, by subsequent verses but he accepts five such verses as against many more by others.

As for the fourteenth principle Sir Syed says that what Allah states in the Qur'an cannot contradict what He does. Or what He has created cannot go against what He has stated in words. It has also been put by him as 'the word of God and work of God cannot go against each other'. He also says under this principle that if some word of God contradicts the work of God, it cannot be the word of God. This clearly means that there cannot be any contradiction whatsoever between the holy Qur'an and the laws of nature or laws of science. They must conform with each other if both are related to God. This approach revolutionized the very understanding of the holy Qur'an. Subsequently, many rationalists of course adopted this approach in understanding the Qur'an, but when first stated by Sir Syed, it really brought about a revolution in understanding of the Qur'an.

In the fifteenth principle Sir Syed maintains that speech, be it of Allah or of human has to be understood in the light of some rules applicable to the language in which the speech has been delivered. For example, if a word has been devised to convey certain meaning in that language it will have to be understood in that meaning only. Also, in every language and also in Arabic language there are allegories, similes, symbols, idiomatic expressions, rhetorical expressions, retaliatory expressions, inductive phrases, promises in words, deeds, etc. which are used to convey certain ideas and expressions. These specificities of the spoken language will have to be kept in mind while understanding the meaning of the Qur'an. Sir Syed then lays down some sub-rules in respect of language like in what way a particular word has been used in that language, or is it used in more than one way and which of the two meanings that word has been used in Qur'an or whether the word has been used in its original sense or in some other metaphorical meaning (*majazi* sense).

Jihad

After having thrown light on the methodology of *tafsir* evolved by Sir Syed we would like to deal with some important issues, which Sir Syed has dealt with while commenting on the relevant Qur'anic verses. Sir Syed has dealt with a large number of issues. We will take up only a few selected one which are of greater significance for us. Sir Syed deals thus, with the issue of *jihad*. It was an important issue then as the 'ulama belonging to Waliyullahi school were giving *fatwas* of *jihad* against the British rule. Naturally Sir Syed was opposed to these *fatwas* and hence, he has written a long note on the subject in his *Tafsir al-Qur'an*.

Firstly, Sir Syed makes a point that Islam does not permit mischief, anarchy (*fasad*), fraud or mutiny (*ghadar*). Islam instructs Muslims to obey (*ita'at*) and feel obligated (*ihsanmandi*) to those who have given them security and peace (*aman*) whether those people are Muslims or *kafirs*. Thus, it is important to note that Sir Syed gives great importance to peace and security for Muslims and requires their obedience and loyalty, even if they be *kafirs*. He also says that Islam has laid great emphasis on fulfilling honestly all the treaties or pacts entered into with *kafirs*.

Islam, Sir Syed maintains, does not permit invading any country to conquer it and to forcibly spread Islam so much so that it does not want to compel even a single person to accept Islam. Islam, according to him, has permitted *jihad* only in two eventualities: one, when *kafirs* take up sword and invade Muslims in order to wipe out Islam out of animosity and not for purpose of conquest because any war for political conquests between Muslims and Muslims and *kafirs* is for worldly matters and has nothing to do with religion. Second, in the country in which Muslims, do not get peace and security and are unable to fulfill their religious obligations (may wage *jihad*). But again Sir Syed qualifies even this permission with the proviso that even in those places in which Muslims live as subjects or where they have agreed to live in peace, and even if they are being persecuted as Muslims, they have not been permitted to take up arms. Thus, it will be seen that Sir Syed put great emphasis on peaceful living under a non-Muslim set up and puts severe restrictions on waging of armed struggle. Sir Syed's agenda was very different from that of the 'ulema. While Sir Syed wanted peace and security for Muslims for their progress, the 'ulama were inclined to wage war and throw the British out of India and hence, many of them issued *fatwas* for waging *jihad*.

Jihad, according to Sir Syed, is permissible only for religious purposes, i.e., when Islam and Muslims are in danger just because Muslims want to fulfill their religious obligations. It is not permissible for any other purposes, certainly not for worldly conquests or worldly purposes. Sir Syed is absolutely right if we take the verse 22-39 into account. The verse says: "Permission (to fight) is given to those on whom war is made, because they are oppressed." The next verse (22:40) made it more explicit when it says, "Those who are driven from their homes without a just cause except that they say: Our Lord is Allah." Despite such clear instructions the concept of *jihad* was much misused for worldly purposes by many Muslim rulers. Also, the concept of *jihad* prevalent in medieval ages cannot hold water in greatly changed circumstances. The nation states are very different from medieval states when religion was invoked for political legitimacy.

Sir Syed also refers to the verse 2:193 which says, "And fight them until there is no persecution, and religion is only for Allah." From this verse some infer that it is duty of Muslims to wage *jihad* until Islam becomes predominant religion. Sir Syed refutes this by referring to the *tafsir* of Imam Razi and says that all this verse means is that Muslims should fight against their persecutors until there is complete freedom for Muslims to fulfill their religious obligations.

Qurbani

He also comments on sacrificing the animals after *Hajj*. There is much for Muslims to learn from Sir Syed's approach to what is called *qurbani* (sacrifice of animals). Sir Syed says that there is nothing in the holy Qur'an to support the concept of *qurbani* in *Hajj*. Mecca was a desolate desert where no agricultural production was possible. When a large number of people collected there for *Hajj* there was no way to feed them all. Therefore, the people going for *Hajj* used to carry their own animals called *Budn* and *Qala'id* and those who could not carry used to buy them in Mecca. They used to slaughter these animals and would eat themselves and distribute among others. This is the only basis of *qurbani* in *Hajj* from the holy Qur'an and he quotes the verses 22:27-28 for this purpose. The verses say, "And proclaim to men the Pilgrimage: they will come to thee on foot and on every lean camel, coming from every remote path. That they may witness benefits (provided) for them, and mention the name of Allah on appointed days over what He has given them of the cattle quadrupeds; then eat of them and feed the distressed one, the needy."

The other verse in the Qur'an about *qurbani* is 22:36 which is also quoted by Sir Syed. The verse reads, "And the *Budn* (camels), We have made them of the signs appointed by Allah for you—for you therein is much good . So mention the name of Allah on them standing in a row. Then when they fall down on their sides, eat of them and feed the contended one and the beggar. Thus, we have made them subservient to you that you may be grateful." Sir Syed also argues that neither there is any god or goddess, nor anything on the mountain on which a goat or sheep or camel be sacrificed. Allah neither likes their smell nor does he drink blood of the sacrificed animal nor he feels pleasure in taking their life. He (Allah) only desires goodness and benevolence. Sir Syed then quotes the verse 22:37, just after the preceding verse to prove his point. The verse says, "Not their flesh, nor their blood, reaches Allah, but to Him is acceptable observance of duty on your part."

Thus, Sir Syed is convinced that there is no concept of the kind of sacrificing of animals prevalent today among the Muslims in Islam at all. They slaughter lakhs of animals and throw them into jungles where vultures and crows eat them. Sir Syed is against such *qurbani*. And undoubtedly, he seems to be much nearer the Qur'anic spirit than those who believe sacrificing animals just for the sake of sacrificing. Needless slaughter of animals is not the intention of Allah. Elsewhere in his *tafsir* he again forcefully argues that sacrifice during *Hajj* is not a religious duty at all. Its obligation (*fardiyyat*), he argues, is not proved decisively either from Qur'an or from any other source.

Polygamy

Sir Syed has also commented on the issue of polygamy while discussing the verse on polygamy (4:3). However, Sir Syed, like other commentators, thinks that this verse requires the Muslims to marry other women up to four if they cannot do justice to the properties of orphan girls or women. If you fear, Sir Syed comments, that if by marrying orphan girls you are not likely to do justice to their properties, you can marry other women. This injunction, according to Sir Syed, implies extreme caution for protection of properties of orphans. He then quotes a tradition (*hadith*) from *Tafsir-e-Kabir* through 'Urwah to prove his point. 'Urwah narrates from A'isha that orphan girls are under protection of their guardians and the guardian is tempted by the property and beauty of orphans to marry them on small *mahr* and after *nikah* the guardian treats the orphan girl badly and there is no one to protect the interests of the orphan girl. It is for this reason that Allah said that you can marry other women if you fear you cannot do justice with orphan girls.

However, some modern scholars are challenging this interpretation of the verse and the tradition on which this interpretation is based. Even if what is stated in the tradition by 'Urwah is true, where was the need to allow men to marry up to four? In that case they would have been asked by Allah to marry one woman of their liking other than the orphan girl. In fact this *hadith* was invented later in order to justify four marriages with any women of their choice. Maulana Umar Ahmad Usmani of Pakistan has discussed this in detail in his book *Fiqh al-Qur'an* and showed that this verse does not at all permit marrying other women up to four.

If this *hadith* is accepted then one will have to insert words in the verse which are not there in it. The fact is that this verse, all commentators agree, was revealed after the battle of Uhud in which about 10% of Muslim men were slain leaving behind large number of widows and orphans. Marriage up to four was basically permitted in order to take care of these orphans and widows as the word *al-nisa* also indicates. The addition 'al' in Arabic is like the addition of the word 'the' in English indicating something particular. Thus, the verse talks of *al-nisa*, i.e., those particular orphans and widows whose fathers or husbands were killed in the battle of Uhud. Muslims were encouraged to marry four from amongst these widows and orphans or only one if they feared that they could not do equal justice to more than one. Thus polygamy is being permitted by the Qur'an in very peculiar circumstances that too with rigorous condition of equal justice.

Sir Syed, though in favour of monogamy, thinks polygamy is justified on certain grounds. He says that nature, if there are no other problems, demands that man should have only one wife. But man, Sir Syed says, who is closer to civilizational matters than woman, has to face such problems because of which he has to deviate from this principle of nature (i.e., monogamy). But in fact it is not deviation, but accepting another principle of nature. If it is the law that one should not marry another woman as long as the relation with the first woman is not cut off, then women would have faced very cruel situations. And if cutting of relations with the first woman depended on her death or on some particular situation, man would have been induced to resort to what has been prohibited or he would have been deprived of his civilizational needs.

If a woman falls ill and her condition becomes pitiable and she is not capable of sexual intercourse or is barren and man's desire for child is not fulfilled, would it be then proper to cut off relations with her and marry another or wait until she dies thus, depriving man of his natural civilizational desire? These are such matters which, because of human nature, cannot wait and if attempt is made to throw obstacle in its way it results in more serious evil.

Sir Syed says that one must, however, take care that except in case of genuine need to fulfill human civilizational urges, polygamy should not become means of fulfilling sexual lust (as Muslims have done it). Thus, Islam puts restriction on polygamy in a very balanced and even manner. He then quotes last part of the verse 4:3 which says 'and if you fear you cannot do justice, then (marry) one'. He further says the words 'in khiftum' (if you fear) are very important since there is not a single man who does not fear breach of justice. Thus, according to the Qur'an, polygamy could be permitted only in case of need and in keeping with the principle of justice. It is only in case of strict justice that one can be free of fear of injustice. Then Sir Syed makes an interesting point that let alone polygamy, Islam has not even made one marriage compulsory.

The word *fankihu* is not imperative (as all commentators accept) but only permissive and not obligatory. Thus, Qur'an has not made it obligatory even to marry one wife, how can it allow number of wives without restriction.

Sir Syed also then goes on to discuss the meaning of the word *'adl* and says that the 'ulama have restricted the practice of *'adl* to giving equal maintenance and equal time to all the wives and do not include equal love for all wives. The 'ulama derive this practice from the Prophet's practice of distributing equal time among all the wives and doing justice. He (the Prophet) used to say, "O Allah, this is my distribution of time (among my wives) which I can do and do not chide me in what I cannot do (i.e., rigorous justice including equal love to all wives)." But Sir Syed says we do not agree with this. Firstly, the authenticity of this *hadith* is doubtful. He then explains the reason briefly why it is doubtful. Secondly, to construe the meaning of the words of *hadith* 'do not chide me for what you possess and I do not possess (i.e., capacity to do justice)' to the inclination of heart to love is not justified. The prophets will not behave this way. It is against their status. The prophets will not say that we will do as our heart desires and do not chide us (O Allah) if we cannot fulfill the function of marriage.

Sir Syed expresses his sorrow that sometimes even the great 'ulama do not understand the greatness and glory of pure souls like of prophets' and what is applicable to ordinary mortals is applied by them to the prophets of Allah. They forget that the status of prophets of Allah is far higher than that of ordinary mortals like us. Sir Syed also says that even if we suppose that the words of above *hadith* are true (which is difficult to accept) how can we say that the words 'what I cannot and you can' may pertain to matters of different nature like someone being afflicted by diseases or someone having child and someone not having a child, etc. It is not necessary that these words pertain to only matters of personal desire as the prophets are far above such lust or desire.

Sir Syed then makes another important argument when he says that the word *'adl* in the verse on polygamy cannot merely refer to equal maintenance as it is not such a difficult thing to do even for ordinary people. It does not require a human person of elevated spiritual status like the prophet to fulfill this condition (of equal maintenance). Fourthly,

Sir Syed argues, it is a great mistake to include inclination of heart in matters of *'adl*. In relations between husband and wife, inclination of heart (love) has high priority and hence, *'adl* is nearest to matter of love with ones conjugal partner and hence, in the above *hadith* one cannot say that the words 'what I cannot and you can' refer to love.

Sir Syed quotes another verse of the Qur'an to show that love between husband and wife has high priority. The verse 30:21 says, "And of His signs is this, that He created mates for you from yourselves that you might find quiet of mind in them, and He put between you love and compassion. Surely there are signs in this for a people who reflect." This is indeed very weighty argument made by Sir Syed and no one can deny its significance as it is from Qur'an itself. Thus, love is most important cementing force in marriage and equal love between all wives becomes most important condition for equal justice.

Yet again Sir Syed mentions another verse from the Qur'an 4:129 which reads: "And you cannot do justice between wives, even, though you wish (it), but be not disinclined (from one) with total disinclination, so that you leave her in suspense." Referring to this verse he says that it clearly says that you cannot do justice even if you want. And if justice meant merely giving equal maintenance and fixing the turn for every wife, it was not so difficult to fulfill that Allah says you cannot even if you like. This also shows that love is an important ingredient of justice in the Qur'anic sense. Then he concludes that the Qur'anic requirement is that one should have one wife and more than one wife could be permitted only in exceptional circumstances when the cultural and civilizational needs might make it necessary and there be no fear of injustice.

Thus, it will be seen that Sir Syed defends monogamy and considers polygamy only an exception rather than the rule. His approach in this matter, to say the least, is highly modern and rational. He is also quite conscious of rights of women and wants no injustice done to them just because they belong to weaker sex.

Though, we have covered very limited issues tackled by Sir Syed in his *Tafsir al-Qur'an* for want of space, it is quite clear that his commentary on Qur'an is not only daringly different from other 'ulama, but also is most modern in its approach. His commentary again is not written merely as an apologia to meet modern requirements, but is undoubtedly based on deeper convictions and is very cogently argued. It is indeed matter of great sorrow and loss that it is not widely known and disseminated. It could not become popular in his own time for obvious reasons. But now it is time it is widely disseminated.

CHAPTER 18

On Religious and Inter-cultural Dialogue

Increasing inter-religious and inter-cultural conflicts throughout the world has made it very necessary to promote inter-religious and inter-cultural dialogue. The reasons of these conflicts are many. The world has been divided into north-south poles, north being highly developed and south afflicted with underdevelopment and mass illiteracy and poverty. The educated youths in the south do not find jobs to fulfill their aspirations. They look towards the north for better paid jobs. Also, most of these underdeveloped countries were once colonies of the North and hence, people from these former colonies are attracted towards the metropolitan countries. When large number of people migrate the native white people resent and racial tensions intensify, specially when there is economic downturn in the metropolitan countries and available jobs are few to go around. Though, the underlying causes may be economic or political, the conflict expresses itself through religious or cultural channels. Though, ultimately tensions could be reduced only by addressing economic causes, its religio-cultural tensions also need to be tackled effectively. The religious and cultural expressions do great deal of damage and spread misunderstanding even among others who are not affected directly by the economic downturn. Due to high-pitched propaganda by extremely vocal sections of fundamentalists, cultural and religious prejudices spread like wildfire.

The media also plays a very important role in spreading these prejudices. The media, needless to say, is more interested in sensational news than sensible constructive news. Repeated negative reportings in the media leads to widespread prejudices against certain religious or cultural groups. It is well-known fact that Islam bashing goes on in the western media. It is very important to understand that the Western countries led by the USA adopt extremely hostile attitude towards certain Islamic countries like Iran, Libya, Iraq who dare to defy the USA authorities. The USA not only punishes them severely (as for example bombings on Iraq or on pharmaceutical factory in Sudan, etc.), but also starts a propaganda war against Islam and Islamic countries in their media. Also, out of sheer frustration, some militant youth carry out violent attacks on some American establishments (for example, explosions in the World Trade Centre or recent past). As a result of all this an average American has terrible prejudices against Islam and Muslims. Islam is thought to be a religion of fanaticism and violence.

Similarly, the internal extremist violence in Algeria has spilled over to France. The Algerian extremists carried out some bombing attacks in Paris too as it believes the Government of France collaborates with the Algerian authorities in wiping out Muslim militants. Naturally this leads to strong prejudices among the French against Islam. The Germans are facing a severe economic recession these days and there is wide-ranging unemployment touching as high a level as 12 per cent. But during the sixties when German economy was booming and foreign labour was needed large number of Turks were brought to Germany. Now with economic recession the Turks are looked down upon and tensions between the Germans and Turks has increased.

Due to ethnic conflict in Sri Lanka a large number of Tamils have also migrated to several European countries including Germany. In last few years quite a few attacks have taken place on Tamils by neo-Nazis. It is strange, but true that it is in East Germany which was formerly under the Communist rule that neo-Nazi movement is spreading and the East German youths are involved in the attacks on the Tamils and Turks. This is because the levels of unemployment among the East Germans are far higher than the national average. It is supposed to be as high as 20-25 per cent. And hence, like an average American, an average German is highly prejudiced against Islam and Muslims as well as against Tamils. The migration of Muslims from Bosnia has further aggravated this religio-cultural conflict.

Apart from the religious and cultural conflict in the West there is increasing number of conflicts among different religious and cultural groups within the developing countries in Asia and Africa. Hindus and Muslims in India (and now Hindus and Christians too), Muslims and Christians in some African countries like in Nigeria and Sudan are embroiled in conflict. Similarly, various ethnic and cultural groups within these countries are involved in mutual violence, for example, Bodos versus other tribals in Assam, Nagas and Meitis in Manipur, Bengalis and tribals in Tripura and so on. There are also prejudices against South Indian in North and Western India. The Shiv Sena is a militant Maharashtrian Hindu organization in Mumbai which attacks both Muslims and South Indians. It has spread militancy among the Maharshtrian youth.

There are various reasons for such conflicts mainly political and also economic in some cases. The developmental processes are quite uneven and leads to inmigration from rural to urban and from less developed urban to more developed urban areas. Thus, one finds different religious and cultural groups jostling with each other in these urban areas. And, one witnesses more conflict in urban than rural areas. Rural areas are more homogeneous and less ameneable to such conflicts. Many urban areas have become real hotbeds of ethnic or religious or cultural turmoils. Each religious or ethnic group wants to establish its own domination in a particular area and wants to cleanse it of other 'polluting' groups. And to mobilize members of their own group and for this religious or cultural discourse is used, thus creating strong prejudices in the minds of the other religious or cultural groups.

It should, however, be noted that it is not a new phenomenon. Throughout history there have been such migrations from one country to another and from one area within a country to other areas. These conflicts are also not new. The Christians and Muslims fought on the question of control over Palestine and these wars in history are known as the 'crusades'. The zeal with which these wars were fought between Christians and Muslims made 'crusade' synonymous with zeal and a new phrase 'crusading spirit' came into existence.

It was these crusades which caused great deal of misunderstanding about Islam in Western countries during the medieval period. The image of Muslims 'Qur'an in one hand, and sword in the other', was creation of these crusades. Similarly, the Muslim invasions on North India led to image of Islam as violent religion in the minds of many Hindus (though quite a few Hindus were collaborators in these invasions for fulfillment of their selfish political ambition). These images are being revived in the modern context to serve contemporary political interests.

However, due to propaganda hype an average Hindu thinks of Muslims as fanatic and violent. The media again plays an important role in spreading such ideas and images. The whole Ramjanambhoomi-Babri Masjid movement drew its vigour and zeal from such images. Muslims were seen as fanatical Hindu temple bashers by an average Hindu. The BJP, itself a Hindu fundamentalist party, played an important role for mobilizing the Hindu electoral support. In medieval ages such mass mobilization for political purposes was not required and the monarchs could maintain inter-religious balance in their own interests. In modern times compulsions of democratic mobilization has its own logic. Masses are sought to be manipulated by political interests. This manipulation is easier by the might of mass media. Such medium did not exist in old times. Thus, we see that need for manipulation of the masses and the role played by the media—and now not only print, but also electronic —plays great role in spreading inter-religious and inter-cultural prejudices.

The images about some religion or culture built by media may not be true, but can play absolute havoc by spreading strong prejudices against particular group. The role of media has become extremely crucial in modern times. The media can play very constructive role with the interest in promotion of better inter-religious or inter-cultural understanding. It should also be pointed out that entire media is not responsible for sensationalizing the conflict. A section of print and electronic media does play a very positive role in this regard. It is for those interested in inter-religious or inter-cultural dialogue to make proper use of both print and electronic media. We have to do everything possible to promote this dialogical spirit among the conflicting groups.

Inter-religious and Inter-cultural dialogue

Now is 'dialogue' the only way left out for promoting better understanding between the conflicting groups. As the spread of mis-information through whatever means is largely responsible for misunderstanding, dissemination of correct information is highly necessary to contain the conflict. This can most effectively be done through dialoguing. We would like to throw light on the rules and processes of such inter-religious and inter-cultural dialogues.

The dialogue can take place between different kinds of groups: (1) political groups; (2) religious groups and (3) supporters of political or religious groups. Also, there are different levels of dialogue and a comprehensive process of dialoguing will involve all these levels. It can take place at the level of political or religious leaders; at the level of intellectuals from different groups and also at the level of masses. The nature of dialogue will vary at all these levels.

At the level of intellectuals it will be more of analysis of events and understanding of the nature of forces involved in promoting conflict. At this level the dialogue will also deal with the strategies of promoting inter-religious and inter-cultural harmony. At the political level the dialogue may deal with those politicians who believe in secular politics based on ideological convictions, and oppose the politics of religious or cultural confrontation. The dialogue may comprise ideas and strategies of bringing secular alliances to isolate the communal and fundamental forces.

At the religious level, the dialogue, will have to deal with religious and theological aspects. A religion too has to be understood at different levels, i.e., at the level of rituals, theology, institutions and values. While rituals, theologies and institutions might vary from religion to religion, values are bound to be complementary. For example, Hinduism emphasizes non-violence and Buddhism compassion; Christianity emphasizes love and Islam justice and equality. It will be seen that all these values are complementary to each other.

Rituals, theologies and institutions are unique to every religion and this often leads to misunderstandings. Each religious tradition emphasizes on importance of certain rituals and theological dogmas as central to that religious tradition and also exerts superiority of its own rituals and theology. For example, the Islamic system of worship prohibits worshipping or bowing before idols. Islam lays central stress on unity of God and considers associating any other being with Him as a sin. The Hindus believe in idol worship and bow before idols. These differences often lead to violent conflict between the two communities in India. However, it is also to be noted that this conflict is not promoted by religious leaders as much as by political leaders who hardly care for religious rituals and dogmas.

That does not mean that religious leaders do not differ. These differences, for a proper dialogue, have to be understood and appreciated rather than fought about. Many Sufis and *bhakti* saints did precisely that. They not only tried to appreciate these differences, but also often tried to even reconcile them. Guru Nanak, the founder of Sikhism, for example, showed great respect both for Islam and Hinduism and worked out a creative synthesis between the two. He had great regard for Sufis of Islamic tradition and included the verses of Baba Farid, a great Sufi saint from Punjab, into his Adi Granth.

Dara Shikoh, the Moghul prince who was greatly interested in Sufi traditions had also deep appreciation of Hindu religious traditions and he wrote a treatise called *Majma' al-Bahrayn* (i.e., meeting of two great oceans Hinduism and Islam). He compared, in this treatise, the terminologies of both the religions and showed striking similarities between the two. He also believed, and believed so on the basis of comparative study of Islamic and Hindu scriptures that Hinduism though apparently polytheistic, was not; and quoting *Upanishads*, the sacred Hindu scriptures, showed that basically Hinduism too is a monotheistic religion.

Another Sufi saint of eighteenth century India, Mazhar Jan-i-Janan believed that idol worship among Hindus is not essentially polytheistic as idols are a way to reach God, not God by themselves. Much earlier, Muhiyuddin Ibn Arabi, an 11th century Sufi saint from Spain laid central emphasis on love of God and considered his heart as centre of love and hence, centre of God. According to his doctrine of *Wahdat al-wujud* the entire creation is the manifestation of God and hence, all barriers between human beings following different religious traditions are artificial and needed to be demolished. His was truely a universalistic approach. These Sufi saints laid more emphasis on spirituality rather than rituals and hence, they could visualize the basic unity among all faith traditions.

The Hindu scriptures also talk of equal respect for all religions and religious traditions. The *bhakti* saints in the Hindu tradition laid great emphasis, like the Sufis, on intense love in the form of *bhakti* i.e., devotion to God, the Supreme Being. For them too rituals were secondary and it is spirituality which was fundamental. In the Christian traditions too, the mystics stressed spirituality and devotion to God.

But this does not mean that rituals and theologies do not matter for the people. There are millions of people who give great importance to their respective ritual and theological systems. An inter-religious dialogue should, as the very basis of the dialogue accept the central importance of the ritual and theological systems. Here I would like to lay down some ground rules for inter-religious dialogue. The following rules would be of great help:

(1) Those who enter into dialogue should be firmly rooted in their faith tradition and should have inner conviction. It is true conviction without being sectarian which becomes the firm ground for dialogue.

(2) There should not be any feeling of superiority of their respective traditions in the minds of dialogue partners. The feeling of superiority can mar the very spirit of dialogue.

(3) Dialogue should never become polemics. Polemical style is very anti-thesis of dialogue. Polemics try to prove the other wrong.

(4) Dialogue should not only be conducted to understand the other, but also should respect the integrity of the other. No dialogue can be successful if there is no respect for integrity and convictions of the other.

(5) The idea of dialogue should be to explain ones point of view and not to convert the other to ones own point of view. Even a slightest attempt to convert the other will destroy the spirit of dialogue. It will then be an attempt at conversion and this will lead to resentment. Attempt at conversion also implies that the person sought to be converted has belief system not as good as that of the convertor.

(6) The dialogue partners should be prepared to recognize the uniqueness of the others belief, ritual or theological systems. It is this uniqueness which makes it different. It is not the question of right or wrong, but rather of uniqueness and diversity.

(7) The dialogue partners should also recognize that diversity is the very basis of life. Without diversity life will become drab and would loose all its charm. The Qur'an not only accepts this diversity, but also legitimizes it. It is Allah's desire to have diversity (5:48; 2:148). Lack of diversity and enforcing one faith system or one ideological system can ultimately lead to fascism and authoritarianism. Thus, theological states, like ideological ones, tend to be highly authoritarian.

(8)   Dialogue should promote the spirit of accommodation and adjustment to minimize conflict in the society. The dialogical spirit consists in appreciating others difficulties and complexities of their situation. Accommodation is the very essence of dialogical culture.

(9)   One has to understand the difference between dialogue and monologue for effective dialoguing. The desire to dominate in the dialogue leads to monologue. Each dialogue partner should get equal opportunity to explain her/his point of view. Dialogue can take place only in true democratic spirit recognizing the rights of all concerned in the dialogue.

(10)   Lastly, one must understand that an effective dialoguing is possible only when one not only listens to the others point of view, but understands and appreciates it in the given context. Even the scriptural text has to be situated in a particular context unless it be a value-statement. Criticism of the text is often based on ignorance of the context.

If these ground rules are followed in inter-religious and inter-cultural dialogues the result will be quite encouraging. No country today can boast of being strictly mono-religious and or mono-cultural. The rapid means of transportation have brought most diverse religious and cultural groups together in every country. And one wants it or not one has to live with such diversity. One cannot wish it away. Some groups will be in numerical majority, others in minority. Or several minorities put together can constitute majority as is likely to happen in Canada in near future. The mosaic model of society can retain its beauty only in harmony; conflict will only reduce this mosaic into complete disjunction due to stress and strain.

Finally, I would also like to refer to what is called the dialogue of life and this dialogue is continuously taking place at the level of the masses. The dialogue of life consists in living together with all its problems, stresses and strains and sharing each others joys and woes in human partnership. We witness this living in togetherness and celebration of life at the level of masses. There are no theories, theologies and concepts to quarrel about; there are only problems and difficulties to be shared together. This is real dialogue of life, a dialogue through living together and sharing together.

CHAPTER 19

Islam and the Concept of Jihad

The concept of *jihad* in Islam has been grossly misunderstood both by Muslims and non-Muslims. It is thought that Islam encourages violence and force and that Allah wants to spread Islam with sword or at the point of gun. The acts of some Muslim extremists and terrorists provide proof for this violent image of Islam. Some Muslims who have very superficial knowledge of Qur'anic pronouncements and injunctions reinforce such an image. The truth is, however, quite otherwise. We would like to examine this question in detail in this Chapter.

Religion is always a spiritual force and Islam much more so. And spiritualism always lays emphasis on peace and inner contentedness, never on violence and strife. Inner contentedness has been termed as *sakinah* by the holy Qur'an. It is this *sakinah* that in fact reinforces inner faith. Thus, the Qur'an says, "He it is who from on high has bestowed inner peace (*sakinah*) upon the hearts of the believers that they might grow, yet, more firm in their faith." (48:4) Thus, it can be seen that the faith depends on inner peace and tranquility. *Iman* (faith) itself means sense of inner security which can only be born out of peace and harmony, not of violence and strife.

Also, there is no question of force or violence in spreading Islam. This was popularized by the West after the crusades which again had nothing to do with spread of religion. They were, in fact, the wars of territorial conquest. As far as spread of religion is concerned, Qur'an rules out violence completely through number of pronouncements. It very forcefully states, *"la ikrah fi'al-din* (there is no compulsion in religion)"* (2:256). Also, it makes it plain that one can invite to the path of Allah through wisdom and goodly manner (16:125). It is no less important that the Qur'an accepted the truth brought by prophets before Muhammad and even emphasized that Islam has come to confirm the existing truth brought by other prophets (see 3:50 and 61:6). As for the Christians and the Jews, the Qur'an says, "Argue not with the People of the Book (the Jews and the Christians) except by what is best save such of them as act unjustly." (29:46)

Thus, the Qur'an requires even the Prophet to argue with the people of the Book in a manner which is the best. The Qur'an even admonishes the holy Prophet not to bother about success of his message. The Qur'an says, "And if thy Lord had pleased, all those who are in the earth would have believed, all of them. Wilt thou then force men till they are believers?" (10:99) The message is very clear. The Prophet's duty was to preach peacefully and not to worry whether people believe or not. There is no question of using force for making people believe. It is against the very spirit of the core message of the Qur'an.

Then what about *jihad*? Is it not obligatory on Muslims? Yes, it has been included in the five pillars of Islam (and according to the Isma'ili Shi'ahs seven pillars). Does it not mean then that every adult Muslim should wage war to spread Islam? Certainly not. Here we would like to throw light on the real concept of *jihad* in Qur'an and how it was understood during the life-time of the Prophet and his immediate successors. First of all it should be noted that it is a popular misconception both among Muslims and non-Muslims that *jihad* means hostility or fighting, warfare and war in particular against infidels. The Qur'an itself never uses it in such a sense. The Arabic terms for warfare or fighting are *harb* and *qital*.

The words *jahada* and *jàhada*, Moulvi Chiragh Ali points out, signify that a person strove, laboured or toiled, exerted himself or his power, or efforts, or endeavours, or ability; employed himself vigorously, diligently, studiously, sedulously, earnestly or with energy, was diligent or studious, took pains or extraordinary pains.(Moulvi Chiragh Ali, 1984, p. 163) He quotes these meanings from number of authentic dictionaries like *The Sihah of Jouhari*, *Lisan al-Arab* of Ibn Mukarram, *The Asas* of Zamakhshari and *the Qamoos* of Fyrozabadi. For example, the term *jàhada fil amr* signifies that a person did his utmost or used his utmost powers, or efforts, or endeavours, or ability in pursuing an affair (see Lane's *Arabic-English Lexicon Book* I, part II, p. 473). The Moulvi also points out that Jauharee, a lexicologist of great repute, whose work is confined to classical terms and their significations, says in his *Sihah* that *jàhada fi sabilillah* or *mojàhadatan* and *jihàdan* and also *ajtahada* and *tajahada* (all derivatives of *jihad*) mean expending power and effort. Also Fayoomee, author of *Misbah al-Muneer*, which contains a very large collection of classical words and phrases of frequent occurrence, also says that *jàhada fi sabilillah jihàdan* and *ajtahada fil amr* means he expended his utmost efforts and power in seeking to attain an object. (Moulvi, 1984, p. 164).

Imam Raghib is another authority on the Qur'anic words and their significations. He also says that *jahd* means difficulties and tribulations, efforts and power. He quotes the Qur'anic verse 79:9 to prove his point. It also means the best of efforts and quotes the verse 38:16 for illustration. Then he goes on to explain the meaning of *al-jihad wa al-mujahidah* and says that this means to make utmost possible efforts in the face of enemies of Islam. He says there are three types of *jihàd*: (1) to face the enemies of Islam; (2) to fight against ones self (to control selfish desires) and (3) to strive in the way of Allah with ones life and wealth (41:9, 20:9). Raghib also quotes a *hadith* "fight against your desires as you fight against your enemy" He also quotes another *hadith* that "fight unbelievers with your hands and tongues". (Raghib, 1971, p. 199-200).

Thus, it becomes clear from Imam Raghib's explication also that *jihad* does not mean war or hostility, but utmost efforts for a cause. Moulvi Chiragh Ali maintains that "It is only a post-classical and technical meaning of *jihàd* to use the word as signifying fighting against an enemy. Mr. Lane says *jahada* came to be used by the Moslems to signify generally he fought, warred, or waged war against unbelievers and the like.' This signification is now given by those lexicologists who do not restrict themselves to the definition of classical terms or significations, like the author of *Qàmoos*. Mr. Lane, the celebrated author of *Maddool Qàmoos*, an Arabic-English lexicologist, clearly shows that the definition of *jihad*, as the act of waging war, is only of Moslem origin and is not classical". (Ibid, p. 164)

The Moulvi tries to show that the Muslim usage of *jihad*, as signifying the waging of war, is a post-Qur'anic usage, and that in the Qur'an it is used classically and literally in its natural sense. What the Moulvi says is that the Qur'an does not use it in the sense of waging war, but in the sense of making utmost efforts in the way of Allah. It is important to note that if one wishes to understand the Qur'anic terms it is highly necessary to have the knowledge of classical usage of those terms before, during and after the process of revelation. The later changes occurred under pressure of circumstances and often changed the entire meaning of the Qur'anic verses.

Moulvi Chiragh Ali maintains that after the death of the Prophet the language was "rapidly corrupted by introduction of foreign words. This was doubtless owing to the great extension of the Mohammadan power at this period. The classical poets are those who died before these great conquests were effected and are the most reliable authorities for Arabic words and their significations, and they are called *jahili*". (Ibid, p. 165) Thus, the *jahili* (i.e., pre-Islamic) poetry was often quoted to fix the meanings of many Qur'anic words also. The earliest classical poets date only a century before the birth of the Prophet, and the latest, about a century after his death. The period of Islamic poets, is the first and second centuries (of Islamic era) and include those who lived after the first corruption of the Arabic language, but before the corruption had become extensive. Thereafter, there took place what can be said as 'the general and rapid corruption of language'.

The Qur'anic verses use the word *jahad* and *johd* and its derivatives both in Meccan period and Madinese period. In the Meccan period when Muslims were being severely persecuted and had not taken arms in their defense, all Muslim commentators as well as some Christian scholars take *jihad* in its literal sense, i.e., making utmost efforts, exertion, energy, etc. But the problem arises in the Madinese period when Muslims had taken up arms in their defense. As regards this period, the words are considered to have an entirely a new and altogether fortuitous meaning, i.e., a religious war of aggression. But even some verses pertaining to *jihad* of this period (i.e., Madinese period) are taken in their literal sense.

It must be admitted, however, that in the post-classical period which began after the death of the holy Prophet, when the language was 'rapidly corrupted' according to Chiragh Ali, the word '*jihad*' came to mean warfare or fighting in the military sense. 'Since that period', the Moulvi maintains, "the word has one to be used as meaning the waging of a war or a crusade only in a military tactics and more recently it found its way in the same sense into Mohammadan law-books and lexicons of later dates. But the subsequent corrupt or post-classical language cannot be accepted as a final or even a satisfactory authority upon the point." (Ibid, p. 168).

Let us now take the Qur'anic verses on what came to be understood in post-classical period as 'jihad' As I said earlier the holy Qur'an does not advocate policy of aggression. It also does not advocate, however, non-violence in absolute sense. The historical legacy of the society being directly addressed by the Qur'an was highly violent one. Both Mecca and Madina, specially Madina, had witnessed high degree of inter-tribal wars before appearance of Islam and such a society could not be transformed into a non-violent society in absolute sense. The Qur'an, therefore, chose a middle path in this respect. It did not allow aggressive violence, but approved of defensive one. The permission for defensive violence also does not mean that Qur'an institutionalizes violence in any sense. As far as norm is concerned, it is non-violence and peace. Defensive wars are permitted only if the context so demands. Violence, in other words, is permissible like polygamy, in a given context, not obligatory.

It is *jihàd* which is one of the pillars of Islam precisely because it does not necessarily mean war. *Jihàd*, as pointed out above, means utmost efforts, not violence and it is obligatory on Muslims to make utmost efforts (in a wise and goodly manner) to spread the message of Allah so as to create a just and compassionate society. This is what is obligatory, not waging war at all. It has been exemplified by the Prophet himself on many occasions specially at the time of *Sulh-i-Hudaibiya* (peace of Hudaibiyah and *Fath-i-Mecca* (conquest of Mecca)).

Sulh-i-Hudaibiyah is a landmark of peace in the history of Islam. The Prophet accepted all the unfavourable terms dictated by the leaders of unbelievers of Mecca in order to avoid prospects of war. Many of the Prophet's followers were not happy, but the Prophet remained firm and entered into the peace treaty with unbelievers of Mecca and avoided needless bloodshed. Similalry, the conquest of Mecca was absolutely peaceful and the Prophet set a record by announcing general pardon of all his former persecutors. He even pardoned Hind, the wife of Abu Sufyan, who had bitten off the liver of the Prophet's uncle Hamza who was great supporter and soldier of Islam.

Also, the Prophet of Islam did not fight any war of aggression. He fought wars in defense. All the major battles Badr, Uhud and Khandaq were fought near or around Madina because the unbelievers of Mecca were the invaders and the Prophet and his followers were defenders. The battle of Khaybar was also forced on the Prophet as the Jews of Khayber, specially the exiles from Madina were conspiring and becoming threat to the security of Madina. The battle of Hunayn too, after the conquest of Mecca was forced on the Prophet as the Thaqif of Ta'if and the tribe of Hawazin refused to accept the changed power equation in Mecca and declared war against Muslims.

Let us now examine certain verses of the Qur'an in which the believers have been asked to fight and also as to what norms have been laid down in this respect. There is not a single verse in Qur'an which urges Muslims to commit aggression. They have been urged to fight in defense. The verse 4:75, for example, says, "And what reason have you not to fight in the way of Allah and of the weak among the men and the women and the children, who say: Our Lord, take us out of this town, whose people are oppressors, and grant us from Thee a friend and grant us from thee a helper."

This verse urges upon the oppressed to fight in their defense as they have been severely persecuted by the people of Mecca (*min hazihil qaryati*). So it is fight against the oppressors and not fight to force others to accept Islamic hegemony. It is the discourse of the weak, not of the hegemonic forces. Maulana Muhammad Ali has made the following observation on this verse: "This verse explains what is meant by fighting in the way of Allah. While most of the believers who had the means had escaped from Mecca, which is here spoken of as the city *whose people are oppressors*, there remained those who were weak and unable to undertake a journey. These were still persecuted. Fighting to deliver them from the persecution of the oppressors was really fighting in the way of Allah." (*Holy Qur'an*, Lahore,1973, p. 211).

The fundamental project of Islam is to establish a just society by empowering the weak and the oppressed and putting an end to oppression and exploitation. The holy Prophet's *hadith* that a society can survive with *kufr* (unbelief), but not with *zulm* (oppression) epitomizes the socio-political philosophy of Islam. The above verse 4:75 also refers to unjust social situation in which the oppressed are intensely suffering and fighting against oppressors becomes necessary to liberate them from oppression.

The other verse (22:39) permitting war also refers to oppression of the weak. It says, "Permission (to fight) is given to those on whom war is made, because they are oppressed, And surely Allah is able to assist them." All the traditions quoted by Tabari and Ibn Kathir, the two noted commentators on the Qur'an maintain that this verse is the earliest Qur'anic reference to the problem of war in Qur'an. This verse, according to Abd Allah ibn 'Abbas, a prominent companion of the Prophet, was revealed immediately after the Prophet migrated from Mecca to Madina which means at the beginning of the year 1 A.H.

The above verse also permits war for the liberation of the oppressed and makes clear the defensive character of war in Islam. Again the verses 2:190-193 also permit war only in defense. These verses state: "And fight in Allah's cause against those who wage war against you, *but do not commit aggression*—for, verily, Allah does not love aggressors. And slay them wherever you may come upon them and drive them away form wherever they drove you away—*for oppression is even worse than killing*. And fight not against them near the Inviolable Hosue of Worship unless they fight against you, slay them: such shall be the recompense of those who deny the truth. *But if they desist— behold, Allah is much forgiving, a dispenser of grace.* Hence, fight against them *until there is no more oppression* and all worship is devoted to Allah alone; *but if they desist, then all hostility shall cease*, save against those who (wilfully do wrong)." (emphasis added)

If we carefully read the portions emphasized it becomes abundantly clear that Qur'an does not believe in war of aggression at all. The words like "but do not commit aggression", or "oppression is worse than killing" or "But if they desist—behold, Allah is much forgiving" do not need any explanation. They are crystal clear. Thus, according to the Qur'anic injunction fight is permitted only and only to end oppression and injustice. Islam does not believe in quietly submitting to gross injustices and oppression. Its aim is to liberate the oppressed. Also nowhere in these verses any mention has been made about the spread of religion. There is not a single verse in the Qur'an which urges upon the believers to wage war or to fight for spreading Islam.

Muhammad Asad, a noted modern commentator of the Qur'an, while commenting on the above three verses says: "This and the following verses lay down unequivocally that only self-defense (in the widest sense of the word) makes war permissible for Muslims. Most of the commentators agree in that the expression *la ta'tadu* signifies, in this context, "do not commit aggression"; while by *al-mu'tadin* 'those who commit aggression' are meant. The defensive character of a fight 'in God's cause'—that is, in the cause of the ethical principles ordained by God—is, moreover, self-evident in the reference to 'those who wage war against you', and has been still further clarified in 22:39—'permission (to fight) is given to those against whom war is being wrongfully waged'—which according to all available traditions, constitutes the earliest (and therefore fundamental) Qur'anic reference to the question of *jihàd*, or holy war (see Tabarì and Ibn Kathìr in their commentaries on 22:39). That this early, fundamental principle of self-defense as the only possible justification of war has been maintained throughout the Qur'an is evident from 60:8, as well as from the concluding sentence of 4:91, both of which belong to a later period than the above verse." (*The Message of The Qur'an* Gibralter, 1980, p. 41).

The verse 60:8 also is very important to understand the Qur'anic philosophy of war. This verse makes it absolutely clear, if any further clarity is required, that no war of aggression is at all permitted by the Qur'an. The verse says, "As for such (of the unbelievers) as do not fight against you on account of (your) faith and neither drive you forth from your homelands, Allah does not forbid you to show them kindness and to behave towards them with full equity: for verily', Allah loves those who act equitably."

This Chapter 60 was revealed, all commentators agree, after the *Sulh-i-Hudaybiyyah*, i.e., in the 7th year after the Prophet's migration and hence, it cannot be argued that the Qur'an speaks of war of defense only in the earlier period when Muslims were oppressed and then permits war of aggression when they became dominant. The above verse is quite vital to the understanding of the philosophy of the Qur'an in respect of use of violence. The earlier verses permit Muslims only to fight for liberation from oppression and here in this verse it is required of them not to fight against those unbelievers who do not persecute the Muslims on account of their faith nor drive them away from their homes and asks Muslims to "show them kindness and to behave towards them with full equity".

The Qur'an repeatedly advises the Muslims not to continue to fight if the unbelievers lay down the weapons. Thus, we find in 4:90, "if they withdraw from you and fight you not and offer you peace, then Allah allows you no way against them." Or as we find in 2:190, "And fight in the way of Allah against those who fight against you, but be not aggressive. Surely Allah loves not the aggressors." This verse also forbids war of aggression and calls upon Muslims to use violence as long as they are aggressed against, not otherwise. And in 9:36, "And fight the polytheists (Mushrikin) all together as they fight you all together."

Whenever the Qur'an urges believers to fight it is only where the enemy is violating social norms and persecuting the Muslims or breaking the treaty or throwing Muslims out of their homes just because they follow a different religion. Thus the verse 9:13 urges Muslims to fight with these words, "Will you not fight a people who broke their oaths and aimed at the expulsion of the Messenger and they attacked you first? Do you fear them? But Allah more right that you should fear Him, if you are believers."

Those of the unbelievers who are not prepared for cessation of hostility they must be fought against with all the might. Thus, the Qur'an says, "So if they withdraw not from you, nor offer you peace and restrain their hands, then seize them and kill them wherever you find them. And against these We have given you a clear authority." This verse seems rather harsh, but seen in the background of betrayal of peace by two tribes Asad and Ghatfan one will understand and appreciate its harshness. These two tribes promised peace to Muslims, but went back on it when their tribesman urged upon them to fight against Muslims.

All these verses about qitàl (war) relate to unbelievers (kuffar) and polytheists (mushrikin). There is, however, a verse on hostility with Ahl al-Kitab. Among Ahl al-Kitab, i..e., Christians and Jews, Muslims had to encounter more hostility with the Jews than with Christians during the Prophet's life time. But towards the end there was clash with the Roman empire and hence, the expedition of Tabuk. The relevant verse is as follows: "Fight those who believe not in Allah, nor in the Last Day, nor forbid that which Allah and His Messenger have forbidden, nor follow the Religion of Truth, out of those who have been given the Book, until they pay the exemption tax (jizyah) with a willing hand after having been humbled (in war)." (9:29)

It is important to note in this verse that Qur'an is not urging Muslims to fight against People of the Book because they do not accept Islam, but because they do not follow their own 'religion of truth'. Thus, the Qur'an accepts validity of other religions. Another controversial matter in this verse is the concept of *jizyah* (compensatory tax). This is thought to be humiliating tax on non-Muslims. This is not true. Firstly, it is levied in lieu of participation in the war obligatory for Muslims. This tax entitles non-Muslims, particularly the People of the Book, exemption from military duty. It is the responsibility of the Muslims (*dhimma*) to protect the life and property of payers of *jizyah*. Also, there is no fixed rate; it is to be negotiated as per the capacity of the payer. Rashid Rida, in his *Tafsir al-Manar* (Volume.X, p. 342) maintains that the words of the Qur'an *'an yadin* (from hand) indicate ability to pay. And hence, Muhammad Asad translates it as 'with a willing hand'. Not only this those who do not earn or discharge religious duties are exempted from paying *jizyah*. For example, women, old men, males who have not attained full maturity, all sick and crippled men and priests and monks are exempt from this tax. And those who volunteer to render military service will also be exempted from *jizyah*.

It should also be born in mind that during the Prophet's time when the holy Qur'an was being revealed there was no regular military or civil police. It was the enjoined duty of every Muslim to offer himself for military duty and hence, it was more ideological in character, i.e., those who embraced Islam considered it their religious duty to protect it from aggression from hostile elements. It does not at all mean that every Muslim is obliged to fight for spread of Islam with the help of sword or guns. As pointed out above there is overwhelming evidence in the Qur'an about the defensive nature of war. *Jihad*, in fact should be considered as obligation on Muslims to make utmost efforts to end hostilities and promote peace in the world.

CHAPTER 20
On Methodology of Understanding Qur'an

There have been numerous interpretations of the holy Qur'an. This itself shows the great significance of this scripture revealed to the holy Prophet of Islam. The Qur'an has inspired millions of people across the globe and continues to do so and will continue to do so. Many enemies of Islam attack this great scripture and try to 'prove' in their own way that it (the Qur'an) spews hatred against non-believers. It provides very rigid and even fanatical system of beliefs and it is because of the Qur'an that Muslims have been fanatics and have shed so much blood on earth. Unfortunately, many rationalists, though not inspired by hatred of the Qur'an, but by their aversion to religion, have often bought these arguments. In a rationalists' conference some Egyptian delegates who happened to be Muslims, also raised such objections against the Qur'an and maintained that its teachings are against rights of women. It is also maintained that the Qur'an requires all believers to wage *jihad* against unbelievers and continue to wage it until all have embraced Islam. It is also believed by many that the revelation is against reason and that the Qur'anic pronouncements are irrational.

It is in view of these objections and misinterpretations of the Qur'an that it is necessary to develop proper methodology of understanding the scripture of such immense significance. Firstly, can there be only one sort of interpretation? Secondly, can any particular interpretation of the Qur'an be binding on subsequent generations, or even for the people of same generation, however, eminent the interpreter may be? Thirdly, did all companions of the holy Prophet agree on a particular interpretation or meaning of a verse of the Qur'an? If not, why did they disagree with each other? Fourthly, what is the role of *ahadith* in understanding the Qur'an? Can one understand the Qur'an without the help of *ahadith*? And fifthly, are those *ahadith* employed for explaining the meaning of the Qur'an are unanimously agreed upon by the interpreters and commentators?

These are very crucial questions for developing proper methodology for understanding the Qur'an. These questions must be satisfactorily answered. It is a fact that there has never been unanimity between different commentators and interpreters of the Holy Book. Since there have been differences between various interpreters and commentators, there is no question of any particular interpretation being binding on all the contemporaries much less all the subsequent generations. However, there are people who think so. But such an approach will not only interfere with the comprehensive understanding of the holy Qur'an, but will also limit it to the understanding of a few individuals. No interpretation, however, important or significant it might be, can be the sole interpretation. This is very fundamental in understanding various aspects of the Qur'anic pronouncements.

A commentator could have primarily a theological perspective, or sociological perspective, or scientific perspective and so on. Each one will have a contribution to make from ones own perspective. In this respect it is important to note that the Qur'an uses words which are pregnant with several meanings or even symbolic language and these symbols or words could not only be understood from different perspectives, but also unfold their new meanings with passage of time and new experiences. Thus, to limit the understanding of the Qur'an to a few interpreters or commentators would seriously limit the scope of the scripture and it would make it relevant only to a period in the past and that interpretation may not be satisfactory from future generations' point of view. We as Muslims do believe that the Qur'an is eternal in its relevance and for it to be so, future generations will have right to interpret the Qur'an in their own light, in the light of their own experiences and the problems they face. The problems and challenges faced by Muslims in the past may not be same as faced by present generations. Thus, in order to derive guidance and inspiration from the Qur'an, the people belonging to the new generations, will have to interpret it from their own perspective.

It is absolutely true that *hadith* plays an important role in understanding of the Qur'an, but there are several problems with the *hadith* literature which need to be sorted out in order to weigh its role in interpretation of the Qur'an. First and foremost problem is of the authenticity of *hadith*. There are serious controversies about various *ahadith* which are employed in the interpretations of various Qur'anic verses. And these *ahadith* make crucial difference in understanding the verses of the Qur'an. Here also there are two things worth noting: first, if these verses pertain to what we call metaphysical beliefs ('*aqa'id*) and '*ibadaat*, such controversies will not have any social impact. But if these matters pertain to socio-economic matters, personal laws and what we call *mu'amalaat* then interpretation of these verses will have great social impact and will affect the lives of people here on earth.

Also, there are several *ahadith* which are often in conflict with the pronouncements of the Qur'an. In deriving *shari'ah* laws many Islamic jurists have employed such *ahadith*. Employment of such *ahadith* definitely affects the understanding of the Qur'an. This is also a highly controversial area. Some scholars have proposed that those *ahadith* which are directly in conflict with the pronouncements of the Qur'an may not be employed in understanding the Qur'an at all. This will be greatly helpful in understanding the inherent meaning of the verses of the Qur'an. Such *ahadith* instead of being helpful in understanding the verses of the Qur'an, have created intense controversies.

Secondly, if one studies the various classical commentaries of the Qur'an, one comes to know the extent of different understandings of these verses by the companions of the holy Prophet. Tabari, the great commentator of the Qur'an, quotes several different understandings of these verses by the *sahabah kiraam* (the companions of the Prophet). It shows the extent of differences among the companions of the Prophet himself about various Qur'anic verses. In some cases Tabari has given more than fifty different meanings of a verse as understood by the companions of the Prophet or their followers.

The fact is that the companions of the Prophet came from different backgrounds as well as different social origins. Also, they had their own differing mental capacities and social prejudices. Also, there were references to the past Prophets and the stories associated with them. As we know these factors play very crucial role in understanding the text of any book and much more so in the case of the revealed scriptures like the holy Qur'an. Thus, the understanding of the verses by the companions of the Prophet will have to be seen in their own background and we must refrain from absolutizing this understanding. In fact many people who could not understand the biblical references in the Qur'an imbibed whatever was told to them by the Jews and Christians and used such information to understand the relevant Qur'anic verses.

And when the Greek knowledge was transferred to Arabic language during the Abbasid period and became available to the Arabic knowing people, it was used by many commentators to understand the Qur'anic verses as many people in our own time try to understand the Qur'anic verses in the light of contemporary developments in the field of science. The belief that sun goes round the earth or that earth is flat and not round were imbibed from Greek thinkers and scientists and from Ptolmian astronomy and they became "Islamic beliefs". Many of our 'ulama vehemently opposed the concept that earth goes round and considered it "un-Islamic" and condemned it as sheer heresy. Thus, the Greek knowledge became sacrosanct for these theologians and any thing contradicting it was considered heresy. Today those very verses are understood very differently in the light of contemporary scientific discoveries. In fact many Muslim scientists are quoting those very verses to prove that the Qur'an maintained that the earth rotates and is not static. Thus, our own system of knowledge and mental background is very crucial to understanding the verses of the Qur'an. No single interpretation of the Qur'anic verses can be privileged or absolutized.

New meanings of these verses dawn upon us with new developments. As pointed out above, the Qur'anic terminology is rich and multi-dimensional and can yield different meanings with more developments and newer experiences. Those who want to limit the understanding of the Qur'an only to certain *ahadith* however genuine and authentic, miss the richness of the Qur'anic text and its various levels of meanings. The religious text is always complex, multi-faceted and multi-dimensional. No interpretation of such a text should be absolutized.

If one carefully studies all the commentaries of the Qur'an written during this period it becomes obvious that they were written under the influence of medieval knowledge systems. However, these commentaries were not only absolutized, but also given quasi-divine status by the followers of these commentators. This is, however, not to suggest that these commentaries were not of significance or that they are not relevant today. Whatever, their importance for study of the Qur'an, they cannot be given quasi-divine status.

Another thing which must be pointed out is that the Qur'anic verses can be divided into three categories: (1) the verses pertaining to '*ibadat* which include *salah* (prayer), *saum* (fasting), *haj* (pilgrimage), *zakah* (poor tax) and similar other practices pertaining to this category. (2) verses pertaining to *mu'amalat* which include, among other things, marriage, divorce, inheritance, evidence, business deals, contract, properties, agriculture and so on; (3) verses pertaining to metaphysical beliefs like oneness of God, day of judgment, hell and heaven, angels and so on; (4) verses pertaining to general guidance; and (5) verses which are value giver like justice, equality, truthfulness, etc.

The verses pertaining to '*ibadaat*, can be understood in the light of authentic *hadith*. The Prophet himself explained how to pray, how to perform *haj*, the matters pertaining to fasting, etc. There is no question of any reinterpretation or rethinking on these verses. They must be understood as explained by the Prophet. It is the concept of '*ibadaat* and rituals associated with them that provide uniqueness to any religion. Each religion has developed its own spiritual system and system of prayer, worship, meditation etc. To rethink on these issues is to tamper with this uniqueness and to destroy its spiritual aesthetics, if I can so describe it. Thus, the understanding of the verses pertaining to '*ibadaat* cannot change. But of course the sectarian differences in this respect will persist. There are many differences, some times even of significant nature, in matters of *salah*, etc., between various schools of jurisprudence within Sunni Islam and (Hanafis, Shafi'is, Malikis, Hanbalis, Zahiris) and Shi'ah Islam (Ithna Asharis, Zaidis, Isma'ilis, etc.). These differences have remained and will remain in future also. In a way these different sectarian practices also provide uniqueness to each sect and even become identity signifiers. These differences are also based on *hadiths* acceptable to every school of thought. Some *madhahib* (schools of thought) accept some *hadiths* as authentic whereas, some accept others as authentic and doubt the authenticity of other *hadiths*.

Then we come to the verses pertaining to *mu'amalaat* which include, as pointed out above matters like marriage, divorce, inheritance, business deals and so on. Here some rethinking is advocated by modernists and they argue, rethinking is necessary in view of the emerging problems and challenges. For example, the Qur'anic permission to marry four wives stands in need of rethinking. This was understood under the medieval ethos and prevailing Arabian practices of the time. The women, who have become much more conscious of their Islamic rights, are in the forefront of this demand. Same thing can be said of the verses pertaining to divorce. Some *ahadith* which are contrary to the spirit of the Qur'anic verses pertaining to divorce have been used to interpret these verses and hence, there is need to restore the spirit of the Qur'an in reinterpreting these verses or enforcing these verses.

As for the third category of verses, i.e., those pertaining to metaphysical beliefs like oneness of God, day of judgment, heaven and hell, angels, etc., are part of what we can call *'aqa'id* (faith and *imaan*). These verses too, like those belonging to the first category, are beyond any change and pertain to the very fundamentals of religion. Belief in oneness of God (*tawheed*) is most fundamental to Islamic teaching. Similarly, the beliefs in the day of judgment and Prophethood and angels also belong to the basic teachings of Islam. The belief that the Prophet Muhammad is the last prophet is also very fundamental to the Islamic belief and is integral part of the Qur'anic teachings. These beliefs are beyond any re-interpretation and must be accepted without any question. These beliefs are also part of uniqueness of Islam and distinguishes it from other religions.

However, there are differences regarding the exact meaning of *tawheed*, for example, the M'utazila concept of *tawheed* varies from that of other Islamic sects. The Ash'aris differ significantly from the Mu'tazila on the understanding of *tawheed*. The M'utazila think that Allah has no attributes (*sifaat*) whereas, the Asha'ira maintain that Allah has attributes and also believe in his physical existence with all the organs like eyes, ears, hands etc. and that the believers will see Him on the day of judgment. These differences are also based on various *ahadith* current in their times.

The Isma'ilis who believe in *ta'wil* (the hidden meaning of the Qura'nic verses) also have very different understanding of the nature of Godhood and *tawheed*. They also believe that Allah has no attributes and that He is beyond all comprehension and intellectual discourse and His existence can only be affirmed by referring to Him as *huwa* (He) and nothing more. Assigning any attribute to him deviates from the concept of real *tawheed* and amounts to *shirk* (associating partners with Him). The Isma'ilis maintain that He cannot be described as 'one' as He is beyond any concept of number and to attribute number to Him is to limit Him. We are just hinting at the Isma'ili beliefs here to show how there are vital differences in understanding such fundamental concepts as *tawheed*. These discussions are, of course, philosophical in nature and do not touch the understanding of an ordinary believer. But nevertheless these different understandings of fundamental teachings of Islam do exist in the Islamic world. And what is important to note is that these differences in understanding the basic concepts of Islam are not of recent origin but pertain to the classical period of Islam. These differences arose mainly during the beginning of the Abbasid period.

Initially the Abbasid rulers were the supporters of Mu'tazila theology which differed significantly from the orthodox positions. There was also a fierce controversy about the nature of the Qur'an—whether it is created or coeternal with God. The Mu'tazila of course maintained that the Qur'an is created (which implies that its text can be destroyed like any other creature at some point of time) and the orthodox maintained that it is coeternal with God (implying that its text can never be destroyed and will exist along with God). The M'utazila who are also known as the rationalists in Islam were part of the Abbasid establishment and they persecuted the eminent jurists like Imam Abu Hanifa who refused to accept the Mu'tazila position on the createdness of the Qur'an. The Imam was imprisoned and was lashed every Friday after the noon prayer. Thus, in the Islamic history it is rationalists who persecuted the orthodox.

The fourth category of the Qur'anic verses pertain to general guidance and to spreading what is good (the Qur'anic term for this is *ma'ruf*) and contain what is evil (the Qur'anic term for this being *munkar*) and stand in no need of change. These are universal truths and these universal truths are shared by other religions also. Of course the understanding of *ma'ruf* and is *munkar* may differ from time to time and place to place and to that extent there may be differences of opinion. But there can be a universal approach regarding *ma'ruf* and *munkar* that is what promotes betterment of God's creature can be universal good and what negates it can be described as universal evil. But there can be differences again on what promotes betterment and what negates it. *Ma'ruf* and *munkar* will continue to be relativized. Also, there can be sectarian differences among Muslims. *Muta'* marriage, for example, is considered *ma'ruf* by Ithna 'ashari Shi'ahs and *munkar* by the Sunnis and Isma'ili Shi'ahs. But there are certain *munkar* (evil) practices like eating pork and drinking and gambling on which there is complete unanimity among all sects of Islam. There is no question of any differing interpretations.

The fifth category of the Qur'anic verses those pertaining to the values like justice, equality, compassion, creation of just social order, etc., are of course eternal in nature. The Qur'an lays great emphasis on these values. One can say that these values are most fundamental to Islam. There is again no question of rethinking about these values as these are universal and eternal. Also, there has been complete agreement among the Muslim theologians and jurists on these values and these are reflected in all theological and juristic formulations in Islam.

However, there can be and are, differences on what is just and what is not or what constitutes equality and in what sense. And what it means to be compassionate. For example, is it enough to treat a slave in a just manner or is it necessary to emancipate a slave for meeting the requirement of justice. The medieval Islamic thinkers felt that to treat a slave in a just manner fulfills the requirement of justice and it was not thought necessary to abolish slavery as to meet the end of justice. Similarly, the verse 4:129 about treatment of wives was so interpreted that equal maintenance for all four wives was thought enough to meet the end of justice. But the Mu'tazila who were also described as the party of *tawheed wa al-'adl* (party of unity of godhood and justice) did not agree with this point of view. Their reading of the verse 4:129 required that equal love along with equal maintenance, was also necessary for meeting the requirement of justice. The modernists would tend to agree with the Mu'tazila view on this question and would even plead for abolition of polygamy to meet the end of Qur'anic justice. Similarly, in contemporary situation simply just treatment of slaves would not satisfy any one. The abolition of slavery will.

Thus, it will be seen that the values though immutable and unabrogatable, are interpreted differently in different periods of time. What appears to be just today may no longer be thought to be just tomorrow. But what is most important is justice, not its understanding in given circumstances. Thus, the interpretation of Islamic jurists of the Qur'anic verses relating to justice, or any other similar values, will have to change in keeping with the ethos of time. This is an important element of the methodology to be used to understand the Qur'anic verses. In other words, there has to be an element of dynamism in understanding the Qur'anic verses.

The *hadith* literature too requires similar approach. Even the most authentic *hadith* on which there is complete unanimity, should not constraint us from discovering new meanings or potentialities of the particular Qur'anic verse. The holy Prophet could not have ignored the constraints of his own time in respect of certain practices, even, though reluctantly. Though, personally he set example by emancipating slaves, he could not have abolished slavery. Islam was probably the first religion to preach equality of all human beings with the Qur'anic proclamation that all children of Adam are honoured, yet, the institution of slavery was so deeply entrenched in the social structure of the time that it could not be abolished completely. But it does not mean it could be perpetuated by quoting some Qur'anic verse or *hadith*.

Here we should consider another important element of the Qur'anic methodology that is putting normative verses above contextual verses. Some Qur'anic verses proclaim norms and values whereas others permit certain practices or institutions in the given context. In other words normative verses are more fundamental than the contextual verses. The normative verses are eternal in application.

While developing methodology for proper understanding of the Qur'an we will always have to bear in mind that Islam was much more than a set of beliefs or rituals; it was proclamation of social revolution, creating a new humane society based on equality, justice and human dignity. It believed in overthrowing any status quo based on hierarchy, discrimination on the basis of tribe, caste, creed, race or nationality. There is a transcendental dimension to the Islamic teachings which can never be ignored. But the interpretation of the Qur'an which we have inherited is sunk deep in medieval values. We thus, have to mount efforts to rescue it from this nedievalism while of course recognising its historical importance. We must go back to the Qur'an and the normative verses to create a new just and humane order in this twenty-first century.

The new methodology of understanding the Qur'an should enable us to shake the present unjust structure of our society, should enable us to transcend our social situation, give a new hope and build a new future for humanity. Presently, we have been caught in the cobweb of status quoist interests which do not permit new understanding of the text of the Qur'an. Any deviation from the early or medieval understanding of the Qur'an is construed as the deviation from divine injunctions. Today for us these old commentaries on Qur'an have greater sanctity than the Qur'an itself. Let this truth dawn on us sooner than later.

CHAPTER 21

Qur'an and Isma'ili Ta'wil

Qur'an is divine, but its interpretation is humane and hence, there have been different interpretations of the Qur'anic verses. The differences in interpretation of the Qur'anic verses was not a later development, but began shortly after the death of the holy Prophet. Different prominent companions of the Prophet began to differ from each other and with the passage of time these differences also deepened in their scope. There were various reasons for these differences. First and foremost was the differences due to understanding. Any text and much more so the divine text which also tends to be symbolic, is understood depending on ones own mental and intellectual capacity. Also, the understanding of these verses depends on ones own personal or family background. The tribal background and the community ethos also would play an important role.

The Muslims were also embroiled in political disputes with the passage of time and these disputes also got reflected in interpretation of the Qur'anic verses. The disputing parties tried to legitimize their respective positions through either *hadith* or interpretation of the Qur'anic verses which suited their position. Also, many sects came into existence in the early period of Islam and every sect tried to prove its authenticity by interpreting the Qur'anic verses in keeping with their doctrines. The formation and doctrinal differences of these have been dealt with in various early books like *Al-Farq bayn al-Firaq* of Baghdadi and others. Each of these sects tried to interpret various Qur'anic verses in their own way. And it became impossible to resolve both political as well as doctrinal differences. There also evolved differences between the jurists (*fuqaha'*). These jurists also interpreted the Qur'anic verses in keeping with their understanding of juristic issues. Thus, within the Sunni Islam there developed four major schools of *fiqh* (jurisprudence). The same is true of *hadith* literature with which we will deal with in another paper.

Among other reasons for different interpretations of the Qur'anic verses the sectarian differences play most important and interesting role. And among other sectarian differences the differences between Sunnis and Shi'as assumed much more controversial role. No other two sects of Islam have differed as much as the Sunnis and Shi'as in understanding and interpretation of certain Qur'anic verses. It was on account of this that the Sunni corpus of *hadith* developed separately from that of Shi'as.

The Shi'as also subsequently subdivided into number of subsects, the main division being between the Ithna Asharis and Isma'ilis. The Isma'ilis developed their own independent interpretation of the Qur'anic verses which radically differs from not only the Sunni interpretation, but also from the mainstream Shi'a interpretation. It is the Isma'ili interpretation that we would deal with in this paper. We have broadly referred to the Isma'ili doctrines in one of our earlier papers. We would briefly summarize it here for ready reference of our readers.

The Isma'ilis branched off from the Ithna Ashari Shi'as on the question of succession to the fifth (and according to the Ithna Asharis the sixth) Imam Ja'far al-Sadiq. It should be noted that the doctrine of imamah is very central to the Shi'a Islam as the doctrine of *khilafah* is to the Sunni Islam. According to the Shi'a belief the imam must belong to the progeny of Fatima and 'Ali and thus, son will always succeed the father. This doctrine remains central whichever the Shi'a sect. And most of the differences among the Shi'a sub-sects, though not always, have been on the question of succession as to which son succeeded the previous Imam.

The Hanafiyas believed that it was Ali's son Muhammad bin Hanifa who succeeded as Imam. Similarly the Zaidi Shi'as believed that it was Zaid, the son of Imam Zain al-Abidin who succeeded him. The Zaidi Shi'as are found mostly in the Yemen. Similarly, the Isma'ili Shi'as believe that it was Isma'il who succeeded Imam J'afar al-Sadiq, whereas the Ithna Asharis believe that it was Musa Kazim who became Imam after Imam Ja'far al-Sadiq. The chain of Imam as far as the Ithna Asharis are concerned stopped with the seclusion of the 12th imam whose reappearance is awaited by them. And as far as the Isma'ilis are concerned the office of imam continued in the progeny of Isma'il and the 21st Imam Taiyyib went into seclusion. But unlike the Ithna Asharis the Isma'ilis do not believe that 21st imam will reappear; they, on the other hand, believe that the imamah continues in his progeny and that the imam of the time from his progeny will appear one day. It is also to be noted that the Isma'ilis also split on the question of succession of imam after Imam Mustansir Billah. A section of the Isma'ilis believed that Mustansir had nominated his younger son Must'ali as his successor and the other section believed that Nizar, his elder son, was nominated as Mustansir's successor. And Imam Taiyyib belongs to the Must'alian stream.

Here in this Chapter we will be dealing mainly with the interpretation of the Qur'an by the Isma'ilis before the split between the Musta'lians and the Nizaris. The Druzes are also basically Isma'ilis and will deal with them in a separate chapter. The Druzes split off from the Isma'ilis after the death of Imam Hakim. The Druzes developed their own interpretation of the Qur'an which again radically differs from the mainstream Isma'ilis.

The Isma'ilis, like all other Shi'as believe in the hidden meaning of the Qur'an which they refer to as *ta'wil*. In the *tafsir* literature of Sunni Islam the words *tafsir* and *ta'wil* are used almost synonymously. But in the Shi'a Islam both have distinct meaning. *Tafsir* in Shi'a Islam refers to the manifest meaning of the Qur'an and *ta'wil* refers to its hidden meaning. The Sunnis and Shi'as differ on the meaning of the sixth verse of the Chapter three, i.e., the chapter on 'Ali Imran'. According to the Sunni commentators this verse means that, "None knows its interpretation (*ta'wil, i.e., the hidden meaning*) save Allah and the *rasikhun fi' al'ilm* (i.e., those firmly rooted in knowledge) say: We believe in it, it is all from our Lord." Thus, according to the Sunni commentators of the Qur'an Allah alone has the knowledge of *ta'wil* and the *Rasikhun fi' al-'ilm* (the great 'ulama) do not possess that knowledge and they only believe that it is known only to Allah.

The Shi'as, believe that the knowledge of *ta'wil* is possessed by the *al-rasikhun fi' al-'ilm* also and these *rasikhun* in *'ilm* are nothing, but the imams from the progeny of Fatima and 'Ali. Not only Allah, but the holy Prophet, his legatee (*wasi*) and imams from his progeny also possess the knowledge of *ta'wil*. Now the most important question is what is this *ta'wil*? In the Isma'ili literature it is also referred to as *'ilm al-ladunni* which passes orally from Prophet to his *wasi* and from *wasi* to imam and from one imam to another.

But, if we go historically then one finds the exposition of *ta'wil* literature much later, i.e., during the Abbasid period, in fact, after the controversy about the appointment of Isma'il and the subsequent split in the Shi'a community. The hidden meaning of the Qur'anic verses is attempted by the Isma'ili imams and da'is (i.e., missionaries and summoners to the Isma'ili faith) after the spread of Greek knowledge in the Islamic world. We have already written about *The Rasa'il Ikhwanus Safa*, i.e., the Epistles of the Brethren of Purity in a separate chapter. These epistles are of great importance in the Isma'ili literature. Though, these epistles do not attempt exposition of *ta'wil* systematically, but do contain elements of it and could be taken as the beginning of the exposition of the discipline of *ta'wil*. Its fifty-third epistle supposedly deals with this.

The Isma'ili da'is particularly Saiyyidna Yaqub al-Sijistani, Saiyyidna Ja'far Mansur al-Yaman, Saiyyidna Qadi al-Nu'man, Saiyyidna Hamiduddin Kirmani, Saiyyidna Muayyad Shirazi, Saiyyidna Hatim, and several others have played great role in developing this unique discipline. It will be no exaggeration to say that *'ilm al-ta'wil* is really unique to the Isma'ili sect and it was a grand attempt to synthesize the all available knowledge of the time—particularly the Greek knowledge popularized by the Abbasids through, translations of the Greek classics into Arabic— with the Islamic teachings.

Of course the Isma'ilis believe that the *'ilm* of *ta'wil* did not develop with the popularization of the Greek knowledge, but is part of the *'ilm al-nubuwwat* (i.e., the prophetic knowledge) passed on from imam to imam as referred to earlier. But, historically speaking we do not find its record before the Epistles of *Ikhwanus Safa* were compiled. One can say that this knowledge of *ta'wil* among the Isma'ilis was reduced to writing only when faced with the challenge of the Greek knowledge. Ash'aris among the Sunnis met this challenge by totally opposing the Greek philosophy (though, using its tools to refute it) while the Isma'ilis among the Shi'as met this challenge by attempting a creative synthesis of the Greek knowledge including its cosmogony with the basic teachings of Islam. Thus, the Ash'aris and the Isma'ilis carved out different ways of meeting the challenge of the Greek philosophy and its great impact on the Islamic world. This impact should not be underrated.

The Ismai'ili *ta'wil* is based on reason. The word *ta'wil* in Arabic means to go to the first, primary or basic meaning of the word. According to the Isma'ilis each and every verse of the Qur'an has basic meaning or hidden meaning apart from the manifest or secondary meaning. According to them a *mu'min* is one who knows and believes in the hidden or original meaning (*batin*) of the Qur'anic verses. The Isma'ilis maintain that there is difference between a Muslim and a *Mu'min*. One who recites the *kalima* and performs all the manifest rituals (*zahiri*) like offering prayers, fasting, giving zakat, performing *Haj*, etc., is a Muslim. But a *mu'min* is more than being a Muslim. A *Mu'min* is one who not only performs the *zahiri* rituals, but also believes in *batin*, the real, the original, the intended, meaning of these rituals.

The Isma'ilis quote the verse 14 of the Chapter 49 which reads as follows: "The dwellers of the desert say: We believe (*amanna*). Say: You believe not, but say, We submit (*aslamna*); and faith (*iman*) has not, yet, entered into your hearts". Thus, this verse, the Isma'ili theologians point out, clearly makes distinction between Islam and Iman, between those who submit, Muslims and those who believe Mu'min. Iman, according to them is not mere acceptance of what is manifest *zahir*, but sincere belief in *batin* (the hidden, the original).

Before we proceed further, it is necessary to throw light on what is *batin* or what is the way *ta'wil* is done? It is also important to note that ordinary people are not supposed to know the original meaning or the *ta'wil*. It is only the chosen few or the initiated who are entitled to know. The contents of *ta'wil* was kept a strictly guarded secret even from ordinary believers. The reason was obvious. The Isma'ilis were looked upon as heretics by the orthodox Muslims. Imam Ghazali also wrote a book on *Batinis* and condemned them. They were accused of believing in *hulul* and *tanasukh*, i.e., belief in Imam being God and transmigration of souls, though it is not true. Even Dr. Kamil Husain, who was chairman of the Department of Isma'ili Studies, Al-Azhar, Cairo, strongly refuted such allegations. But the Isma'ilis were greatly misunderstood about their real beliefs.

Previously the Isma'ilis, for fear of such condemnations had to hide their beliefs in *batini* theology from general Muslims and reveal it only to the chosen or initiated few. The knowledge of *batin* was revealed to a person only after ensuring his/her sincerity and faithfulness. Even today the ordinary Bohras do not have any knowledge of *ta'wil*, though there is no such fear as it prevailed in those days from the Sunni orthodox 'ulama.

According to the Isma'ilis there is whole ideal system called *mathal* and here on earth there is a corresponding system called *mamthul* (representative of the ideal). To understand this it is necessary to know that Allah is a totally transcendent Being who cannot be comprehended by human mind at all. He transcends everything conceivable and is just incomprehensible. He has no attributes whatsoever. He is also not actively involved in creation of the universe. He only created the *'uqul* (intellects made of pure light). The intellects are fine beings made of light. The matter, as opposed to light, is *kathif* (i.e., heavy and dark) Allah or the Ultimate Being has no role in creation of matter. He is referred to by Saiyyidna Yaqub al-Sijistani as *Mubd'i al-Mubdi'at* (the creator of the creators. His role ceased with creation of the *'Uqul* (the intellects). Allah created only light, not darkness. One cannot attribute creation of darkness and *kathafat* (heaviness) to Him.

Matter was created by the tenth intellect also called *'ashir-i-mudabbir* (the tenth intellect managing the universe). All the matter representing *kathafat* (heaviness and darkness). Since the tenth intellect (*'ashir-e-mudabbir*) is responsible for creation of matter and this universe, it is his responsibility to reconvert this darkness and heaviness into light (*nur*). The corresponding being on earth to the tenth intellect is the Prophet. Thus, the Prophet is the *mamthul* of *'ashir-e-mudabbir* on earth. He assists him (the tenth intellect) in transforming the *kathafat* (darkness and heaviness) into *latafat* (*nur*).

The Prophet shows the right path to the people and has been described by the Qur'an as *sirajan munirah* (i.e. the lighted lamp) for this reason. He transforms the human beings into light (*nur*). After the Prophet it is the Imam who performs this function. And as there cannot be any Prophet after Muhammad (PBUH), he is succeeded by Imams from the progeny of Fatima, his daughter and 'Ali, her husband. According to the Isma'ili beliefs this earth can never remain without Imam, a spiritual guide, an active agent (*mamthul* of *Ashir-e-Mudabbir*) on earth. An Isma'ili da'i wrote an epistle *Ithbat-ul-Imamah* to prove this.

Thus, Imam on earth is the representative of the tenth intellect and hence, commands highest respect of the believers. He has all the attributes of the tenth intellect and since Allah has no attributes (He transcends all attributes and is beyond them), these attributes apply to the Tenth Intellect. Therefore, Imam who is *mamthul* of the Tenth intellect on earth also has these attributes on earth. It is this theory of attributes which was misunderstood by the opponents of the Fatimi Imams as the belief in *hulul*, i.e., descent of God into the person of Imam. Dr. Kamil Husain has discussed this in detail in his *Muqaddimah* (introduction) to the Diwan of Saiyyidna Mua'yyad Shirazi. The person of Imam does not correspond to Allah, but to the tenth intellect, as pointed out above.

The Isma'ilis (also referred to as the Fatimids or those following the Fatimi Da'wah) also believe in the cyclical theory of history. Since it is the duty of the tenth intellect to covert total darkness and *kathafat* in the universe into light in every cycle of history a portion of darkness is reconverted into light and these cycles will continue until entire matter is reconverted into *nur* (light) and there is no more *kathafat* in this universe.

In every cycle an Adam is created and the chain of Prophethood ends with the last Prophet who is in turn succeeded by imams and lastly, in every cycle there appears what is known as *Qa'im al-Qiyamah* (i.e., one who brings about the Day of Judgement, the *Qiyamat*). The cycle ends with the *Qa'im al-Qiyamah* and a definite portion of dark matter is converted into light in that cycle. Thus, according to this theory, these cycles will continue until there is no more matter in this universe and all matter therein is transformed into *latafat*, i.e., light and it is light which will ultimately prevail. This, in short, is the Isma'ili cyclical theory of history of this universe.

Some of the important books of *ta'wil* and *batini 'ulum* are the *Kitab al-Shawahid wa al-Bayan* of Saiyyidna Mansur al-Yaman, *Ta'wil al-Da'a'im* of Saiyyidna Qadi al-Nu'man *Rahat al-'Aql* by Saiyyidna Hamiduddin Kirmani, *Al-Majalis* of Saiyyidna Mua'yyad Shirazi, etc. These books contain the highest achievements of the Isma'ili or Fatimi missionaries as far as the knowledge of *batin* is concerned. We will give some examples of *'ilm al-ta'wil* from these books.

Saiyyidna Qadi al-Nu'man who compiled the celebrated book of Isma'ili jurisprudence *Al-Da'a'im al-Islam*, also compiled *Ta'wil al-Da'a'im*. In this latter work Qadi Nu'man describes the original meanings of all the elements of shari'ah and all the related rituals. Qadi Nu'man first emphasises that a true believer has to strike balance between the *zahir* and *batin* i.e., what is manifest and what is original intent of the shari'ah rituals. Qadi Nu'man had to lay this emphasis on the balance between *zahir* and *batin* because some extremists among the Isma'ilis had declared that the shari'ah is suspended (*ta'til al-shari'ah*) and it is no more necessary to observe the external rituals for those who know *'ilm al-batin*. The Qaramitah, an extremist sect of the Isma'ilis had ceased to observe the *zahiri shari'ah*. The Nizaris later did the same.

The Isma'ilis, as pointed out in an earlier paper, believe in seven pillars of Islam as opposed to other Muslims who believe in five pillars. The two additional pillars are *walayah* (the love of the family of the Prophet—*ahl al-bayt*) and *taharah* (cleanliness). *Taharah* really means spiritual cleanliness and removal of all spiritual pollutants. The Qadi describes in his *Ta'wil al-Da'a'im* the hidden meaning of all the seven *da'a'im*, (pillars) one by one.

The very first pillar according to the Isma'ilis is *walayat* (love of the family of the Prophet). According to the Qadi each pillar represents one of the great prophets from Adam to Muhammad. Adam represents *walayah*. Adam was the first Prophet whose *walayah* was made obligatory on the angels and the angels were made to prostrate before him or perform *sajdah* before him. *Sajdah* in reality implies obedience. And this is *walayah*. Adam's *walayah* is the *walayah* of all the succeeding Prophets and Imams. Those who do not have love of Adam cannot achieve salvation.

The second pillar, according to the Isma'ili theology, is *taharah* (i.e., purity). The second Prophet Nuh (Noah) represents *taharah*. Nuh was sent for purification of mankind. Whatever sins were committed during and after Adma's time Nuh came to purify them and he is one of the great prophets, a prophet with his own shari'ah. The flood water which is associated with Nuh, symbolizes purity as water is needed for purity from dirt and water in *batin* means *'ilm* (knowledge of ultimate reality) and it is through knowledge that spiritual purity can be attained.

And the third pillar is *Salah* (prayer) and Qadi Nu'man ascribes it to the prophet Ibrahim. It is he who constructed *Baytullah* the House of Allah in Mecca and Allah made this House the *Qiblah* (the direction in which the Muslims turn to pray). Hazrat Ibrahim also has great status among the prophets and he is also described as *hanif* in the holy Qur'an, i.e., one who is inclined towards truth.

And it is the prophet Musa who represents *zakat*. He is the first prophet who is said to have asked Pharaoh (Fir'aun) to purify himself (*tazakka* (see the verse 79:16). Musa was the first prophet whom Allah called upon to preach to Fir'aun purity of self (*tazkiyah*). Zakat has essentially to do with purification. It is through *zakat* that one purifies ones wealth by giving away one portion of it to the needy and poor.

The *saum* (fasting) is related to the prophet Isa (Christ). *Saum* in *ta'wil* actually means keeping silent about the *batin* (i.e., hidden truth of the injunctions of shari'ah). It was Isa's mother Mariyam (Mary) who was asked by Allah to say to her people that, "I have vowed a fast to the Beneficent, so I will not speak to any man today." (19:26). Thus, it will be seen that in this verse fasting is directly related to keeping silent (about the knowledge of *batin*).

Similarly *Haj* is related to the last of the prophets Muhammad (PBUH). It is he who first required Muslims to perform *Haj* and expounded all its related *manasik* (i.e., rituals pertaining to *Haj*). Though the Arabs used to perform *Haj* before Islam, but the *manasik* appointed by Allah in the Qur'an did not exist. Allah says about the pre-Islamic Arabs and their prayer near the Ka'bah, "And their prayer at the House is nothing, but whistling and clapping of hands." (8:35). And the disbelievers used to circumambulate around Ka'bah in a state of nakedness. It is the holy Prophet who abolished such abominable practice. They had also installed idols all around Ka'bah whom they used to worship. It is Prophet Muhammad who demolished these idols. He then appointed the rituals for the *Haj*.

And the last of the pillars of Islam is *jihad* and it is related to the seventh of the chain of imams. The Isma'ilis (or the Fatimids) give great importance to every seventh imam in the chain of Fatimi imams. The seventh imam is also called *natiq* (i.e., Speaker). Thus, every seventh imam will speak with the permission of Allah about His injunctions and give them a new interpretation through his exertions or through waging war to purify His religion. The Qa'im al-Qiyamah, referred to above, will also be the seventh of the chain of imams and he will be the last of the seventh imams and through him the imams will be unified on the shari'ah of the Prophet Muhammad. Thus, Prophet Muhammad has merit over all other prophets in the sense that two pillars of Islam—*Haj* and *jihad*—have been related to him and his progeny.

Saiyyidna Qadi Al-Nu'man in his *Ta'wil al-Da'a'im* lays great stress on *'ilm* (knowledge). *'Ilm* is very fundamental to the Isma'ili system. *'Ilm* is *wazir* (minister) to *iman* (faith). Faith draws sustenance through *'ilm* (knowledge). The Qadi says that *'ilm* applies to both *zahir* (manifest) and *batin* (hidden). Thus, a *mu'min* becomes true person of faith through *iman* and *'ilm*. As the human body can be purified only by water, the soul of a *mu'min* can be purified only by knowledge. And as *amwal* (material wealth) cannot be given to undeserving persons or those weak of understanding (*sufaha'* see verse 4:5), knowledge also cannot be imparted to those who do not deserve.

Thus, one who has been favoured by Allah through knowledge, he should not impart it to undeserving persons. In other words the knowledge of *batin* can be imparted only to deserving persons whose *iman* (faith) is strong and unwavering and it will become even more stronger through such knowledge. But, if it is imparted to undeserving person, his faith may be weakened and his doubts might increase. Also, one should not be miserly in imparting knowledge of *ta'wil* to deserving people and he should not be extravagant with the undeserving.

Prayer system (*salah*) in its essence means establishing the system of *da'wah*. Wherever the Qur'an speaks of *salah* it does not say 'read prayer', but says 'establish prayer' (*aqim al-salah*) which in fact means establish the *da'wah* headed by the imam who is, after the Prophet, the highest representative of the community of the faithfuls. As one is required to come to prayers at appropriate time, one is required to devote ones energy in establishing the *da'wah* (mission) at suitable times and make all possible efforts for it. As the soul enriches itself through prayers, a faithful enriches one self by his/her efforts to establish the mission for the faithfuls.

In short these are some of the prominent features of the Isma'ili *ta'wil*. In this brief essay we cannot do full justice to it. But an attempt has been made here to throw light on its essential features. The Fatimi Da'is have written hundreds of books on this subject which are available to the scholars. This essay can only initiate those interested in the subject.

CHAPTER 22

Reconstruction of Islamic Thought

How do we look at a religion? As a set of rituals, dogmas and institutions? Or as values and thought system? Some emphasize the former and others the latter. Generally the masses of people are more concerned with rituals dogmas and institutions whereas, the intellectuals lay more emphasis on thought system and values, particularly on the thought system. For the masses religion is nothing, but performance of certain rituals as laid down and to have belief in certain dogmas formulated by the learned scholars. For them anyone who deviates from performance of these rituals or questions against any of these dogmas is a 'heretic' worthy of condemnation.

The intellectuals may lay more emphasis on the thought system of a religion, but there are those who accept the thought system as inherited and there are those who are intellectually quite active and consider it necessary to rethink the thought system of the religion they have inherited. In a dynamic society, there are much greater possibilities of rethinking the thought system. In a stagnant or a closed society such possibilities are smothered. The early Islamic society was highly dynamic and full of vitalities. Islam was a great revolution, not only religious but, also social and economic. It had upturned all old ideas and ideologies. It gave human society a new value system and heightened the human sensitivity for change for the better. Islam put greater emphasis on change and called everything old into question. It encouraged people to rethink the beliefs of their ancestors. All that their ancestors believed in was not necessarily right and beneficial.

Thus, in early Islam change was never thought to be a 'sin' as it is today. The Qur'an laid great emphasis on *'ilm* as well as *'amal* (knowledge and practice). The Arab peninsula was an area of darkness in many ways. Only poetry was their passion. The other area of information they were proud of was what they called *ansab* (the family tree). For them the nobility (*sharf*) of ancestors was more important than their own. They were greatly proud of their ancestry. Islam changed all this. It brought about complete revolution in the Arabian mind set, which spread to other areas conquered by them. The emphasis was put on present and future, not on the past. The individual was brought at the centre, not the tribe. The individual was made responsible for everything, not the tribe one belonged to.

There was no quest for knowledge in the pre-Islamic Arabia. In fact any knowledge except that of ones tribal ancestry was derided upon. However, the Qur'an, put all the emphasis on *'ilm* (knowledge), which is a very comprehensive work in Arabic. *'Ilm* is used for science as well. It includes knowledge of everything created by Allah including the knowledge of creator himself. Allah invites human beings to think, to brood and to reflect on the whole universe, on the creations of Allah, the stars, the earth, the plants and the animals. Also, the Qur'an lays great emphasis on induction rather than deduction. The former leads to objective knowledge of the universe and latter to speculation. Modern science is based on induction rather than deduction.

Also, knowledge was given further practical orientation by laying equal emphasis on *'amal* (practice). *'Ilm* without *'amal* was projected as bereft of any benefit to humanity. Correct knowledge (*'ilm al-yaqin*) and healthy practice (*'amal salih*) is the most desirable synthesis. The word *'ilm al-yaqin* (i.e., knowledge with conviction) is of great value. It is thus, clear that the Qur'an neither encourages superficial knowledge nor allows its instrumentalization. Qur'an has been described as *hudan lil muttaqin,* i.e., a guide for the God fearing or the pious. Thus, the term *'ilm* is not only comprehensive but also value-oriented. Knowledge must not only be true, but should also be based on conviction; it should not only advance the state of information about the universe, but should also serve the humanity.

Similarly, *'amal* (practice) as pointed out above, has to be nothing, but *salih* (healthy). The practice, based on knowledge and conviction, must promote the health of society. The modern capitalist society often exploits knowledge for private gain. Knowledge as an industry for private gain is negation of all human values which leads humanity astray and hence condemnable. Such a knowledge and wrong practice (*'amal ghayr salih*) will be harmful to humanity and will distort all values. Knowledge *per se* is desirable but it should be essentially value-oriented in order to benefit the human society.

In Greece as well as in Persia, knowledge, at the time of rise of Islam, had become quite speculative and devoid of external observation. Such a knowledge may be useful in its own way, but it fails to advance our knowledge about the creation, of the universe. The Greek and Persian knowledge had, therefore, become stagnant and mere speculative exercises. The Qur'an, while not rejecting the importance of philosophy, speculation and knowledge of inner self, lays even more emphasis on objective knowledge which is even more beneficial to humanity.

What kind of revolution it was in a stagnant society of Arabian peninsula whose whole universe was its own tribe cannot be easily imagined by us today. It was nothing short of a total break from the past; a break which changed the whole quality of social life and brought about tremendous advancement in knowledge. The ritual system of Islam—*'ibadat*—was also not devoid of value-system. The French revolution had given important values to modern society—equality, fraternity and liberty. Islam had given these values to humanity much earlier and had devised its *'ibadat* (ritual system) to reflect these values and hence these rituals were also made part of *'amal salih* (practice leading to social health).

Take for example the prayer system (*salat*) of Islam. Since Islam's whole emphasis is on equality and dignity of all human beings and to create a society without any hierarchy, all Muslims have to stand in one line for prayer. In this there is absolutely no distinction of caste, race or social status. Since slavery was initially permitted by Islam (though, to be ultimately abolished) even their human dignity was duly recognized by making it obligatory on them to stand in one line with their masters. In this respect no discrimination was allowed between masters and slaves as both are human beings and both possess the same degree of human dignity.

Islam strictly forbade a human being prostrating before another human being, not even before the Prophet. It is only Allah before whom one could prostrate (perform *sajdah*). It is only unseen Allah who is the greatest and human rulers are His creation and hence equal to other human beings. Thus, Islam wipes out, in one sweep, all distinctions between the ruler and the ruled. Islam does not even recognize, let alone allow to be practised, the institution of monarchy.

Similarly, Islam does not accord any priority whatsoever to race, tribe, language, creed or colour. The Qur'an makes categorical statement to this effect (see 49:13 and 30:22). It also strictly forbade the Muslims from making any distinction between an Arabian and non-Arabian and a white and a black. The Prophet, in order to effectively demolish any such hierarchical distinctions, appointed a black liberated slave from Ethiopia, Bilal Habshi, to give *azan* (call Muslims to prayer), a distinction, many Arabians close to the Prophet, intensely desired. But the Prophet accorded this distinction to a black slave to emphasize the importance of equality of all human beings.

No social or political system had put so much importance to the idea of human dignity and equality until the French Revolution of 1789, i.e., until the close of eighteenth century. And as pointed out before, this concept of equality was also spiritualized by integrating it with the prayer system of Islam. Thus, equality found its place in the spiritual realm too. But it is a matter of shame that Muslims did not steadfastly adhered to this concept of equality and adopted the caste and other hierarchical systems including the institution of monarchy under alien influences. The Islamic teachings were discarded and yielded to other pressures.

The other slogan of the French Revolution was fraternity. The Prophet of Islam when migrated to Madinah devised the institution of *ukhuwwah* (fraternity) and made every Meccan migrant a brother of the Medinese Muslim. The Qur'an also declared that all faithfuls are brothers (49:10) and included women too in this category. The word *mu'minun*, as all commentators of the Qur'an agree, is inclusive of both sexes.

The third part of the French Revolution was 'liberty' which essentially means freedom of conscience. The Qur'an accepted this freedom of conscience as declared in the verse 2:256 and Chapter 109. It is, in fact, erroneous belief that Islam does not allow freedom of conscience.

It is again the later Muslim juristic formulations and practice which is responsible for such an impression. If one goes by the Qur'anic pronouncements it is crystal clear that freedom of conscience is quite central to the Qur'anic thought. In fact every individual is free to do what he or she likes and reward or punishment will entirely depend on individual actions. In the tribal universe of Arabia it was the tribe which decided individual actions denying him completely the freedom of conscience. However, Islamic revolution put individual at the centre, not the tribe or any other collectivity. The individual was made answerable for all his deeds—good or bad. It was a revolutionary step in a tribal society where individual was only a part of collectivity totally subordinate to it.

Also, as anthropologists tell us, in a tribal society the main fulcrum of knowledge is knowledge of received traditions and tribal customs. Any other knowledge which is not related to the tribe is totally meaningless. The ideas of cosmos, creation and all related notions originate from the tribal practices. The frontiers of knowledge, in other words, cannot transcend the boundaries of the tribal universe. Islam, however, broke these tribal boundaries and made knowledge coterminous with the universe, i.e., the entire creation of Allah.

It is also very interesting to note that the Arab world which had never known beyond tribal customs and traditions, became the forerunner in the world of jurisprudence. We may have several problems today with the Shari‘ah formulations. But, the *juris corpus* of Islam, was a highly progressive body of laws in those days. The French Revolution, as pointed out above, had talked of liberty, equality and fraternity, but had no reference to justice. Islam, made justice as central as equality, liberty and fraternity.

The notion of justice is very central to Islam (5:8). And it is justice in its absolute and varied sense. The Qur'anic notion of justice is quite comprehensive. No Muslim jurist could ever ignore the significance of justice in his legal formulations. But how justice was understood to have been done has of course been debatable. There may be arguments about how justice was thought to have been done in medieval ages and what is modern notion of justice. But that does not reduce the significance of justice as a Qur'anic doctrine. The relativity of medieval notion of justice and its modern notion is understandable.

The Qur'anic notion of justice was not tribal, but universal. And this made all the difference. The Qur'anic notion of justice is so universal that it laid down that even the enmity with any one else should not come in the way of dispensing justice (5:8). In a tribal society justice was confined within the tribal limits. There was no question of justice vis-a-vis other tribes. Islam lays down that justice be done even to an enemy. The Qur'an gives the principle of justice as a norm; the legal doctors applied it to various issues which arose from time to time, according to their own ability, understanding and socio-cultural background.

It is necessary to understand that it is justice which has to be rigorously applied to all the issues in framing laws. It is the very foundation of the *juris corpus* of Islam. It is more central than the corpus of laws inherited by us. As the legal doctors applied the notion of justice in keeping with their own circumstances we must rethink the issues in Shari'ah laws based on the notion of centrality of justice particularly in the sphere of family laws.

Here we would like to point out that the position of women in the Qur'an is not subordinate to that of man. Certain verses (like 4:34) are used selectively and out of context, to project subordination of women to men ignoring several other verses (like 2:228, 9:71, 33:35 and others) which clearly indicate equality of men and women. The verses 9:71 and 33:35 are quite central in this respect. In verse 9:71 men and women are not only shown each others friends, but also charged with equal responsibilities of enjoining good and forbidding evil, keeping up prayer and paying the poor-rate (*zakat*). How could then women be inferior to men?

Thus, we should not hesitate in having a second look at the Shari'ah laws which have inbuilt medieval biases towards women. The Qur'an accord equal dignity to men and women. Prior to Islam even great Greek philosophers thought that animal and women have no soul and hence women deserve no legal rights. Women could not inherit, let alone holding property in her own right, even in Roman law, prior to Islam.

The spirit of the Qur'an is more important than the opinions of medieval legal doctors and hence, entire corpus of Shari'ah laws in this regard should be re-examined and re-thought. Also, as pointed out in some of my books (*Rights of Women in Islam, The Qur'an, Women and Modern Society* and *Status of Women in Islam*) there never was unanimity on these issues among the legal doctors themselves. The opinions differed from one legal doctor to another and on several issues even the disciples differed from their masters. While some legal doctors do not even admit women's evidence on *hudud* matters, others, like Imam Abu Hanifa, maintain that a woman can even become *qadi* on the basis of verse 9:71. The Shari'ah laws as formulated by early Muslim *fuqaha'* (legal doctors) need to be thoroughly reviewed. The centrality of justice must be asserted.

Knowledge, as pointed out above, was quite central to Islam. Some of the 'ulama', however, confined the knowledge to knowledge of *din* (i.e., religion of Islam). But there is no strong evidence in the Qur'an or sunna in this respect. It is a product of theologians' own mind. Since theologians were primarily concerned with religious or theological matters, they tried to confine knowledge to theological issues alone. Imitating these theologians many people still argue that *'ilm* should be confined to the *'ilm al-din* and reject other spheres of knowledge. But this view is no more a central view in the world of Islam today.

In fact this view that knowledge in the Qur'an is confined to the knowledge of *din* did not go uncontested even in the early history of Islam. Knowledge from different sources and from different fields was not only accepted by early Muslims, but was also creatively advanced by them. The entire corpus of Greek knowledge in various sciences, mathematics and philosophy was transferred into Arabic language and passed on to Europe. No wonder than that H.G. Wells, the noted British historian, has described Arabs as foster father of knowledge. The Europe had lost contact with the Greek treasure of knowledge and they re-established contact with it only through the agency of Arabs. The House of Wisdom (Bait al-Hikmah) established by the Abbasids fulfilled this task.

The Muslims assimilated this knowledge and also enriched it immensely. Their own contribution in enriching the Greek knowledge acquired by them was no mean contribution. Also, they imbibed knowledge from other sources as well, i.e., Persian and Indian sources, besides their own Islamic sources. The Mu'tazila were a party of rationalists who gave primacy to reason. For them reason was the test of faith and not vice versa. Thus, if reason holds something good, Shari'ah will also hold it good. The Asha'irah, on the other hand, held something good, because Shari'ah held it good even if reason contradicted it.

The Mu'tazila also gave primacy to justice along with reason. This is what the modern rationalists also plead. Thus, the Mu'tazilah were as fervent advocates of reason and justice as the modern rationalists are. But the modern rationalists tend to be atheists which Mu'tazilah were not. Mu'tazilah were also known as the party of *tawhid wa al-'adl* (party of unity of Godhood and justice). Thus, Mu'tazilah were essentially theists, but also rationalists.

Islam, as all of us know, had arisen in Arabian peninsula and had its vitality and practicability. Practical rationality remained quite central to it. But when it spread to the ancient centres of great cultures like parts of Eastern Byzantian empire, or Persian empire and India, it was confronted with entirely different mindset. These great civilizations were based, as pointed out before, on speculative reason and sophisticated intellectual achievements. This had both positive and negative impact on Islamic thought.

The Islamic thought became inward looking and lost some of its most fundamental concerns like justice for weaker sections of society. These centres of civilization were centres of feudal culture and along with feudal sophistication, feudal values were also imbibed. Thus, what Islamic thought gained in swing, lost in its sweep. Islam spread with great rapidity because of its great concern with justice for weaker sections of society, but now it became an integral part of a huge Islamic empire and nearly lost its sensitivity towards suffering of the downtrodden of the society.

The Qur'an which was so direct and simple in its teachings, became a target for exercises in sophisticated inner meanings justifying hierarchical values which came to be acquired through feudal cultures of Roman and Persian empires. Monarchy became an acceptable institution and blind and uncritical obedience to the ruling monarch and religious establishment of the time, became very common. Disobedience to them was construed to be disobedience to Allah and His Book. The earlier critical faculty and concern for justice was totally lost. It was in this atmosphere that Islamic thought became totally stagnant and part of oppressive establishment. There is great need to recapture its earlier vitality, dynamism and sensitivity. Critical evaluation, and not blind obedience, is closer to the Islamic spirit. What predominates today, however, is Islamic theological thought, and, the age-old Shari'ah formulation, on the other. It has made Islamic thought totally stagnant.

What is to be noted is that, what goes in the name of theology is human construct and divine commandments as understood by human agency under a set of socio-cultural influences. For example, *'Ilm al-Kalam* (Islamic dialectics) came into existence as a reaction to the widening influence of Greek philosophy and sciences during the Abbasid period. This became an integral part of Islamic theology. *Kalam*, undoubtedly influenced the great minds of Islamic world of the time and also the succeeding generation for several centuries. But now *Kalam* cannot be treated as unchangeable and reified. There is urgent need for a new *ilm al-kalam* in the light of modern corpus of scientific knowledge.

A religion consists of several sub-systems like ritual system (*'ibadat*), institutional system (like *zakat*, *'ushr*, etc.), thought system and value system (like equality, justice, compassion, etc.). Of these, ritual and value systems are permanent and cannot be changed under any circumstances. But the thought system could and must change, if religion has to keep pace with time. There is misconception among Muslims about the Qur'anic verse 5:3 (i.e., This day have I perfected for you your religion and completed My favour to you...). They think that now what we have inherited is perfect in every respect and there is no need for rethinking in any sense at all. Our *din* is perfect. The *din* is undoubtedly perfect, but the meaning and significance of *din* should be understood properly. One cannot include the *kalam*, for example, in *din*. The Islamic thought system has been evolved by theologians who are human beings and no human person can ever be perfect. Human beings think under certain influences, which they cannot transcend as human beings. All divine commands are sought to be understood by human agents under certain socio-cultural influences and these influences are reflected in the religious-thought system. Once we understand this there will be no resistance to change in the thought system. This will bring about a great revolution.

The Islamic *shari'ah* is also an embodiment of Islamic values. Islamic *shari'ah* is nothing, but a sincere attempt by the *fuqaha'* (Islamic jurists) to apply divine commands and the Islamic values to a number of issues like marriage, divorce, inheritance, nature of evidence, crimes like theft, rape, adultery, division of property, etc. This attempt to approach these issues in the light of Islamic values and divine commands was also influenced by the socio-cultural circumstances of the time. They could not have applied Islamic values and divine commands to these issues in vacuum. There is great deal of change in these external influences and hence, many of these *shari'ah* formulations stand in need of change. This change does not amount to tempering with the divine commands, but yet making, another human attempt in the light of our own experiences and circumstances.

If we evolve this understanding of religion the dynamics of problem changes and religion will be an even greater force to bring about spiritual transformation for the better. Naturally, there will be differences in opinion while bringing about these changes. We should not be afraid of differences. These differences, if honest and sincere, provide greater vigour to human thought. The founders of the different schools of jurisprudence during the second and third centuries of Islam were not afraid of differences. Why should we be?

CHAPTER 23

WHAT I BELIEVE

I have completed sixty-one years of life in March, 2000 and I thought it was time to state what my beliefs are. I have spent many years reflecting on various issues related to philosophical and spiritual nature, which kept me troubling for long. I was born in a Bohra orthodox priestly family. The Bohras are Shi'ah Isma'ili Muslims. My father was a learned scholar of Islam and served the establishment of the Bohra head priest who holds the office of Da'i and popularly known as 'Saiyyidna' (i.e., our Lord).

My father, who was firm believer in the Shi'ah-Isma'ili Islam had somewhat open mind and showed great patience when persons of other persuasions entered into dialogue with him. In my childhood a Hindu Brahmin priest used to come and have talks with my father and both used to exchange views on each others beliefs. I was brought up in this religious environment. My father taught me Arabic and also *tafsir* (commentary on the holy Qur'an), *hadith* (reports on sayings and doings of the holy Prophet) and *fiqh* (Islamic jurisprudence).

He also sent me to a municipal school and saw to it that I acquire modern secular knowledge. In fact he persuaded me to go for either engineering or medical course but I chose to opt for a degree course in civil engineering and later chose to settle down in Mumbai where my father joined me.

I have seen exploitation in the name of religion from very close quarter since my father was a Bohra priest himself. He inwardly resented this exploitative system strongly, but found himself helpless as he had no alternate means of livelihood. He had to serve the system or starve or even face severe persecution as I discovered later when I challenged the system. There was no trace of spiritualism in the Bohra priestly system. The system was nothing, but a huge machinery for collection of money from its followers and which was controlled by one priestly family of the Da'i. This machinery had total grip over the life of a Bohra. An ordinary Bohra lived in the fear of the system. Any trace of disobedience could ruin his/her life. The vice-like grip of the Bohra priestly establishment over the lives of ordinary Bohras had reduced them to mere slaves.

I, therefore, came to the conclusion at an early age that an organized religion can become totally subservient to the powerful vested interests. It no longer remains a means of enriching inner spiritual life, but only an instrument of exploitation and servitude to vested interests. Thus when I read and reread the Qur'an I was more and more convinced that the real purpose of religion is to enrich inner life and to seek closeness to God. The Qur'an emphasizes that it is in remembrance of Allah that ones heart finds inner peace (13:28). There are several such verses in the Qur'an which strongly emphasize the richness of spiritual life.

The gross exploitation, which I saw at close quarter in my childhood and also part of adult life made me seriously rethink the fundamentals of religion. I also read avidly literature on rationalism in Urdu, Arabic and English. I also read writings of Niyaaz Fatehpuri—a noted Urdu writer and a critic of religious orthodoxy when I was studying in my first year of inter-science. It was that time that I also read writings of Bertrand Russell, a rationalist Brtisih philosopher. I also studied the Das Capital of Marx. Though I was influenced by the writings of these great thinkers I never ceased to study the Qur'an and its *tafsir* by great scholars of Islam. It is during that period that I read Sir Syed's and Maulana Azad's commentaries also. I also delved deep into *Rasa'il khwanus Safa* believed to have been compiled by the Isma'ili Imams during the period of their concealment in late eighth century AD. It is the philosophical tract of great significance and has been described by scholars as an encyclopaedic work. These epistles of the Brethren of Purity (*Ikhwanus Safa*) are great works of synthesis of reason and revelation. I also kept on studying the science of *ta'wil* (the inner meaning of the Qur'anic verses developed by the Isma'ili scholars).

All this combined gave me a new vision of life and its meaning. I came to the conclusion that reason is very crucial for human intellectual development, but not sufficient. Revelation is also a very important source of guidance and inner development. Reason plays very crucial role in human life and its significance can never be underestimated, but it has obvious limits and cannot answer the ultimate questions regarding the ultimate meaning and direction of life. It is revelation, which is more helpful in this respect. I also came to believe that revelation cannot be contradictory to reason as many would like to believe. Revelation can and does go beyond reason but does not contradict it. Dr. Mohammad Iqbal, the noted poet-philosopher, has also thrown light on this question in his *Reconstruction of Religious Thought in Islam*.

A careful study of the Qur'an makes it very clear that revelation in no way is contradictory to reason. Both, in fact, are complementary to each other and one is incomplete without the other. While reason helps us understand the physical aspects of this universe (whole development of natural sciences depends on human intellect), revelation helps us find the ultimate answers to our origin and destination. While reason is an important source of enrichment of our material life, revelation is necessary for our spiritual growth.

I believe that religion is an instrument and not a goal and like any instrument it can both be used and misused. It has often been misused by the vested interests to serve their own ends. This is what led many rationalists to believe that religion is not only unnecessary for human beings, but also a great obstacle in the way to progress. It was because those, who controlled religious establishment, opposed any change as change threatened their interests.

I believe that religion should not be equated with superstitions and dogmas. Each age has its own superstitions and with progress of science these superstitions are called in question. An honest intellectual quest is very vital not only for material progress, but also for healthy spiritual life. Superstitions thrive in the absence of knowledge and enrichment of knowledge punctures superstitious beliefs and it is an ongoing process.

I believe that dogmas are product of human urge for security rather than that of spiritual quest for inner certitude. Dogmas can satisfy only those who have given up any quest for intellectual and spiritual growth. Ghalib, the noted Urdu poet of nineteenth century India, describes dogma in a very picturesque manner as 'reflection of repetition of desire (for security)' and 'a refuge of the tired mind'. I fully endorse this view and feel that a dogma negates the very spirit of quest, which is inculcated by the inner urge to know the truth. Dogmas do lead to a sense of mental security for many, but it brings about total stagnation in their life.

I believe that there is vital difference between urge for mental security by believing in dogmas and search for inner certitude, which is the result of faith in higher spiritual values. The Qur'an calls this inner certitude *imaan*, which is usually translated as 'faith'. This inner certitude, I believe, is highly necessary for healthy spiritual growth of human beings. This should not be confused with belief in dogmas. The two are qualitatively different. While one leads to stagnation of intellectual and spiritual life, the other is vital for its growth. The sense of commitment is also born as a result of this inner certitude. The absence of which these can lead to mere scepticism and cynicism and paralyze the urge for any positive action.

Inner certitude is a must for action. A human being will act with enthusiasm only when one possesses the quality of inner confidence about his/her action. It is this inner strength which inspires a person to make great sacrifices for higher causes. Life acquires great sense of dynamism because of this inner conviction (*imaan* in the language of the Qur'an). In all ages human beings have been inspired by this sense of inner certitude to act to renew and reconstruct the world. Any noble act, even an act to defend ones country or to fight against corruption, or to work for the upliftment of the weaker sections of the society or to bring about revolution requires the state of inner certitude. It makes action itself its own reward and that is why people make sacrifices, even if immediate success is not in sight. Only those who look for material benefit act in the expectation of immediate result and not on account of their conviction.

I believe that dogmatism is not only associated with religion, but it is an attitude of mind rather than a set of immutable beliefs. One can find dogmatism in any sphere of life including social, political and cultural. Even rationalists can be dogmatists and many of them actually are. It is as difficult to discuss with them with an open mind on religion as with any person with orthodox views. I also distinguish between 'dogmatism' of common people and that of many learned scholars. The common people tend to be more 'dogmatic' because they need some firm beliefs and a sense of certainty rather than an attitude of mind or because of some interests associated with it. The scholars or educated orthodox believers defend religious dogmas not because of inner conviction, but more because of either laziness of mind or some interests associated with it. Whatever it is to hold on to dogmas results in negativity rather than positivity.

I believe that any act, which leads to general good of the human beings is a spiritual act. The Prophet of Islam is reported to have said that to feed a hungry soul is more meritorious than praying throughout the night. He is also reported to have said that the angels do not descend in a locality where people are starving. Thus, the real spirituality lies in serving the people, in fact serving the whole creation. Therefore, the act to protect environment from destruction is also a spiritual act. It is only in proper environment that life—whether it be human, animal or plant—can thrive. Any act to destroy the environment is an irreligious act.

I believe that religious sectarianism is very harmful and is a negative attitude. It is based on the view that what one believes is final and the only truth and what others' believe is based on falsity and is the root cause of sectarian conflicts. One should have a open mind, and respect the integrity and sincerity of other believers. I even believe that one who cannot respect others' beliefs is not capable of having genuine respect for his own beliefs. Respecting others beliefs is more important than mere tolerance.

I, therefore, believe that change of conviction should also be respected. It is more often than not, a result of quest for truth. I, therefore, strongly believe that every individual must have a right to convert to any other religion or point of view without let or hindrance. Those who penalize others or attack others for change of conviction are far from defenders of their own faith. Therefore, I believe that the fanatics and fundamentalists do more harm to their own religion than to that of others. A true lover of his own religion will always respect others faith. Deep and true conviction of ones own faith would never evoke hatred and disrespect for others' Belief.

I believe that religious authoritarianism is more worse than political authoritarianism though both are equally condemnable. Political authoritarianism leads to suppression of freedom of expression; religious authoritarianism, stunts the growth of spiritual life, evokes hatred and contempt for others and totally destroys true spirit of commitment to higher values. Similarly combination of wealth and religion on one hand and that of political power and religion on the other, is destructive of all. Both power and wealth not only corrupts, but also produces arrogance which leads to oppression. That is why the Holy Qur'an strongly condemns Pharoa who represents arrogance of power (*istikbar*) and supports Moses who symbolizes liberation from oppression and sensitivity towards sufferings of weaker sections of society (*istid'af*).

I believe that one who is truely religious is highly sensitive towards others sufferings, particularly sufferings of the weaker sections of society. Thus the feeling of compassion is very fundamental to being religious. In all religious traditions, particularly in Buddhist and Islamic traditions God is embodiment of compassion. No one who lacks compassion and sensitivity towards others sufferings can ever claim to be a full human being, let alone a religious person.

I believe that the Qur'an emphasizes four most important teachings without which, one cannot be a good Muslim. These are '*adl, ihsan, rahmah* and *hikmah*, i.e., justice, benevolence, compassion and wisdom. Thus, a person must in order to be a good human being. Mere performance of certain rituals cannot qualify one for being a spiritual person. One must inculcate these qualities.

I believe that a truely religious person is quite subversive of the unjust established order. One who supports an unjust order, or remains silent in view of gross injustices is, in my opinion, not at all a religious person. It amounts to collusion with the oppressors and exploiters. A religious person must continue to wage *jihad* against all forms of exploitation and injustices. Even a religious establishment can become highly oppressive and one must fight against such oppressive religious establishment. One who compromises with such establishment pollutes his/her own soul and does so either out of fear or lust for power. Both fear and lust for power destroy human sensibilities. Fear leads to cowardice and lust towards insensitivity and oppression and exploitation.

I believe in non-violence and totally oppose any form of violence. Resort to violence is destructive of all human values. Violence could be the last expedient in once own defence. Even defensive violence should not be treated as a licence to kill. If one cannot create life, then he has no right to destroy it. The respect for life is the rudiment of human sensitivity. In my opinion violence should not be used licentiously,

even for liberative purposes. The liberative violence soon degenerates
into oppressive violence. Once you take up a gun you do not want to
lay it down. Gun empowers you and you want to enjoy that power over
others.

Liberative violence soon results in killing spree against ones' own
revolutionary colleagues. The history is full of such instances. Be it
French revolution or Russian revolution, though they were undoubtedly
liberative, resulted in needless killings of hundreds of thousands of
innocent people. It is true that hunger and deprivation (of basic
necessities or even of freedom) are form of violence, but violence
perpetrated by weapons is any time worse than that of hunger and
deprivation. Any social or economic order based on violence cannot
lead to a just order.

The extremists in Kashmir resorted to violence to achieve so-called
'azadi', but only ended in the death of more than 50,000 people either
at their own hands or at the hands of the army and security forces. And
they are nowhere near the objective. Democratic and peaceful methods,
though at times frustratingly long in yielding results, are much more
healthier for society and for the ultimate objective. I, therefore, strongly
believe in democratic transformation. Kashmir problem would have been
nearer to solution had the extremists not resorted to indiscriminate use
of violence. And same is true of North East and other parts of India.
The Khalistanis also killed a large number of innocent Sikhs and Hindus
in Punjab. The LTTE has killed thousands of innocent Tamils and
Sinhalas and has spread culture of violence through political killings.
And yet, the LTTE is nowhere near its goal of the Tamil Ellam. And
even, if such a goal is realized it will be highly oppressive and exploitative.
Violence destroys all human sensitivities and turns a human into an
insensitive killing monster.

Nuclear explosion is the worst crime against humanity. Nuclear
weapons have the highest potential for killing. No person with any
human sensibility would ever support a nuclear weaponization project
even in the name of security. All weapons can at best create only an
illusion of security, never a real security. Real security comes only
through peace and well-being of people. History also has proved time
and again that highly weaponized states, with discontented population,
collapsed like house of cards at the hands of much less powerful

attackers. Real movement should be to destroy all modern weapons, nuclear or otherwise and use resources for building peaceful and contented society throughout the world. Higher cultural values can be based only on culture of peace and non-violence. It is unfortunate that while we pay lip service to non-violence we glorify as 'heroes' those who waged wars and killed.

I strongly believe in pluralism and diversity. I believe that uniformity, be it of religious or political beliefs or of cultural practices, result only in suppressing human creativity. Human creativity can thrive only in the situation of freedom and diversity. Democratic freedom has meaning only if diversity is allowed to flower. Strict uniformity can and often does, lead to fascism. A truely democratic society can be promoted only if diversity is allowed to flower. I, therefore, believe in three 'ds', i.e., democracy, diversity and dialogue. It sustain and strengthen each other. If there is no diversity, then there can be no democracy and if there is no dialogue, diversity cannot be strengthened. Dialogue is the very spirit of religious and cultural diversity. A genuine dialogue can be conducted only in the spirit of democracy. Firstly, dialogue recognizes the right of others to believe what they think is based on their own inner convictions. Secondly, dialogue is conducted not to convert others to ones own viewpoint, but to understand others viewpoint. Also dialogue can be conducted only in a spirit of humility. I believe that while arrogance dictates dialogue discusses. In a democratic set-up differences should be resolved only through dialogue and discussion.

I believe in essential unity of all religions. The differences are more apparent than real. The Qur'an not only accepted the truth of all religions preceding it but also emphasized that it has not brought any new truth, but has come to confirm the truth that exists. I accept the Upanishadic doctrine that reality is one, but its manifestations are many. I believe that all religions are source of highest and most exalted values and these values are more fundamental to these religions than their rituals and theological doctrines.

Every major religion be it Hinduism, Buddhism, Jainism, Judaism, Christianity, Islam or Sikkhism, emphasizes certain values which, compliment rather than contradict each other. For example, Hinduism and Jainism emphasize non-violence; Buddhism emphasizes compassion, Christianity love and Islam equality and justice. All these values are complementary to each other and hence, supportive of each other. The rivalries between these religions are promoted by those who control respective religious establishments. Those who do not aspire to control religious establishments do not promote any hostility against others. For example, the Sufis and Bhakti saints who were more interested in spiritual exercises and never aspired to control any religious establishments and hence, they did not involve themselves in religious polemics. They showed respect towards each other.

I believe that religious plurality enriches spiritual life and promotes human creativity. God is the creator of this plurality and hence, those who seek to destroy it act against His will. Thus, a truely religious person should have liberal disposition and should be far from being fanatical about his beliefs. He should accept plurality as a boon from God. Each religion has made a unique contribution to human culture and civilization through its own spiritual milieu, theological concepts and value-orientation.

I, therefore, totally reject the theory of clash of civilizations and believe that it is not civilizations, but barbarians who clash. There can be power struggle between those who aspire to control one or the other civilizational-based institutions, but there can never be clash of civilizations. This doctrine has been formulated deliberately to promote Western hegemony and should not be taken seriously. The peace-loving people belonging to different civilizations would refute such superficial doctrine by living in harmony and cooperative spirit with each other enriching human civilization as a whole.

I believe in unity of entire humanity and integrity of entire creation. If we love God we must love the entire universe. The Qur'an has described Allah as sustainer of entire universe *Rabb al-'Aalamin* and hence, it is our duty to submit humbly to the will of Allah and be His humble servant in maintaining and sustaining integrity of His creation.

CHAPTER 24

The Intra-Community Violations of Rights— The Bohra Case

The concept of perfect democracy can rarely be achieved in practice. In fact, if perfect form of democracy could be realized in practice the concept of religious or linguistic minority-majority also would be superfluous. Many scholars argue that in democracy there could be nothing like religious minority or majority, but only political minority or majority. The underlying assumption for such formulation of political minority-majority is that a perfect form of democracy is realizable. Human nature being what it is, nothing is realizable in its perfect form. Vested interests, prejudices and will to dominate always lead to 'majoritarianism'. The religious majority tries to dominate and deny religious or linguistic minorities their due.

It is for this reason that constitutional safeguards are provided to protect rights of racial, religious or linguistic minorities. All democratic constitutions make such provisions in greater or lesser degree. Only authoritarian societies might deny its minorities such rights and perpetuate domination by racial or religious or linguistic majorities of corresponding minorities. In fact it is a well-known fact that India got divided because a section of the Muslim minority could not be ultimately satisfied with respect to the constitutional arrangements to protect their political interests. Had such an arrangement been successfully negotiated our country would not have been divided.

It is also wrong on the part of some scholars to argue that Muslims are inherently separatist or that Islam requires that Muslims carve out a separate Islamic regime. Undoubtedly, there is a small fanatical section among the Muslims who keeps on arguing on these lines. But the reality is far more complex. Such a fanatical fringe does not reflect the whole reality, much less its central core. There are several examples that other

Rational Approach to Islam

non-Muslim minorities also have waged separatist struggles. Two examples are quite prominent in this respect—the Catholic Christian minority of the Southern Ireland refuses to be integrated with the Protestant Anglican Britain. The Catholics of the Southern Ireland has been waging struggle for more than sixty-five years for its separate existence. The second example is that of French Speaking minority of Canada, which feels suffocated within the English speaking Canada and often comes close to separation. Two years ago in a referendum, the unity of Canada came close to peril and could be saved only by one per cent vote. The minorities do have real or imaginary grievances and special provisions have to be made in the constitution to resolve them.

Though, a section of Muslims insisted on a separate homeland and got it, all Muslims in India were not in favour of vivisection of the country and after its vivisection refused to migrate and voted with their feet against creation of Pakistan. Thus, those Muslims who had remained behind had to be satisfied with proper constitutional provisions for their rights as a religious minority and to protect their identity and culture. The Constitution did make these provisions in the form of Articles from 25 to 30. The article 25 guarantees, "subject to public order, morality and health and to other provisions of this Part (Part III on fundamental rights), all persons are equally entitled to freedom of conscience and the right freely to profess, practice and propagate religion"

In fact this Article 25 is applicable to all citizens of India and is not applicable only to minorities. Nevertheless, it does provide a constitutional guarantee to minorities to "profess, practice and propagate their religion." It is, needless to say, very significant fundamental right available to all the citizens of India and to minorities, in particular. Similarly the Article 26 relates to freedom to manage religious affairs. This right relates to "establish and maintain institutions for religious and charitable purposes, to manage its own affairs to matters of religion, to own and acquire moveable and immoveable property; and to administer such property in accordance with law. And the Articles 29 and 30 relate to cultural and educational rights. The Article 29 empowers any section of citizen to conserve its distinct language, script or culture and that no citizen shall be denied admission into any educational institution maintained by the State or receiving aid out of State funds on grounds of religion, race, caste, language or any of them."

And finally the Article 30 guarantees "Right of minorities to establish and administer educational institutions." The Article states that "All minorities, whether based on religion or language, shall have the right to establish and administer educational institutions of their choice" and "the State shall not, in granting aid to educational institutions discriminate against any educational institution on the ground of that it is under the management of a minority, whether based on religion or language."

These are important fundamental rights meant, specially for the minorities. And as pointed out above, no democratic society can flourish without such constitutional guarantees to the minorities. The Indian Constitution thus, is, highly democratic and has provided lead to many other countries in Asia and Africa.

However, there is one vital question, which relates to minorities within minorities. As a minority wants certain constitutional guarantees to protect its religious, educational, linguistic and cultural rights vis-a-vis a majority, a minority within a minority also wants to secure these provisions. But, it has been seen and experienced that while a minority is anxious to secure these rights vis-a-vis a majority, is not in turn, as anxious to impart these rights to a minority within its own fold. This 'majority' within a minority is, on the contrary, quite ruthless in denying or suppressing these rights of the minority within its own fold. Not only this, there is another important question to be dealt with. Even within the 'main minority', the constitutional provisions are, more often than not, monopolized by a small coterie denying their enjoyment to a wider variety of elements within its own fold in true democratic spirit.

The Case of Bohras

We would like to illustrate our above thesis with the help of the case of the Bohra community. The Bohras are close to one million in India and are spread in several states particularly in Gujarat, Maharashtra, Rajasthan and Madhya Pradesh. Besides these they are also found in Calcutta, Hyderabad, Coachin, Calicut, Madras and several other cities of other states. The Bohras are shi'ah Isma'ilis' but differ from the Agakhani (or Nizaris) who too, are Isma'ili Shi'ahs. The Nizaris, as the name itself indicates, accepted Nizar as their 19th Imam on the death of Imam al-Mustansir, the 18th Fatimid Imam. The Bohras accepted Musta'li as the 19th Imam. They can also be referred to as Musta'lians.

The word 'Bohra' is, however, of Indian origin. The Bohras, are originally from Gujarat and were converted in 12th-13th centuries AD mostly from middle caste Hindus, especially from trading castes. These trading castes are often referred to as 'Vohras' in Gujrat. This caste appellation stuck to them and in the course of time 'V' was replaced by 'B' and they came to be known as Bohras. As they are primarily a business community, they migrated to different parts of India and abroad in search of better prospects for business. But wherever they went they preserved their Gujarati language and culture.

The Bohras are a highly well-knit and inward looking community. It is tightly controlled by religious leader known as the 'Da'i', which literally means 'summoner to the faith.' In fact the Da'i is not the highest authority in the Shi'ah Isma'ili hierarchy. It is the Imam from the progeny of Fatima, the daughter of the Holy Prophet (PBUH) and 'Ali, his cousin and son-in-law. But since the Imam is supposed to be in seclusion, the Da'i deputizes for him. In past most of the Da'is were highly religious and God-fearing and looked after the welfare of the community. But the things began to change gradually with the onset of the British rule and consequent improvement in the prospects of trade. The Bohras became more prosperous and the Da'is began to attract a part of this wealth by devising new methods of taxation.

As the Da'is grew richer their lust for power and money also increased and in order to extract more and more money they began to tighten their control over the community. The spread of modern education also increased their fear. They thought modern education will intensify critical thinking and lessen their influence and hence, they began to persecute those who began to establish modern educational institutions. The first four persons who became victims of persecution in the form of ex-communication (called salam band) were those who tried to establish modern school in Burhanpur.

This control by priesthood increased so much that it became impossible for any Bohra, even to raise any question about the monstrous powers assumed by the priesthood. Also, the large priestly family, began to live in high style like princes. Not only that each male member of the family began to describe himself as prince. Any Bohra who addressed them otherwise, was severely punished. This went to such an extent that the Da'i began to insist that a Bohra is his 'slave' ('abd) and that he/she must describe himself/herself as 'abd-e-Syedna/amat-e-Syedna i.e. slave or slave girl of Syedna, Syedna being the Bohra high priest. It was also made compulsory that on every marriage invitation card one must write 'abd-e-Syedna' or 'amat-e-Syedna' and if one did not, the marriage function will be forcibly annulled.

Again, it is not the matter of describing oneself as abd or amat (slave or slave girl) as mere formality, but it is expected of the Bohras that they literally behave as slaves. They are not free to undertake any activity of their own free-will. They have to obtain permission for every thing from Syedna or his representatives posted all over India from birth to death be it marrying, or burial, or naming a child or for business or starting any institution. Also, he has to pay up about seven taxes whenever demanded and particularly during the month of *Ramada*. Non-payment of these taxes can result in severe repercussions.

A regular tab is maintained on every individual Bohra. One is required to fill up a certain kind of forms every year declaring his/her assets and an account of his/her activities such as membership of various committees, attendance of study circles (Daris) regularly conducted by the authorized representative of the da'i. If one is not regular in these matters he/she will not be issued green card, which is necessary for entry into Bohra mosques/mausoleums/jamaatkhanas, etc. In short, one can say that the way a Bohra's life is controlled and strictly regimented, even the most authoritarian state does not regiment its citizens' life.

If one dares to disobey Syedna's regulations or fails to pay the dues demanded, he/she is put under socio-religious boycott. A boycotted person is shunned by all Bohras including his own parents or children or brothers and sisters. No one can maintain relations with such an ex-communicated person. If one does, he/she will also face the same consequences. Such an ex-communicated person cannot attend funeral of his/her near and dear ones or participate in their marriage functions or on any family occasions. Only a Bohra can feel and knows what kind of curse it is to live under the authoritarian regime of the Syedna.

One can say that the Bohras, though formally governed by the Indian Constitution, enjoy no fundamental rights at all. What the Indian Constitution guarantees and implemented by the Government of India, is taken away by the Bohra high priest in the case of the Bohras.

Normally a Bohra has neither freedom of speech nor freedom to act according to his conscience. The Bohra Da'i's establishment is a government within the country's government. And as far as the Bohras are concerned, the Da'i's government happens to be much more powerful than the country's government. In any case a Bohra cannot escape the wrath of the Syedna's government. He/she can avoid payment of income tax, but cannot avoid paying the taxes imposed by the Da'i. If he does, his/her entire socio-religious life will be ruined. He may end up getting completely isolated from entire community including his own family.

It is against this authoritarian regime of the Bohra Da'i that some conscientious Bohras raised their voice and struggled to retrieve their lost fundamental rights guaranteed by the Indian Constitution. In order to dilute the Da'i's authoritarian regime the reformist Bohras demanded that (1) the functioning of local Bohra jamat's be democratized; 2) the Da'i should be made accountable for the funds collected from the community; (3) that the payment of money should not be compulsory, but voluntary in the form of donations and (4) that the Da'i should act merely as a religious guide and should not interfere in personal and secular matters.

The reformist Bohras and their supporters were inhumanly persecuted for making these elementary democratic demands. They were not only ex-communicated (or put under barat or social boycott), but many of them physically assaulted. This writer was nearly fatally assaulted five times including once in Egypt. However, he had miraculous escape. Many long-standing marriages were dissolved because either husband or wife supported the reform movement. Many children were lost to their parents or vice versa in this struggle.

The Nathwani Inquiry Commission which was appointed by Citizens For Democracy headed by Shri Jayprakash Narayan, inquired into the violations of human rights of the reformist Bohras. The Commission headed by a retired high court judge shri Narendra Nathwani and comprising legal experts and eminent academics concluded that: "The inquiry has shown that there is large-scale infringement of civil liberties and human rights of reformist Bohras at the hands of the priestly class and that those who fail to obey the orders of the Syedna and his Amils, even in purely secular matters, are subjected to Baraat resulting in complete social boycott, mental torture and frequent physical assaults.

The Misaq (the oath of unquestioning obedience to the Head Priest), which every Bohra is required to give before he or she attains the age of majority, is used as the main instrument for keeping the entire community under the subjugation of the Syedna and his nominees."

The report further continues: "On the threat of Baraat (social boycott) and the resulting grave disabilities, Bohras are prevented from reading periodicals, which are censored by the Syedna (such as the *Bombay Samachar, The Blitz* and the *Bohra Bulletin*); from establishing charitable institutions like orphanages, dispensaries, libraries, etc., without the prior permission of the Syedna except by submitting to such conditions as he may impose; from contesting elections to municipal and legislative bodies without securing beforehand the blessings of the Syedna; and above all, from having any social contact with a person subjected to Baraat, even if the person is one's husband, wife, brother, sister, father or son. The weapon of Baraat has been used to compel a husband to divorce his wife, a son to disown his father, a mother refuse to see her son and a brother or sister to desist from attending the marriage of his or her sister or brother. An excommunicated member becomes virtually an untouchable in the community, and besides being isolated from his friends and nearest relatives, is unable to attend and offer prayers at the Bohra mosque. Even death does not release him from the taboo, for his dead body is not allowed to be buried at the community's common burial ground."

The Commission could also establish on the basis of oral and documentary evidence that: "Bohra jamaats in India and abroad are not allowed to frame their own rules and regulations, but are subjected to authoritarian constitutions granting absolute power to the Syedna and his nominees. Millions of rupees are collected every year from Bohras in India and abroad as customary taxes and Nazranas by the Syedna and his nominees, but the Syedna is not accountable for them to any one. The Syedna also claims to be the owner of all the Bohra mosques and the sole trustee of all Bohra trusts and where the account of any of these trusts are audited, the work is done by a firm composed of some members of the Bohra Community who are also bound by the Misaq given by them to the Syedna."

Thus, the inquiry commission headed by Justice Nathwani has presented the true picture of the authoritarian regime of the Syedna.

Thus, it can be seen that a minority of reformists within the minority Bohra community are suffering intensely and are denied all the rights guaranteed by the Indian Constitution. It is a typical case of a minority within a minority community being deprived of enjoyment of the fundamental rights. In fact the whole Bohra community also does not enjoy these rights. But a powerful coterie tightly controlled by the family of the Bohra high priest, really enjoys these rights and denies the Bohras in general and the reformist Bohras in particular, enjoyment of these fundamental rights.

In fact the Bohras themselves are a small minority within the Muslim minority in India and the reformist Bohras are a minority within that minority. But the powerful coterie headed by the Syedna also is adept at maneuvering the leaders of the Muslim minority. The Muslim leaders, instead of sympathizing with the plight of the reformist Bohras, have always (of course with few honourable exceptions) stood in defence of the Bohra high priest in the name of safeguarding the minority rights. The reformist Bohras are thought to be those who are instrumental in 'opening the floodgates of governmental interference' in the affairs of minority community. For this fear almost entire Muslim leadership vehemently opposed appointment of Nathwani Commission.

The Commission had made it absolutely clear that they are going to inquire only the violations of human rights of reformist Bohras at the hands of the Bohra priesthood and not into their religious beliefs and practices. Some of us also met the top Muslim leadership and tried to explain the situation and even agreed to withdraw from Nathwani Commission if they have grave apprehensions against it provided that they agree to constitute an inquiry commission themselves to inquire into the allegations of violations of civil liberties and human rights. They did not agree to this request and only insisted on withdrawing from the Commission unconditionally without providing any relief against the authoritarian priestly set-up.

Thus, it can be seen that the larger minority suppresses rights of smaller minority within and denies it what it claims for itself. The Articles 25 to 30 of the Indian Constitution and particularly the Article 25, guarantees the freedom of conscience to all the citizens. However, the reformist Bohras and their supporters cannot enjoy this very vital right. The Syedna invokes this right for himself even in legal suits; but denies its enjoyment to other Bohras. Unfortunately, even the Supreme Court, in its 1962 judgement, invoked the Article 25 for safeguarding the Syedna's right to excommunicate, though, at the same time admonishing him to use it judiciously and in a way which will not violate the process of natural justice. (The Syedna, however, ignoring the Supreme Court directive, continues to use it most arbitrarily). The reformists have filed a review petition before a larger Bench to get the 1962 judgement reviewed in the light of two inquiry commissions having established the reformist case. Another Commission, headed by Justice Tewatia (the retired Chief Justice of the Calcutta High Court) examined the continued violations of human rights of the reformist Bohras in the post-Nathwani Commission period and found all allegations to be correct.

Thus, there is a strong case for devising a mechanism whereby a minority within the minority community is not deprived of enjoyment of all the rights guaranteed in the Indian Constitution. What that device could be is for the Constitutional experts to formulate. But the severe persecution of the reformist Bohras and their continued sufferings makes it very urgent. The reformist Bohras are crying for justice. The benefits of the Constitutional rights must reach each and every member of the minority community and not only the powerful coteries among them. The Government of India turns a blind eye towards sufferings of minorities within minorities for political reasons. The vote-bank politics has its own compulsions as the top priority of the ruling party is to win elections rather than enforce constitutional provisions.

It is important to note that the Article 25 is preceded by the qualification "subject to public order, morality and health". What the Bohra priesthood is doing is the very negation of this important condition. He is disturbing the public order, morality and health of the society. The very community he heads, is going through great turmoil because of the Syedna's authoritarian ways. It is for the law courts, the Minorities Commission, the National Human Rights Commission and human rights organizations and activists to safeguard the rights of minorities within minorities by insisting on proper enforcement of the preceding condition of the Article 25 ensuring the public order, morality and health before enforcement of its operative part. This alone seems to be the remedy to safeguard the rights of the reformist Bohras.

CHAPTER 25

Imam Bukhari—His Life and Contribution to Science of Hadith

Imam Bukhari' has made immense contribution to the world of Islam. His services to the cause of Islam can never be forgotten even by his opponents. His contribution to the science of *hadith* is so great that it would have been incomplete without him. He not only collected *ahadith* (the holy Prophet's sayings and doings), but evolved a rigorous methodology of accepting or rejecting true and false *ahadith*. He also evolved the science of *Rijal*, i.e., criterion about the integrity and honesty of the narrators of *ahadith*. But more of it later.

First we would like to throw some light on the life of Imam Bukhari was born in 194 AH after the Friday prayer. His name was Muhammad bin Isma'il. His father Isma'il was also a great *muhaddith* (master of the science of *hadith*). Imam Bukhari achieved such excellence as *muhaddith* that he came to be known by various epithets like *Imam al-muhaddithin, Amiru'l mu'minin f'il hadith, Syed al-fuqaha,'* etc. Muhammad bin Isma'il, popularly known as Bukhari was born in Bukhara, then a great centre of Islamic learning, where the illustrious philosopher, also known as second Master of Greek Philosophy Ibn-e-Sina (known in the West as Avicenna) was born in 428 AH. The Imam became popular only as Bukhari and hardly anyone knows him as Muhammad bin Isma'il. Also, his collection of *ahadith* is known as *Sahih Bukhari*, a reference to the town of his birth. Thus, he gave eternal fame to this centre of learning in the Central Asia.

Imam Bukhari's father died when he was quite young and the burden of bringing him up fell on his mother. He was brought up in the atmosphere of Islamic learning. Thus, says Imam Qastallani about his upbringing: "He was brought up in the lap of learning. He grew up and was nursed with the milk of education and scholarship. And his weaning took place at it." His biographer Muhammad bin Abi Hatim Warraq says, "I myself heard Imam Bukhari say 'Allah gave me the desire to memorize *hadith* at the time when I was in the primary school'". Warraq further says, "I asked Imam Bukhari about his age at the time when he felt the longing to memorize *hadith* and he replied, 'ten years or less than that.' It was at this age that he began participating in the teaching circles of *muhaddithin* (specialists in the science of *hadith*)."

It would be interesting to quote an event from the early age of Imam Bukhari. This event has been quoted by Mohammad Abdus Salam Mubarakpuri in his *Life and Work of Imam Bokhari* (Idaratul Buhusil Islamia, Varanasi, India, 1984). Allama Dakhili who was a *muhaddith* of a high stature in Bukhara and whose seminary was of great eminence, was giving lessons as usual. Allama Dakhili narrated the testimony of one *hadith* (through chain of narrators). As he erred in naming narrators, Bukhari, at a very early stage of his education, said, "Abu Zaid did not report from Ibrahim." This startled Dakhili and he, in his disturbed mood, rebuked Bukhari. But Imam Bukhari submitted with great suavity 'if you have the original kindly refer to it'. And he was right. Allama Dakhili went home and checked with the original. When Dakhili came out of his house he asked, "Boy! What is the correct testimony?" And Imam Bukhari promptly replied, "Zubair bin Adi and he from Ibrahim." This shows the extraordinary power of memory the Imam had been gifted with and it is this immense power of memory which enabled him to memorize and remember thousands of *ahadith* at a time with their chains of narrators.

This power of memory was almost unbelievable. It is said that Imam Bukhari had already memorized about 70,000 *ahadith* in his boyhood. Here I would like to refer to what Allama Salim bin Mujahid said about him. He says, "One day I came to the presence of the *muhaddith* of the time Muhammad bin Salam Bekandi. The *Muhaddith* (Bekandi) said, 'If you had come a little earlier you would have seen a boy who remembers 70,000 *hadiths*.'" When Salim bin Mujahid checked with the boy, to his astonishment he discovered that not only he remembers 70,000 *ahadith* but also names, dates of birth and residences of narrators of these *ahadith*. Even if there is exaggeration in this, it is certainly true that the Imam could remember large number of *ahadith* in his childhood itself alongwith its narrators. This itself is no mean achievement. As far as the science of *hadith* is concerned Bukhari was a child-prodigy and has remained unparalleled in the world of Sunni Islam.

Allama Bekandi, the great *muhaddith* of his time used to acknowledge the prowess of Imam Bukhari who was his student by asking him to correct his (Bekandi's) book of *hadith*. One of the Bekandi's disciple asked him who is this boy. You are the Sheikh of the time and leader of the discipline of *hadith*, and yet, you are asking a mere boy to go through your book in order to correct errors? In reply Allama Bekandi said, "He is matchless". Allama Bekandi used to say, "When Muhammad bin Isma'il comes to my class I am astonished and feel afraid of narrating *hadiths* lest I should commit a mistake in his presence". And these words of Allama Bekandi pertain to the period when Bukhari had not migrated to Hejaz for acquiring higher knowledge of Islamic sciences.

Imam Bukhari of course later went to Mecca and Madina for acquisition of much sought after Islamic knowledge, particularly of *hadith* and spent years of his life in these holy towns collecting *hadiths* from various sheikhs of *hadith*. However, many authorities on *hadith* including the *sahabah* (the companions of the holy Prophet), *tabi'in* (the followers of the companions) and *tab'a tabi'in* (followers of the followers of the companions) scattered all over the Islamic empire, it became very difficult to find the whole treasure of *hadith* at any one place. Thus, for the collector of *hadith* in those times when long distances had to be traversed on camel or horse back it was no easy thing. They had to face undescribable hardships in the process. And if they had no adequate resources for travel and food it was even worse. It required strong will and high degree of courage to undertake such hazardous journeys.

Abdus Salam Mubarakpuri points out in this connection, "Not to be disheartened with hardships of journey, not to allow ambitions to be frustrated even after starving for days together, walking on foot by wrapping rags around the feet in the absence of a ride, keeping the mind undistracted even after hardest difficulties, maintaining the zeal and enthusiasm of the heart undiminished even while leaving on barks and leaves, keeping alive the fire raging in the heart even after thousands of adversities, considering the hardships of the journey as pleasures, sacrificing one's own wealth and welfare for this work, were not the work of a man of ordinary heart and soul, and of normal courage and conviction. These are the qualities which raised Imam Bukhari to the stature of the earlier Imams who occupied far more important positions in their times than Imam Bokhari". (See Muhammad Abdus Salam Mubarakpuri op.cit. p. 22).

Qutaiba bin Sa'id Thaqafi used to say, "If Imam Bukhari were among the *sahaba* (companions of the Prophet) he would have been one of the major signs of Allah." But the common notion is that if Imam Bukhari were among the *tabi'in* (followers of the companions of the Prophet), he would have been a major sign of Allah.

Imam Bukhari went to Hejaz at the age of sixteen, according to his biographer Warraq. Ibn Hatim Warraq states that the Imam used to say, "When I had learnt by heart the works of Abdullah bin Mubarak and fully understood the positions of *Ahl al-Ra'i* (people of opinion in matters of *din* and *shari'ah*) I traveled to Hejaz. At that time I was of 16 years of age." According to Warraq Imam's first *rehlah* (travel) took place in the year 210 AH. After performing *Hajj* he did not return with his mother and elder brother to his native place, but stayed on to acquire higher learning. The historians are unanimous that his total stay in Hejaz which included Makkah, Ta'if, Jeddah and Madina, was for six years.

In addition to staying in Hejaz, the Imam went to Kufah and Basrah several times. Kufah and Basrah were also great centres of Islamic learning as they were important centres of political power, trade and intellectual activities. In Basrah he benefited from Imam Abu Asim Annabil, Safwan bin 'Isa, Badil bin Muhabbir, Hamri bin Umara, Affan bin Muslim and several others. After Basra he visited Kufah repeatedly as well as Baghdad. Warraq quotes Bukhari about his journeys to Kufah and Baghdad, "I cannot count the number of times I entered Kufah and Baghdad with *muhaddithin*. Baghdad during the reign of Abbasids was the great centre of learning, religious as well as secular. Imam visited it frequently in search of knowledge and also to teach. He also visited Syria and Egypt. In Sham he studied under Allama Yusuf Firyabi, Abu Nasr Ishaq bin Ibrahim, Hatim bin Suraih and others. He also visited other places like Khorasan, Merv, Balkh, Herat, Nishapur, Ray, and Jabale Khorasan. And of course he visited places like Tashkand and Samarkand in the neighbourhood of Bukhara. In all these travels the Imam acquired *hadiths* from several sheikhs of *hadith*. Jafar bin Muhammad bin Hattan says, "I heard Imam Bukhari say, 'I noted down *hadith* from more than·one thousand teachers. And I do not remember a single *hadith* without due ascription'".

Muslim and Tirmidhi, the other collectors of *hadith* among the authentic six collectors of Sunni Islam, have also paid rich tributes to Imam Bukhari. For example, Muslim says, "Only that man will have animus with you (Imam Bukhari) who is jealous of you. And I bear witness that there is no one to match you in the world today." Imam Bukhari's great contribution to the cause of Islam is obvious from the fact that his ·collection of *hadiths* popularly known as *Sahih Bukhari* is considered next only to Qur'an in Sunni Islam as *Nahj al-Balaghah*, the sermons of Ali, the son-in-law of the Prophet, is considered next to Qur'an in Shi'ah Islam.

Imam Bukhari was so devoted to his cause of collection of authentic *ahadith* that he neglected everything including his own well-being. Though, he was not a man of no means, yet, he lived an exemplary life of austerity, totally devoted to his own cause. Abul Hasan Yusuf bin Abi Zar of Bukhara says that once Imam Bukhari fell ill. His urine was examined by physicians. After examining his urine they opined that his urine resembles of those hermits who eat nothing with bread. So the treatment proposed was that he should eat something with the bread. When Imam was asked to eat something with the bread he said that he had not eaten anything with bread for last 40 years. First he refused to accept the prescription to eat substantial food, but when eminent 'ulama insisted, in the interest of his health, he consented to eat little sugar with bread.

The Imam's task of collecting *ahadith* and verifying them from authentic sources was so difficult and demanding that one day he was in the hills of Khorasan and other in the mountains of Lebanon. Either he is journeying to Basra or teaching in Kufah, or is compiling the authentic *ahadith* between the arches and pulpits of Prophet's mosque. Once it so happened that he forgot to take expenses for his journey while going to a sheikh for collecting *hadith*. He had to starve and eat leaves in the forest. But the Imam felt proud walking in step with the companions of the holy Prophet who had survived on leaves in the battle of *Zatul Khabt*. Once he sold off all his clothes except his *tahmad* and could not come out of his room for three days until his admirers arranged for clothes.

He was always trying to act according to the holy Prophet's *sunnah*. When he was building a guest house for the comfort of travellers he carried bricks and mortar on his head. When he was requested not to do this he said that it is inspired by the act of the Prophet of Allah as the Prophet (S) himself carried the bricks and mortar while constructing his mosque in Madinah or which he did while digging the trenches on the day of battle of Ahzab. He even acted according to "Prepare yourselves according to your ability and the availability of horses" He, in keeping with this *hadith* of the Prophet practiced marksmanship on a horseback.

He considered even intention to do something as his promise to himself and fulfilled it. We find in the *Muqaddimah* of *Fath al-Bari* that once Abu Hafs who was an especial disciple of Isma'il, the father of Imam Bukhari, sent some goods to Imam Bukhari. A trader came in the evening and wanted to buy the goods by offering a profit of five thousand (Imam Bukhari was a trader in his own right). The Imam asked him to go back as he would confirm the sale next morning. On the next morning other traders came and they offered a profit of ten thousand. However, the Imam turned down other traders saying he has made an intention to sell it to other trader who came to him last night and sold goods to him. Thus, he did not mind loosing additional five thousand as he had made up his mind to sell the goods to the first trader. "I do not like to violate my own intentions", he said.

Also, the Imam was very meticulous about *ahadith*. Once he was convinced it was an authentic one, he would not hesitate to include that *hadith* in his collection even if it went against his own creed. Thus one will find the narrators in *Sahih Bukhari* who are Shi'ahs. Though, the Imam was charged of being Shi'ah as he included these narrators.

Imam Bukhari believed in keeping away from the company of *amirs* and sultans who violated injunctions of the faith and acted only in their own interests. He believed that in the company of such unscrupulous rulers it is not possible to observe injunctions of ones religion. While making concessions to them a faithful strays far away from his true beliefs. Bukhari did not act in this way of his own, but he was acting according to the *hadith* of the Prophet (S). Thus, we find it in *Mishkat*, *Kitab al-'Ilm*. From *Muqaddimah* of *Fath al-Bari* we learn one of the statements of Imam Bukhari that "Knowledge is debased in the company of the rich and the faith suffers loss in their flattery".

Imam Bukhari practiced it in his life at his own cost and suffering. Khalid bin Ahmad Zuhli, the Governor of Bukhara on behalf of the Sultanate of Tahiria, sent a word to the Imam, when he had established his own school in Bukhara to which lovers of knowledge made a bee line for admission, to come to the palace and teach him and his princes history and *Sahih Bukhari*. The Imam flatly refused the request and showed that men like Imam Malik who knew how to respect learning were still alive—who never cared for the hostility of the world nor did they strive for wealth, fame and power.

The Imam sent the word through the messenger who had brought the governor's message: "I do not want to become a flatterer in the Royal Palace. Such an act will discredit knowledge." The governor then sent the message that if the Imam cannot come to the palace he should set aside time for teaching the princes in his school. The Imam refused this request also saying, "This is the heritage of the Prophet (S). The general and special all have equal rights in it. The doors of my seminary and the mosque are open to all and at all time. Whoever wants can come and take advantage. No one is prevented. I cannot accept such a request which opens the door for some and bars it for others. If you resent it, stop me forcibly from teaching so that I can make a complaint in the Court of Allah."

This frank and blunt reply made the governor furious and the Imam had to pay a heavy price for his deeply held conviction. The governor conspired with some of his flatterers to bring a false charge against the Imam to persecute him. The governor's men spread the rumour that Imam Bukhari believes that the Qur'an is created and not co-eternal with Allah. This false charge was widely publicized creating public opinion against him and the Imam was asked to leave the town of Bukhara. While going out of the town he cried, "O Allah! Bring upon them and their children the same that these people have intended for me."

Imam Bukhari left the town and reached Bekand. The rumour had reached Bekand too and the people of Bekand were divided into two groups: those who believed the rumour and those who did not. So Imam did not think it fit to stay in Bekand when one group was hostile to him and left for Samarkand as the people of Samarkand had invited him. But in Samarkand too, people were divided in two groups and Imam did not think it fit to go there. On his way to Samarkand he died and was buried there. He died in 256 AH at the age of sixty-two and was buried at the same place. Thus, it will be seen that Imam Bukhari preferred to be exiled, but refused to compromise on his lofty principles.

This persecution of Bukhari by the governor of Bukhara did no harm to his reputation at all. He was greatly revered by his contemporary and later *muhaddithin* and other *mujtahids* of the science of *hadith*. The governor who persecuted the Imam is no more to be heard of, but the Imam is still revered throughout the Islamic world and will continue to be revered as long as the world exists and there are Muslims in it.

There is one controversy about the Imam. Was he Hanbali or Shafi'i? Allama Ujlooni writes, "The Ahl-e-Taqlid have differed from the creed of the Imam. Some think he was Shafi'i for he recorded *hadiths* from Imam Karabisi, Abu Saur, and Zafarani and learnt *fiqh* from Humaidi and all these are disciples of Shafi'i." On the other hand Ibn Iraqi says that the Imam belonged to Hambali sect for he is one of the disciples of Imam Muhammad bin Hanbal. But Imam Bukhari himself says, "I have been to Baghdad and sat with Imam Ahmad each time. The last time when I took leave of him he hesitated in giving permission to leave. He said, 'O Abu Abdullah! You are leaving behind the scholars and knowledge and going to Khorasan?'"

But fact is that Imam Bukhari was neither Hanbali nor Shafi'i. Allama Uljooni also suggests—and this seems to be true—that Imam Bukhari was an absolute *mujtahid*. Allama Taqiuddin bin Taymiyyah has also expounded the concept of his being *mujtahid-i-mutlaq*. He says that Imam *al-muhaddithin*, i.e., Imam Bukhari was an *imam b'il fiqh* and a man of *ijtihad*. This seems to be true as a great mind like that of Bukhari would not confine himself to any particular *madhhab*, i.e., school of *fiqh* and would prefer to draw his own conclusions based on his study in depth of *hadith* and Qur'an.

Imam Bukhari's most famous and abiding work is of course *Sahih Bukhari*. But this is not his only work. He has written several other books though lesser known to the world. He wrote what is known as *Tarikh-e-Kabir* at the age of eighteen. This is counted as an important work by the learned ulama. Imam Abu Ali Ghassani says, "When Imam Bukhari wrote *Tarikh-e-Kabir*, a talented sheikh of the stature of Imam Ishaq bin Rahueh presented the rare compilation to the court of Amir Abdullah bin Tahir, the ruler of Ray, and said, 'Should I not show you a work of magic?' Allama Tajuddin Subki writes about this book: 'The history by Imam Bukhari is such a noble work that no one before it could produce such a book".

Similarly, he also wrote *Tarikh-e-Saghir* which is not extant. Some have expressed doubts about it. But the author of *Sirat al-Nu'man* writes "...I have seen most of the books on *rijal* and works of history in which Imam Abu Hanifa has been mentioned and these include the *Tarikh-e-Saghir* by Bukhari, *Ma'arif* by Qutaibah and so on." Similalrly, he also wrote *Tarikh al-Awsat*.

There are several other books written by the Imam many of which are no more available now. But they have been mentioned in other contemporary works and it is through these sources that we come to know of the Imam's various works. For example, his *Al-Jami' al-Kabir*, though no more available, has been mentioned by Ibn Tahir. Not much details are known about it and no manuscript of this book has been traced so far. He also wrote what is known as *Khalq-u-'Af'al al-'Ibad*. This book adopts same style to refute the false creeds by the Qur'anic verses and the *ahadith* that the *Sahaba* and the *Tab'iin* adopted in this connection. This book contains refutations of false creeds of Tahamia and Mu'attalahs.

He wrote two works on weak narrators of *ahadith Kitab al-Zu'afa al-Saghir* and *Kitab al-Zu'afa al-Kabir*. Also, Allama Ferabri who was a student of Imam Bukhari mentions two other works of the Imam *Al-Musnad al-Kabir* and *Al-Tafsir al-Kabir*. The details about both these compilations also remain unknown as they have been lost over a period of time. Yet, another of his work *Kitab al-Hibah* has been mentioned by his biographer Muhammad bin Abu Hatim. He says that Imam Bukhari wrote a book on the problems of *hibah* and that it is so exhaustive in its sweep that the books by Waqi Ibn Jarrah and Abdullah bin Mubarak bear no comparison to it.

Also we find mention of another important book *Asma' al-Sahabah* by Abul Qasim bin Mandah and he himself reports it from Ibn Faris, and often copies from it. Similarly, he also wrote a book *Kitab al-Uhadan* in which he has collected the names of all those from amongst the *Sahaba* from whom only one *hadith* has been reported. We also find mention of his another book *Kitab al-Mabsut* in which Imam Bukhari has discussed problems of *fiqh* deduced from *ahadith*. Abul Qasim bin

Mandah mentions, yet, another book *Kitab al-'Ilal* from Imam Bukhari. The science of '*ilal* is extremely important, but very complicated. Imam Bukhari had mastered it. Besides these books we find mention of several others like *Kitab al-Fawa'id, Al-Adab al-Mufrad, Birr al-Walidain, Qadaya al-Sahabah wa al-Tabi'in, Kitab al-Riqaq, Al-Jami'i al-Saghir fi'l hadith,* etc., These are all important works of the Imam all of which, as pointed out, are not available in our times. But nevertheless, these works made important contribution to various problems of fiqh in their own time.

Contribution and Limitations of Imam

The contribution of the Imam to the literature of *hadith* was immense and has left its mark on the history of *hadith* literature permanently. No one can underrate his contribution in this respect. He took immense pains in collecting about 600,000 *ahadith* from all available sources and selected, after rigorous critique, about 4,000 of them for inclusion in his *Sahih*. His honesty and integrity in selection of these *ahadith* from amongst 600,000 he collected can never be in doubt. In addition to rigorous selection of *hadith,* through his intellectual faculty he would also perform *wudu'*, offer two *raka'ah* prayer and perform *istikharah* before including any *hadith* in his *Sahih*. Thus, he took not only intellectual care but also invoked spiritual integrity for selection of *hadith*.

And yet, there are problems with the *hadith* literature. The problem is not of mere intellectual and spiritual honesty and integrity, but also of *hadith* literature *per se*. There are differences among Muslims on this question. First of all *hadith* cannot be equated with the divinely revealed Qur'an. The holy Prophet made it obligatory on his companions to carefully collect the verses of Qur'an. And the final collection also known as the *Mushaf Uthman* was unanimously accepted by all Muslims, whatever their sect and doctrinal differences among themselves. No one has seriously challenged this final compilation and no one quoted the verses from any other compilation.

But *hadith* could never achieve this status. Firstly, the Prophet(s) himself discouraged the Muslims from collecting *hadith*. The Prophet's successors also did not approve of such collections. Although many Qur'anic verses required help of *hadith* to comprehend them still collection and compilation of *hadith* was not encouraged for fear that fake one will soon be mixed up with genuine and also loss of memory and comprehension by companions might also create their own problems. Add to this mutual struggles—both doctrinal as well as political and we can realize the grave dimensions of the problem.

Muslims differed among themselves on many issues, and very seriously at that. They derived legitimation for their own doctrinal position by invoking one or the other *hadith*, many of which were fabricated. The Prophet(s) was very well aware of these possibilities and hence he stopped his companions from collecting *hadith*. Anyway *ahadith* were fabricated on a large-scale and used unabashedly for partisan purposes. Within hundred years of the Prophet's death scores of sects came into existence and each sect resorted generously to *hadith* for justification of their doctrinal position. Also, *ahadith* were fabricated in favour or against certain companions among whom there was struggle for power.

Also, by the time Imam Bukhari was collecting *ahadith*, even the time of *tab 'a tabi 'in* (followers of the followers of the Prophet) was over and it was very difficult to ascertain who heard the *hadith* from whom reaching the chain right upto the Prophet. Many ahadith were *marfu'* the chain of narrators reaching right upto the holy Prophet or *mauquf* stopping at some companion or his follower. In order to ascertain the authenticity of narrators the *muhaddithin* (experts on the science of *hadith*) evolved the science of what is called *'Ilm al-Rijal* science of critiquing the narrators of *hadith* as for their integrity, purity, spiritual attainments and honesty.

Many *ahadith* were narrated by weak persons and *muhaddithun* have described many as even *kazzab* (liers). Many *ahadith* were reported by one narrator only and some by several narrators. Also, there was fear of some narrations having been exaggerated and some understated to emphasise or de-emphasize certain aspects. Also, there was question of comprehension as *hadiths* have been reported by all sorts of companions some of whom were highly intelligent while some quite dull, some understood nuances of language some did not. Some were conversant with idiomatic expressions of a language while some were quite unaware of that. Some companions were of Persian and even Roman origin with their own cultural and traditional background. Many companions were slaves of poor intellectual capacities and some had heard from the Prophet from a distance and some had heard him at close quarters. Also some had heard him only at once while others heard him to say the same thing several times.

There were several other problems besides these. There were references in the holy Qur'an to several past events of which most of the companions knew hardly anything. There were also references to Judaic and Christian sources and biblical stories with which many were not conversant among his companions. They approached Christians and Jews for understanding these portions of the Qur'an and often ascribed them to the Prophet to increase chances of their acceptability. Also, many statements of the Prophet were culturally conditioned. The then prevailing cultural and intellectual ethos also deeply affected understanding of the Qur'an and Prophet's statements. The Prophet also had to explain certain things in the light of prevalent cultural ethos.

A *muhaddith* had to grapple with all these formidable problems and no *muhaddith*, however great he might have been could overcome all these severe constraints. They were, after all, despite their deep commitments, product of their own time and space. Even eminent *fuqaha'* (Islamic jurists) differed from each other as they lived in widely differing intellectual milieu. Those living in Mecca and Madina were closer to local traditions in understanding the issues than those who lived in Kufah, Basrah, Baghdad and Egypt. They drew different inferences.

In view of these formidable constraints it is not surprising if we find several problematic ahadith in Imam Bukhari's collection today. Despite his transparently honest efforts he has included some ahadith which will not be acceptable to modern critical mind or which may not be in keeping with the Qur'anic ethos. This, however, does not detract from the eminence Imam Bukhari rightly enjoys in Sunni Islam today. He has bequeathed such rich *hadith* literature to us that we will ever be grateful to his immensely rich contribution to the world of *hadith*.

CHAPTER 26

Sighting of Moon and Problems of Muslim Calendar

The problem of sighting of moon and beginning of a month normally does not bother an ordinary Muslim except at the time of *Eid*. It is the sighting of moon that brings the gravity of the problem to the fore. A Muslim month begins with the sighting of the moon. *Eid* brings greatest spiritual joy to the Muslim community in the world. Most of the Muslims fast during the month of *Ramadan* and hence they are quite anxious to celebrate *Eid* at the end of their fasting. Sighting of moon becomes important on other occasions like *Hajj*. But since *Hajj* is performed in the holy city of Mecca under the domain of Saudis, it is Saudis who decide which day will be 9th of *Dhu'l Hajj* (the day of *Hajj*) and subsequent day the day of *Eid-ul-Adhah*. Any way *Eid-ul-Adhah* being on the 10th of the month, controversy, if any about sighting the moon of *Dhu'l Hijjah* is settled by then. But, since the *Eid-ul-Fitr* is on the very first day of *Sha'ban* the controversy acquires added significance. Also people are anxious to celebrate *Eid* and everyone waits with bated breath for sighting of moon. It is in this atmosphere that the controversy about sighting the moon acquires so much significance.

People differ from each other on the question of sighting the moon. Hilal committee also fail to come up with any satisfactory solution. They adopt even sectarian attitude. If the committee is dominated by Barelvis or Deobandis they give different verdicts. In different parts of Islamic world *Eid* is celebrated on different days and sometimes, even in one city different sections of Muslims celebrate it on different days. And in some extreme cases in one family it is observed a day earlier or later. Even the Government finds it difficult to declare holiday and it has to change the day of the leave depending on whether moon is sighted or not.

The reasons for sighting the moon

Why moon is sighted for starting the month? The Arabs who had not cultivated astronomy, nor did they feel the need for it, found it most practicable to sight the new moon for starting the month. The Arabian peninsula was not primarily agricultural except in certain parts. It grew mostly date palms, which also did not depend on agricultural cycles or seasons. Thus in the absence of agricultural operations the variation of seasons posed no problems whatsoever. A particular month in winter may after the cycle of 11 years fall in summer. Their lunar year has roughly 354 days whereas the solar calendar has 365. Where agricultural operations are basic to the economy of region, lunar calendar will pose certain problems for sowing, rain etc. So it is observed that wherever agricultural operations are involved solar calendar is more functional than lunar calendar. In countries like India where advanced knowledge of astronomy had developed, a combination of lunar and solar calendars were worked out to avoid problems. India could not do only with lunar calendar as it has been primarily an agricultural country. That is why there occurs slight variation in the date of certain festivals like *Deepavali* etc. One year it occurs in October and another year in November. But season does not change.

The Arabs were not, dependent on agricultural operations they did not need any sophisticated calculations for sowing or cutting of crops which very much depend on fixed seasons. They found it most convenient to sight the new moon and begin their month. Moon is much easier to sight the stars. Moon being satellite of earth is closest and hence, quite prominent in size to the naked eye.

The holy Qur'an is not only a book of guidance for humankind, but also a book which tried to cultivate an objective scientific outlook among the believers for this universe. Even those who do not have faith in the Qur'an will be surprised at the description of sun, moon and other stars and their creation in it. It is undoubtedly a book of spiritual guidance, but it also deals extensively with this material world and imparts, at times in symbolic and at times in descriptive way, proper knowledge of this universe and reasons of its creation. The followers of the Prophet is not though not great scholars, physicist or astronomers but were, nevertheless, quite inquisitive about this universe and would ask questions to the Prophet and these questions would be answered by the Qur'an through revelation.

Before we take up the question of sighting of moon I would like to refer to an important verse about creation of the universe and the attitude of the believers. In the verse 3:189-90 Allah says, "In the creation of the heavens and the earth and the alternation of the night and the day, there are surely signs for men of understanding. Those who remember Allah standing and sitting and (lying) on their sides, and reflect on the creation of the heavens and the earth: Our Lord, Thou has not created this in vain! Glory be to Thee! Save us from the chastisement of the Fire."

This verse clearly says three things: (1) in the creation of the heaven and earth and alteration of the night and the day there are signs (*ayat*) for men to understand (*u'lil albab*—people of intellect); (2) those who remember Allah whether standing, sitting or lying on their sides *reflect* on creation; (3) the men of intellect reflect and come to the conclusion that nothing has been created in vain by the Lord and the Sustainer of this universe. Thus, sun and moon and stars and other heavenly objects have useful functions to perform. This verse and similar other verses in the Qur'an praise the quality of *fikr, tafakkur* (thinking, reflecting) which create knowledge and according to one *ahadith'* road to knowledge is road to paradise. Thus it is the duty of the believers that they should continuously reflect on the *ayat* (signs) of Allah.

It was in this spirit that some *m'uminun* (faithfuls) asked the Prophet about various stages of moon (*ahillah*) and the Prophet replied which is the Qur'anic basis of sighting of moon for starting the month. The relevant verse of the Qur'an is as follows: "They ask thee of thy new moon. Say: 'they indicate time (for various things) for humankind including the pilgrimage'". Tabari throwing light on this verse indicates that it refers to sighting of moon for fasting, for breaking of fast, for *Hajj*, for counting *iddah* of their women and other functions relating to *din* of Muslims. (see *Jami' al-Bayan'an Ta'wil Ayah al-Qur'an* by Tabari, Vol.II). The other commentators also hint at this. Thus, Muslim calendar has to be a lunar calendar and moon fulfils an important function of indicating time as per the will of Allah. Thus keeping in view of the changing shapes of moon one can fix time conveniently.

Muhammad Asad, a noted modern commentator of the Qur'an says, explaining this verse, "The reference, at this stage, to lunar months arises from the fact that the observance of several of the religious obligations instituted by Islam—like the fast of *Ramadan*, or the .pilgrimage to Mecca—is based on the lunar calendar, in which the months rotate through the seasons of the solar year. This fixation on the lunar calendar results in a continuous variations of the seasonal circumstances in which those religious observances are performed...." (Muhammad Asad, *The Message of the Qur'an*).

But does it necessitate the sighting of the moon with the naked eye every time or its appearance at the beginning of the month can be calculated through mathematical and astronomical calculations? Here the differences start. The consensus among all Muslims, except the Shai'ah Isma'ilis, is on sighting of the new moon with ones own eye at the beginning of every year. Of course now some liberal Muslims are also insisting on knowing the position of the moon through calculations. All the *ahadith* in *sihah sittah* (the six most authentic collections of *ahadith* of Sunni Muslims) as well as the authentic collections of *ahadith* of Shi'ah Imamiyah Muslims lay down sighting of the moon through ones own eye. It is only in the Shi'ah Isma'ili *ahadith* which do not require sighting of moon directly with ones own eyes. They have prepared a lunar calendar and follow it avoiding all the confusion in determining exact date of appearance of moon.

We would throw light on some of the *ahadith* found in *Sihah Sittah* about sighting of moon. Thus the *hadith* from *Sahih Muslim* narrated by Abu Hurayrah says, "Allah's Messenger (PBUH) said: Whenever you sight the new moon (of the month of *Ramadan*) observe fast and when you sight it (the new moon of *Shawwal*) break it, and if the sky is cloudy for you, then observe fast for thirty days."

Abdullah bin Abbas narrates a *hadith* reported in *Sahih Muslim* which says, "Kurayb said: Umm Fadl, daughter of Harith, sent him (Fadl, i.e., her son) to Mu'awiyah in Syriah. I (Fadl) arrived in Syria and did the needful for her. It was there in Syria that the month of *Ramadan* commenced. I saw the new moon (of *Ramadan*) on Friday. I then came back to Medina at the end of the month."

Abdullah bin Abbas asked me (about the new moon of *Ramadan*) and said: When did you see it? I said: We saw it on Friday night. He said: (Did) you see it yourself? I said: yes, and the people also saw it so they observed fast and Mu'awiyah also observed fast. Thereupon he said: But we saw it on Saturday night. So we shall continue to observe the fast until we complete thirty (fasts) or we see it (the new moon of *Shawwal*). I said: Is the sighting of the moon by Mu'awiyah not valid for you? He said: No; this is how the Messenger of Allah (PBUH) has commanded us. Yahya ibn Yahya was in doubt (whether the word used in the narration by Kurayb was *Naktafi or Taktafi*

This *ahadith* clearly shows that there used to be controversies of the same nature during those days also about sighting of moon. Syrians began fasting on one day and the Medinians on the other day. The Syrians broke fast on one day and the Medinians on the other day. Similarly we find another *ahadith* in *Sahih Muslim* also narrated by Abdullah ibn Abbas. According to this *hadith,* "Abul Bakhtari reported: We went to perform *Umrah* and when we encamped in the valley of Nakhlah, we tried to see the new moon. Some of the people said: it was three nights old, and others (said) that it was two nights old. We then met Ibn Abbas and told him we had seen the new moon, but that some of the people said it was three nights old and others that it was two nights old. He asked on which night we had seen it; and when we told him we had seen on such and such night, he said the Prophet of Allah (PBUH) had said: Verily Allah had deferred it till the time it is seen, so it is to be reckoned from the night you saw it."

This *ahadith* introduces, yet, another problematic. That one should begin the month only after seeing the moon oneself in a place, even if it is two or three days old in another place. This will create complete confusion in reckoning dates. In one place if month begins on a particular day and in another place two or three days later how one will ensure any uniformity in reckoning days? How one will maintain any uniform records? We find a *ahadith* in *Al-Muwatta* of Imam ibn Malik narrated by Abdullah ibn Umar. This a *hadith* says, "The Messenger of Allah, may Allah bless him and grant him peace, once mentioned *Ramadan* and said, 'Do not begin the fast until you see the new moon, and do not break the fast (at the end of *Ramadan*) until you see it. If the new moon is obscured from you, then work out (when it should be)."

Another *ahadith* in Mishkat al-Masabih narrated by Abu Hurayrah says, "Allah's Messenger (PBUH) said, 'Calculate on the basis of the new moon of *Sha'ban* when *Ramadan* begins."

No doubt these *ahadith* require us to see the new moon with ones own eye before starting a month. But we also have to take the context of these *sahih ahadith* into account. It is important to understand why the holy Prophet ordered us to see the moon with ones own eyes? Was there any alternative available from which he chose sighting of the moon giving up another possibility? No *ahadith* tells us of that. As pointed out above in the pre-Islamic period the Arabs also used to begin their month by sighting the new moon which was the only practical method available to them to determine their months. The Arabs were far from developing any calendar, which they did not need also. Firstly, they had no agricultural operations and secondly they had no pressing economic necessity for developing calendar in other economic. field like commerce etc. As we know necessity is the mother of invention, Also, in the pre-Islamic period there was widespread illiteracy and illiterate people could not develop something like a calendar which requires advanced knowledge of mathematics and astronomy.

The Prophet continued the same as during his time also, no advancements either in science or in the field of economy had taken place. He saw no need for developing a calendar. Islam stressed significance of knowledge so much so that the Prophet said the ink of a scholar was better than the blood of a martyr. His companions wanted to learn from the Prophet as much as they could about religion and about Shari'ah. They were not so much interested at that time in physical sciences like mathematics and astronomy. They felt need for physical sciences later when they expanded their commerce, their knowledge of universe and their knowledge of physics, chemistry, geology, astronomy and mathematics. They achieved many breakthroughs in these fields.

Thus, developing a calendar had not much priority during the Prophet's time. There was the prevalent method to determine the beginning of a month and in the absence of advanced knowledge of astronomy the Prophet continued it. He saw no harm in doing so for the people of Arabia. It was, after all, the only practical method available for people without much knowledge. As the Arabs used camel for transportation, as it was the only means of transportation available then, they do not hesitate from using modern means of transportation and communication today. The holy Prophet also used camel, as it was the only available means then. Does any religious leader of the highest significance today in the world of Islam hesitate to use these modern means of transportation and communication? Certainly not. Because be it camel or jet plane, they are the means, not the end. Even today in backward areas most primitive means of transport or communications like camel or bullock or donkey are used. So the most advanced as well as the most primitive can coexist depending on the need of the society. During the holy Prophet's time also advanced calendar existed in India and in the Roman world. But in Arabia the primitive method of sighting the moon was used and the Prophet continued it as it very well served the practical need for determining the month in Arabia. The Qur'an also said that the moon is for determining the time for Hajj and other needs of the people.

However, neither the Qur'an nor any *ahadith* prohibits the believer from basing the calendar on precise mathematical and astronomical calculations. Moreover, there are verses in the Qur'an which clearly indicate that Allah has fixed the movements of the sun and moon and that they cannot defy Allah's appointed course. There are several *ayats* to this effect in the Qur'an. Thus, the Qur'an says, "(He is) the One who causes the dawn to break; and He has made the night to be (a source of) stillness and the sun and the moon to run their appointed courses (*husbanan*) : (all) this is laid down by the will of the Almighty, the All-Knowing" (6:96). Thus, this verse makes it clear that the sun and the moon run on an appointed course fixed by Allah. The word *husban* has same root as *hisab* and means counting, reckoning, calculating, etc.

Thus, the sun and moon run according to an appointed course which can be calculated. The same words we find in the verse 55:5, "*Al-shamsu wa'l qamaru bihusban*" (the sun and the moon follow an appointed course). Again in the verse 13:2 we find that, "He made the sun and the moon subservient (to you). Each one runs to an appointed course (*li ajalin musamman*)." In the verse 21:33 it is stated, "And He it is Who created the night and the day and the sun and the moon. All float in orbits (*fi falakin yasbahun*)."

All these verses are enough to make it absolutely clear that sun and moon and in fact all the stars run their course and move in their own orbits. This is quite scientific observations in the Qur'an and this is what has been observed by the scientists and astronomers for centuries.

And all the calculations of astronomers are based on the fact that these stars or satellites like moons do not deviate from their course nor shall they until Allah desires so. And all the calendars in the world are based on this fact. These calendars, whether solar or lunar, have never been proved wrong. Not only this the orbital course of sun and moon is so precise that solar or lunar eclipses are correctly predicted to a fraction of a second.

To witness moon is not a matter of principle; it is a method and a primitive method, of course. As a matter of principle is that our calendar should be based on the movement of moon, not on sun, i.e., we must follow a lunar calendar, not a solar one. The Islamic calendar is related to our religious rituals. The reason Allah chose a lunar calendar has been very well explained by Muhammad Asad as follows: "The reference, at this stage, to lunar months arises from the fact that the observance of several of the religious obligations instituted by Islam, like the fast of *Ramadan*, or the pilgrimage to Mecca... is based on the lunar calendar, in which the months rotate through the seasons of the solar year. This fixation on the lunar calendar results in a continuous variation of the seasonal circumstances in which those religious observances are performed (e.g., the length of the fasting-period between dawn and sunset, heat or cold at the time of the fast or pilgrimage) and thus, in a corresponding, periodical increase or decrease of the hardships involved." (see *The Message of* The Qur'an, p. 40).

Whether one agrees with Muhammad Asad or not the Islamic calendar will continue to remain lunar as it has been so desired by Allah in the Qur'an and so ordained by His Messenger. But only question is of precise determination of beginning of a lunar month. Whether it should be through sighting of a moon by ones own eye which causes great deal of problems—the altitude of the place of observation, weather condition (cloudy or clear), thinness of the size of moon, etc.—or whether it should be based on calculation. The calculation of a lunar month has no where been prohibited. The Qur'anic verses quoted above lays stress on the fixed and appointed course of the sun and moon and other heavenly bodies. Also, breathtaking developments have taken place in the field of astronomy in our own time. Should we, then not, go for adopting a calendar based on calculation rather than sighting of moon causing great deal of problems? Have we not readily abandoned camel or bullock or horse in favour of car or aircraft for transportation? Can we not choose better and surer means for determining our months?

The Ulama earlier had rejected even use of helicopter for sighting the moon. But now many of them are coming round and accepting the use of helicopter. This is of course one step forward. In western countries the moon cannot be easily sighted due to weather conditions as it is often cloudy, especially in the winter season. The Egyptian calendar, which is a lunar calendar is highly reliable and can be safely used. It has been in use for centuries and its authenticity has never been questioned. This calendar can resolve most of our problems

Index

Abbasids
  capture of power, 116
  and killings of Prophet's
    children, 165
  and political fight with
    Umayyads, 67
  State of, 68
  Caliphate, 82
  decline of, 68, 82
  and philosophical sciences, 76
  downfall prediction in *Ikhwan,* 165
  support to Mu'tazil, 227
Abbas Hamdani studies on
  Ikhwanus Safa, 161
Abraham and Moses, 99
Absolute reality, 39
Accumulation of wealth views
  of Quran, 176
Acceptance of truth of all religions, 36
Accountability, 60-61
Acceptance by Quran of all
  religions, 106
Acquisition of knowledge, 62
Adl/Zulm, 28-29, 121
  emphasis in Qur'an, 120
  in polygamy, 200-01
  and Ihsan, 111
Adultery
  punishment for, 190
Adornment meaning, 144-45
Ahadith, 132-33
  interpretation of Qur'an, 223
  of Christians, Jews others, 154
Alam Khundmiri
  philosophical essays of, 78-80
Alf Mujaddin Thani, 81
Algeria
  Islam in, 47
  globalization–case study, 94
Allah's name according
  to Qur'an, 32, 36
Al-Ghazali, 69

Al-Farabi, 84
  on religion and modernity, 85-86
Ali Shari'ati, 93
Amal, 241
Amal Salih 119-120
Ansars, 114
Appearance of Muhammad
  —social scene, background, 171
Appreciation of religious
  differences
    by Sufis, Guru Nanak, 208
Arabs before Islam
  illiteracy aspect, 169
  women position,
  economic scene,
    political scene, 170
  concept of literacy, 172, 241
  and learning, 75-76
Arabia
  uniting of by Islam, 44
Arguments
  theological and
    philosophical, 69-70
Aspiration for leadership
  in Mecca, 110
Ash'ari doctrine, 81-82
Asha'iras, 98
Aurangzeb's relations with Rajputs, 100
Authoritarian regimes
  and doctrine of accountability, 51
Ayatollah
  Khomeini-Islamic values, 93
  Talequani, 93

Bait-al-Hikmat, 66, 76
  and spread of science
  and philosophy, 66
Bank interest views on, 189
Battle of Camel, 116
Battle of Uhud and justification of
  polygamy, 198

Batin/Batini theology, 235
  knowledge, 239
Bedouins, 115
Bernard Lewis
  definition of modernity, 63
  criteria of modernity, 66, 68
Berbers of West Africa, 106
Bhakti saints
  respect for all religions, 208
Bilalian Society USA, 173
Bohras priest, 251
  case of minorities, 263
  origin, 264
  community as slaves, 265
  and Da' is government, 266
  demands of, 266
Buddhist approach to God, 39-40
Bosnia conflicts, 11
Books written by Muslim
  intellectuals, 184-85

Caliph
  assassination and dissidence, 115
Catholic minority
  separatist struggles, 262
Cancellation of verses of Qur'an, 194
Change in Islamic society in
  19th Century, 184
Change concept of, 179, 241
Characteristics of Islamic State, 117
Charter of Rights of Women
  in Quran, 174-75
Chadar
  significance in Islam, 93
Child marriages, 16
Church role
  in State in West, 46
Christians and Muslims, 99
Cloning, 190
Co-existence of Muslims,
  Jews and Christians, 100
Collapse of Communist rule
  in Russia, 90
Colonial culture resentment,
  independence from, 87-88
Compilation controversy
  of Ikhwanus Safa, 68
Compilation of Prophet's
  sayings (ahadith hadith), 137
Compassion in Islam, 126

Concepts of Human
  Rights and Islam, 52
  secularism, pluralism, 52
Conscience freedom of
  in Qur'an, 151
Constitution of Madina, 153
Conversions categories of, 102
Consumerist values imposing of, 14
Core values of all religions, 15
Conservatism in Islam, 15
Contradiction of Quran, 194
Covenant of Madina, 60
Continuity, 81
Conquest of countries and
  conversions, 102
Criteria for modernity, 64
Crusades, 99, 205
Cyclical Theory of History, 237

Day of judgement, 40
Dara Shikoh appreciation of
  Hinduism, 208
Death of Prophet
  aftermath of, 178, 180
Death penalty, 52
Democratic principles in
  Islam, 113
Democracy
  advent of, 88
  achievement, 261
  in Qur'an, 71
Demolition of religious
  places according to Quran, 49, 103
Differences in Islamic World, 46
Dialecticians vs. rationalist, 78
Different interpretations
  to prophethood and
    receiving of revelations, 57-58
  to Qur'an, 231-32
Different Communities by Allah, 149
Din
  meaning of, 22-23
  in Qur'an, 109, 149
Divine drama on earth, 83
Diverse cultures, 88
Discrimination, 173
  views on, 140
Diversity
  legitimacy of in Qur'an, 152
Doctrine of
  taqlid, 137
  accountability, 51

Dominant civilizations and
    modernity, 64
Dowry deaths, 16
Dream condition, 69
Duties of Muslims, 109,111
Dressing Code, 67

Economic Justice in Qur'an, 176
Education/literacy views on, 65
Egypt gender justice, 73
Election role of women in Iran, 72
Embracing of Islam by non-Arabs, 114
Emigrants Muhajirs, 153
Environment destruction, 17
Equal rights in Muslim
    majority country, 50
Ethical aspects of
    human conduct, 119
Eye donation
    opposition in Islam, 190

Faith in human existence, 18
Farabi view on destiny of man, 84
Fatimid character of
    Ikhwanus Safa, 158
Fatimids (Isma'ilis) believes of, 237
Fanikhu, 200
Fight/war
    concepts regarding, 219
    in Qur'an against
        non-believers, 220
Fiqh Academy of India, 190
Fuqaha, 181, 250
Freedom of conscience, 51-52
French Revolution
    slogans of, 244
    and acceptance by Qur'an, 244
Full witness
    women as, 189
Form of State
    in Islam, 116

Gabriel as
    mode of Wahi, 55-56
    different schools of thought, 56
Ghazali
    and Islam revivalism, 80
    and Kant comparison, 80
    doctrine, period, 82

Gender justice, 15
    in Islam, 129
    and modernity, 70
    in Arabia, Iran, 72
Globalization and western
    values over Asia and Africa, 14
    threat, process in third
        world, 87-89
    and denial of cultural diversity, 91
    in Muslim countries, 92

Haj
    origin of, 239
    qurbani, 197
Hadith, 132
    literature, 25, 75
        107, 132, 222, 229
    justification of polygamy, 198
    role in understanding Qur'an, 222
Half witness woman
    concept of, 188
Hanafiyas
    believe of successor
        to Imam, 232
Hassan bin Talan Prince
    on cause of conflicts, 11
Hazrat Ali
    and succeeding Prophet, 112
    omission of praises of, 53
Hazrat Musa (Moses), 55
Hermeneutics, 43
Henotheism
    (al-Arbabi), 38
Higher human values,
    and Islam, 65
Hijab (veil)
    injunction regarding in Qur'an, 144
Hikmah/Hakim
    hakam, 28, 59-60
Hindu-Muslim
    unity, 34
    relations, 100
Hindu Concept of
    God, 39
Human relations in
    Islam, 111
    values, 111
Humanity
    division of, 105

according to Qur'an, 105
Human Rights
and modernity, 70
in pluralist society, 147
Human situations,
and Shari'ah, 136
Huntington's clash of
civilizations theory, 90-91
Honour killings
Bill against (Jordan), 15

Ibn Arabi's doctrines, 85
Ibadat, 126
types of, 166
Ibrahim
Sufi lore of, 38-39
Id
Ghadir al-Khuman, 162
al-musiba, 162
Ideal individual description, 164
Identity crisis, 90
Idol worship, 170
according to Sufi, 208
in Qur'an, 102
Ihsan, 28-29
Ijitihad
and problem solving, 138, 180
meaning, acceptance,
qualification, 185
Ijma, 131, 180
Ikhwanus Safa, 76
works, controversies,
compiling, origin, 157-58
controversy, 68
period of compilation, 161
Ilm, 75, 171, 239, 241
Ilmal Kalam, 192
Imamah
theory of, 112-13
Imam appointment of in
Shi'ah Islam, 132
Imam Bukhara life of,
271-91
Imaan, 254
Imam Mahdi
appearance of, opinion
regarding, 163
Imam replacement question, 181
India
and socially unjust customs of, 16

Inductive/deductive
approach of reasoning, 66
Inheritance in feudal
lords—Sindh, 15-16
rights of daughters, 144
Inter-religious/cultural dialogues
importance of, 203, 206, 207
intellectual/religious level, 207
rules, 209-10
Inter/Intra religious differences, 99
Injustice/oppression
denouncement of, 177
Iraq, and the Baath party, 47
Iran policies in, 72, 112
gender justice, revolution, 72
Islam
and literacy, 75
compatibility with secularism, 45
term, 24
Islamic
revolution—history of, 94
terminology, 21
countries and secularism, 47-48
modernity, 64
philosophers, 76
State-concept aspects, 107
law-sources, controversies, 132
Isma'ilis (*Batinis*), 84
interpretation to Qur'an, 233
views of man's existence, 84
concepts of God, 98-99
movement, 164
origin of Rasa'il, 159
question of succession to Imam, 232
Jama'at-e
Islami-i-Hind, 52
Jabriyas, 67, 77
Jahilliah period justice
in Qur'an, 186-87
Jannat/Jahannam views on, 193
Jews and Muslims, 99
Jihad, 26-27, 195, 211, 239
Word meaning, 211-216
Jizyah Tax, 103, 220
Jurists
in Sunni Islam,
differences in, 135
Justice in Islam, 245-46
Kafirs, 106, 195,
word, 155

Khilafat model, 45, 115
Khilafat-i-Rashidah, 114
Khundmiri Alam
    on Ghazali, 80
    on Law, 84
Killing of a person
    in Qur'an, 122
Kosovo
    conflict reason, 111
Kufr, 98, 100, 104, 121
Kuwait
    policies in, 72

Learning and scholarship
    in Islam, 75
Legal category, superiority, 83
Legal structure of
    Islam methodology of creating, 131
Liberal secularism, 48
Liberation
    of *Ikhwas,* 164
    of weaker sections, 174
    loss of after
        Prophet's death, 178
    mission of Prophet, 171
    elements of, 171
Literacy concept of
    Arabs, 172
Love
    importance of
        in Rumi's views, 85

Madinah/Madina
    meaning, 23
    migration to, 125
Ma'adh bin Jabal
    hadith of, 138
Man's nature and destiny, 83
Maulana Maududi
    Commentary on Quran, 135
Maulana Husain
    Ahmad Madani, 52
Maulana Abul Kalam Azad
    concepts of, 31-42
Material vs. spiritual existence
    of man, 84
Malak
    derivation meaning of, 56
Mala, 108
Malkae nubuwwat

and revelation, 57
Mamthul, 235
    system, Prophet as, 236
Meccan Stage Islam, 124
Melting Pot Model USA, 89
Methodology of understanding
    Quran/Scriptures, need for, 221
    Hadith role in, 222
Message of Allah
    mode of, 56
Militancy and violence
    in West and South Asia, 204
Minhaj, 148
Miracles
    ridicule in Qur'an, 173
    non-acceptance, 193
Misaq-i-Madina, 153
Mithaq-i-Madina, 51, 60, 108, 125
Mohenjodaro
    connection with oneness
        of God, 36
Modernity, 63-64, 71
Multicultural or
    mosaic model, 89
Muhammad Iqbal on ijitihad, 148
Muhay man, 149
Muhammad Prophet
    liberation movement, 169
Muhiyuddin Ibn Arabi, 208
Mufti al-Azhar measures of, 184
Mujtahid, 184
Music ban in Shari'ah, 98
Mushrik word, 155
Mu'tazila, 98
    and Abbasid, 82
    priority to reason,
        justice, 248
    and doctrine of revelation, 57
    and traditionalists, 77
Mutakallimum, 77
Mushaf-e-Uthman, 53, 55
Muslim and Mu'min
    differences, characteristics, 235
Nature laws of
    and Qur'an, 193
Nathwani Inquiry Commission on
    Bohras, 266-67

Occassionalism doctrine, 81
Oneness of humankind theory, 152

Other religions attitude towards,
  177-78
Organ transplantation views on, 190
Pact of Prophet
  with all religions, 35
Peripheral Islamic empires, 82-83
Persecutions of Muslims, 106
Philosophic year
  festivals of, 162
Pillars of Islam, 237-38
Pluralist way of
  life in Islam, 49
Pluralism
  in Qur'an, 104
  attitude of in
    Qur'an, 147-48
  and diversity, 258
Polygamy
  acceptance, 187-88 ·
  views on, 61
  in Qur'an, 142-43
Political community
  views in Islam, 110
Prajapati or *Vishwakarman*, 38
Pre-Islamic Arab Society, 107-08
Prophet's
  migration, 49, 108, 125, 152
  companions, 136-37
  literacy of, 58-59
  family in Shi'ahs Islam, 180
Prayer system of Islam, 243
Prostrating views on, 243
Priesthood concept in Islam, 179
Prophet Abraham and use of
  reason, 61
Punishment for
  drinking, 180
  crime, 189
Purdah (veil)
  concept in Qur'an, 176
Qadriyas, 67, 77
Qawwali, 98
Qiyas, 180
Qist, 29
Qur'an
  and revelation, 55
  and other religions , 101
  and concept of
    society, 107
  4 important teachings, 256

  marriage to, 16
  terminology of, 21
  teachings, 60
Qur'anic verses
  categories, 225-26
  and principles of Islam, 140
Qur'anic pluralism, 150
Qurbani
  in Hajj, 196-97
Quraysh
  superiority, 110, 114
  division into claws, 114

Ramjanambhoomi
  Movement, 95, 206
Rabbi David Rosen
  and Israel and world peace, 12-13
Raisul Ulama
  Mustafa Cervic
  (Bosnia), 11
  remarks of, 11
Rahmah/Rahim/
  Rahman, 25-26
Reason vs. faith,
  centuries of values, 18-19
  importance, 59
Reasons for conflicts, 203, 205
Reasons
  priority to, 248
  and intellect, 61
  and revelation, 84
Religion and
  conflict, 12-13
  modernity, 85
  world peace, 11
  thought system, 241
  sub-systems of, 249
Religious
  Fundamentalism, 94-95
  Scene before advent
    of Prophet, 169-70
  Leaders views on
    religion and conflicts, 11-14
  Tolerance, 100
Reconstruction of Religious
  Thoughts in Islam, 80
Responsibility of Individuals,
  acts on individuals, 61
Restraining anger in Qur'an, 122
Resentment

against colonial culture-reasons, 87-88

against cultural homogenization globalization, 91-92

Retaliation, 122
law of, 108

Retaliatory violence, 122

Revelation
concept, mode, 53
and reason, 59
of Qur'anic verses, 135

Revivalism in Islam, 80

Revolt among Muslims, 115

Rigidity in
Muslims/Hindus aspects of, 98

Rig Veda
concept of unity of Qur'an, 38

Rights of
conversion, 52
non-Muslims, 50
women in Qur'an, 143

Rituals
emphasis on, 207

Role of media
in conflicts, 203

Rububiyah
concept of Azad, 37

Rumi Jalaluddin, 85

Salam/Saalim, 24

Salamat
meaning, 24

Sati, 16

Saudi Arabia
governance/
women's rights, 71-72
modernity,
parameters, 72

Scientific activities
and early Islam, 66

Scriptural
hermeneutics, 43
injunctions, 129
pronouncements, 130

Sect of Shi'a
compilers of
Rasa'il, 162

Secularism and Islam, 43, 46

Semitic religions/tribes
and Islam, 9

and oneness of God, 36

Sense perception, 69

Sexual equality, 182
verses on, 141-42

Separate electorate for
non-Muslims, 50

Shah of Iran
policies of, 92

Shari'ah
ban on music, 98
formulations, 98
law, 40-41,50, 129-32
and women's rights, 79-80
issues, 181

Shari'ah laws 40-41, 50
and Ahadiths, 223
and bias against
woman, 246-47
need of review, 247
meaning, 250

Shi'ah sects, 131
beliefs, 112-13
division, 113

Share-cropping
denouncement by
Prophet, 177

Slavery
in Shari'ah, 182

Socio-political
doctrines of Islam, 154

Social situations
and liberation
movement, 169
before Prophet, 169

Speech-rules of, 194

Sufis
defiance of fatwa
religious concepts of, 32
and Islam, 52
Islam, 126
literature and
destiny of man, 89
praises for in
Rasa'il, 159

Sunni Islam, 131

Sunnah principle, 80, 154

Superstition
and supernatural beliefs
Prophet's fight against, 173

Supernatural powers
  denial in Islam, 174
Syedna's subjugation
  of Bohras, 267, 269
Syed Ahmad Khan, and principles
  of *tafsir*, 1191
  and English language, 192
  on contents of Qur'an, 192
  on *Jihad*, 195
  On *Qurbani*, 196
  On Polygamy, 197
Tafsir
  literature, 31, 35, 233
  of Sir Syed, 191
Tahafat-al-Falsifa, 69, 77, 80
Tasawwuf, 80
Tarjuman al-Qur'an, 31, 34, 38
Taqlid, 138, 179,
  mindset, 154
Tawhid, 40-41
Ta'wil meaning discipline of
  Qur'an, 233-35
Thinking encouragement to, 180
Territorial conflicts,
  countries undergoing, 13
Terminology, in Qur'an, 21
Theological
  and philosophical debates/
    arguments, 69-70
  doctrine of monotheism, 98
  formulations, 130
Tolerance
  and liberalism in religious, 97, 99
Transportation role in migration, 14
Truth and patience in Qur'an, 120
Triple divorce hadith acceptance, 188
Two-nation Theory, 52

Ulama of India
  Association and effort for
    secular India, 50
  Opposition to Two-nation
    Theory, 50
  and secularism, 52
  need for *ijitihad*, 138
Ulama
  career as, 186
  after fall of Baghdad, 183
Ulama view of Qur'an on women
  rights, 70

Ultimate reality
  concept of, 39
Umayyad, 67
  oppression of, 178
  capture of power, 116
Ummi, *Ũmma*, 58
Ummah, 148, 153-54
Unity of Religion
  belief in, 258-59
  concept of Maulana
    Abul Kalam Azad, 31
Universal moral values, 119
UN Human Rights Declarations 1948
  signing of, 51
USA hostility towards
  Islamic countries, 204

Value based society
  importance in Islam, 117
Values fundamental
  to Islam, 140
Violence
  interconnection with
    Islam, 121
Virtues,
  excellence in
    and Qur'an, 101
Wahdat-e-din, 32-33, 41, 149
Wahdat-al-Wujud doctrine, 81, 208
Wahy,
  and revelation in
    Qur'an, 54
  different meanings, 54-55
Wealth accumulation
  in Islam, 124
Weaker section
  concern for Islam, 140
Western liberal secular model, 46
White revolution in Iran, 92
Women's Role in Conference, 15
Women's rights
  and Qur'anic teaching, 61
  in Islam, 70, 142
World Conference for
  Religion and Peace
    (WCRP) Jordan, 11
WTO meetings Opposition to, 18
Zakah, 127
Zihar, 134
Zulm and *Udwan* opposition to, 107